This book is a masterpiece. It is ... is wider than T'ai Chi. The content is b... is a gift to the world, born of years and ...tion. It comes from the deep cauldron c... pon the wisdom of some of the world's ... and it is an offering of all this back to those who can absorb and appreciate it.

— **Susan Swire,** BSc., PgDip., MCSP,
Author of "Secrets of the Feel-Good Home"
Feng Shui Consultant

In this book, the author guides us back to the Tao of old. For the reader it opens the heart as we move through life's journey, painstakingly examining our first intimations towards the unfolding of wisdom. Undoubtedly, the book reads you, as it explores the fight to survive, evolve and grow, revealing an army within whose combatants are both necessary and recognisable. It portrays the refined essence of all our experiences and interactions, with endearing allegories that will capture the humanity in us all.

— **Leith Brown,** BSc. (Hons.), MCSP, MACP,
Tutor: "The Art of Living Mindfully"

The author has written an eloquent and profound book which, as well as being allegorical, also has practical applications. It is exquisitely written, and on a valued subject, is easy to read and yet thought-provoking. The writing has an air of serenity about it – it flows beautifully and tranquilly and makes the reader want to get up and practise each T'ai Chi stance and experience the flow of energy within. It has much to recommend it.

— **Lorna Howarth**, FRSA,
Founding Editor, The Write Factor

This book is enchanting. As well as being informative and illustrative, it is full of inspiration and is endowed with a wisdom, awareness and 'knowingness' that can only have come from one who has not just learnt and practised T'ai Chi, but who has lived it.

— **Audrey Hyde-Chambers** (Charity Director;
Training and Personnel Manager; co-author of "Tibetan Folktales")

The author brings to this book all the qualities that engaged and enthused her pupils. It is easy to read, whilst being insightful into the underlying truths that T'ai Chi embodies. It reflects the compassion with which she views the world and I thoroughly recommend it to anyone who has an interest in Eastern spiritual teachings and/or T'ai Chi.

— **Fredrick R Hyde-Chambers**, OBE (Chair, the Buddhist Chaplaincy Support Group; author of "Lama"; "The Mouse King" and co-author of "Tibetan Folktales")

Congratulations! "The Tiger's Mouth" is written so beautifully. It is chock-full of wisdom and gems. You have so masterfully linked Taoism and T'ai Chi at philosophical, spiritual, experiential levels. It is also personal and practical. I love it. I will treasure it, enjoy it, and share it with my family. I thank you so much.

— **Ellen Cheng**, daughter of Grand Master, Prof. Cheng Man Ching, CMC Enterprise, Asheville, U.S.A.

The Tiger's Mouth

A Taoist Journey towards the Source

by

Ursula Smilde-Hiatt

First published July 2015
ISBN: 978-1-78324-024-1

Front Cover: author's collection, photo by Barry Windsor
Back Cover: "Berries" by Enid H. Higgs, author's collection, photo by Barry Windsor

Typesetting and cover design by *wordzworth.com*

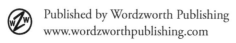 Published by Wordzworth Publishing
www.wordzworthpublishing.com

Contents

PART TWO   ADULTHOOD

Preface and Acknowledgements

I owe so much to the T'ai Chi Ch'üan:

It is a history of Chinese symbolism,
a gentle therapeutic exercise,
a series of movements that clarify and calm the mind,
a meditation for both performer and observer.

It is a visual masterpiece,
poetry in slow motion,
a beautifully-choreographed art form,
a philosophical foundation for life and
a sacred dance.

It also has a story to tell...

The basis for this story began in ancient China when Taoism became its philosophical mainstay and when, over time, physical exercises were devised which related to that philosophy and to observation of Nature. These, in turn, became today's T'ai Chi Ch'üan and its movements, titles and symbolism evolved and spread, not only in China, but throughout the world.

The traditional Yang Style, Long Form, which was established in 1883, has retained much of what was originally offered and, together with its Short Form – as exemplified by the illustrious Grand Master, *Cheng Man Ching* – now shares many of its movements, and the same, or similar titles, with other T'ai Chi Styles and Forms, thus linking its practitioners with a multitude of other teachers and students around the globe.

It was the Yang Style, Long Form which, initially, was taught to me by the late Gerda (Pytt) Geddes and by two of her many pupils who became teachers, Sue Phipps and Beverley Milne. My gratitude, therefore, goes to all three of them. It was Pytt who imparted to her students the foundation for this Journey, however, and I am, therefore, most grateful to her, not only for her wisdom and insight, but because it was she who, whilst studying T'ai Chi in Shanghai, began to source the symbolism in some of the movements which appear in this book.

As well as training in the Long and the Short Form with other T'ai Chi teachers in the U.K. and abroad, and, thereby, travelling further along the T'ai Chi road, I eventually offered the basis of Pytt's Journey to my own T'ai Chi pupils and found that it began to grow, change, and then flourish from the many seeds and flowers inherent in the good soil of Chinese symbolism and mysticism; in Oriental and Indian philosophy and spirituality; in Western psychology; from the fertile and rich minds of many writers and poets, and from my own imagination, for a different approach to the Journey had begun to evolve in my mind, which would give meaning to *all* the movements in the Long Form and still maintain their Taoist symbolic origins. In confirmation of this, I found that, from the way my T'ai Chi teacher in Bangkok, Master *Tang* Liang Tia, performed the movements, I was supplied with more aspects of the Journey, rather in the manner of providing missing pieces of a jigsaw puzzle. It is, therefore, with much gratitude and affection that I give my profound thanks to Master *Tang*, not only for his teaching and for the invaluable photographs he allowed me to take of him, but also because it is due to him that this book could take its final shape.

Inspiration also came from my beloved T'ai Chi pupils. They inherited the harvest this Allegorical Journey produced and gave much in return and, for their intelligent, insightful and highly-varied responses, their continuing interest, and their loving encouragement, I am forever indebted. Many other friends were involved in various stages of this book and, for their time, help and support and for their generous, sensitive and careful reading of some of the chapters, I am, again, deeply thankful. All have been wonderful and none will be forgotten.

Special mention, however, and warm thanks must go to: Chris Coombes for his computer expertise and patient, kindly help over many years; Barry Windsor for his wonderful photography; Anna Leung and Gaia Friedman for their artistic skills; Leith Brown and Christy Georgiades for the loan of their statuettes and much-appreciated input; Ros Tennyson, Rosemary Marshall, Maggie Fealdman, Dennis Huntley and George Piggott for their photographs; Patricia de Mayo Kueckelmann for her musicianship; David Cameron for his Haiku poem; Riki and Audrey Hyde-Chambers for their valued contributions, as well as, with John Ellerton, Maggie Fealdman and Sam Musnier, for the use of photos in which they appear; David Compton for his inestimable assistance; Susan Swire for her encouragement and loyalty; Isabelle Blondiau, Shirley Oomkens, Moya Myers, Betty Law, Jill Ygesias and Bezon Shroff for their kind help and steadfast interest; Sheila Dainton for her highly-valued input, and Maxi Gainza-Bemberg for just 'being there'.

For the reader, whether linked to the T'ai Chi or otherwise, my hope is that some life-enhancement may be furthered by pondering upon the spiritual landmarks offered herein, and that they may produce an even-more fruitful harvest in their own lives.

Hampshire, 2015

Introduction

This book has been written for all who have an interest in self-knowledge and wisdom teachings. It takes the form of an Allegorical Journey which illustrates an imaginary life-cycle and links the wealth of rich symbolism in the titles and movements of the T'ai Chi Ch'üan with our spiritual and psychological development. It is not a treatise on the T'ai Chi itself, however, nor is it a description of any one person's actual inner journey, since our lives do not follow such specific patterns in such a clear-cut linear progression as do the titles in this book. Thus, the journey is different for each of us, with some arriving at wisdom quite early in life and others experiencing their spiritual landmarks at varying stages thereafter. Regardless of what or where we are, however, some aspects of this journey will have meaning for us and may help us along the way, whilst an Allegory, when seen as just that, can offer many opportunities to look at ourselves and, perhaps, recognise some, if not all, of our own experiences.

Traditionally, the Long Form of the T'ai Chi Ch'üan is performed in three parts and this structure lends itself to the three stages of the human journey: that of a child growing into adolescence and young adulthood; adult opportunities for self-knowledge and self-mastery, and the ultimate search for maturity and wisdom. Moreover, the sub-titles in the three parts offer their inner meaning to: the emergence of ego conflict in the child and adolescent; the domination of a damaged ego in the adult, and the ability to overcome that damage through the intensity of the desire for self-knowledge and truth.

The symbolism and philosophy, the psychological and spiritual development of a human being, and the role that ego-conflict plays in our lives, thereby underlie the three basic themes which recur throughout the three-part structure of this story. Nor is the number 'three' haphazard, woven as it is into our perceptions of heaven and earth and all that exists between them; of mother, father and child; of birth, life and death.

But, the predominant feature is the disruption caused by the damaged ego, since, regardless of our beliefs, attitudes, or philosophies, the results of our disruptive ego are obvious. Few escape some consciousness of it, its domination over us varies only in degree, and how we deal with it is considered here to be of paramount importance. Thus, 'egolessness' is seen (as it does in all spiritual teachings) as the birth of Enlightenment and is regarded as the key to self-knowledge and spiritual wholeness, whilst its 'death' – which occurs when we are able to conquer it with the arrows of spiritual wisdom – becomes our spiritual fulfilment.

To illustrate this, the 'Tiger' in the titles is used as a symbol of the ego, because the Tiger movements are so physically powerful and because, especially in Eastern tradition, the tiger exemplifies the ego in human nature. Tiger thus plays a large part in the Allegory, emerging in its most destructive form when the spiritual nature of the child is unable to grow spontaneously; when it is neglected or rejected; when it is given inadequate recognition or respect, or denied full expression. A child's true self is precious and pure, but because it so rarely is allowed to fulfil its spiritual nature, the child's frustration and confusion can result in what we term selfish or anti-social behaviour and the Tiger then dominates many of his or her responses. It is through the interaction between the damaged ego and its environment, however, that opportunities can arise for later self-knowledge and spiritual development and these then can offer some measure of growth towards maturity and wisdom. Moreover, even if the 'human condition' does not allow for any conquest of the Tiger to occur for more than a few moments in a day, those few moments are seen as contributions towards the balance and harmony of what the Chinese term "Tao"* – or "The Universal Way of Life" – as well as being of immense benefit to the individual.

The significance of ego-awareness also derives from three features of the Taoist philosophy: that of 'yielding' to life's circumstances; the application of *wu-wei* (or 'action that is ego-free'), and the *yin* and the *yang* of the duality which forms the many conflicting opposites within our own nature and which, according to Taoism, can be resolved by an

* pron. *dhow*

understanding and acceptance of the complementary qualities of the opposites in our lives and in Nature as a whole.

The first two categories of yielding and *wu-wei* have the same foundation, since both derive from egolessness, but they are considered separately, since the pliability of philosophically-yielding could be termed a *yin* condition. It embodies an attitude of mind that quietly intuits the vast wonder of life and, despite its apparently haphazard manifestations, the depth of its order. To complain and bemoan one's lot, to resist change, or to feel the unhappy victim of fate, is alien to the Taoist philosopher, for such an attitude reveals an inability to appreciate and accept the Universal Laws of life and to comprehend to what degree we have become alienated from them. Thus, flowing with life and moving in harmony with its ever-changing patterns, forms the basis of yielding.

Wu-wei, as activity that is ego-free, indicates what can be termed a *yang* condition. The sage may, on the whole, be liberated from ego-domination, but life goes on. Decisions have to be made and actions taken, but, when they are made in accordance with the dictates of circumstance and for their own sake, they are not governed by ego and their results are beneficial.

Both yielding and *wu-wei* are difficult to achieve consistently on a daily basis, but the process can be facilitated by observing the *yin* and *yang* dualities within our own nature and by recognising that they can be as balanced as they are in Nature. We all experience a multitude of mixed emotional and mental responses and attitudes that vary only in degree of intensity or intuitive understanding and, since every experience has its opposite, every condition its complementary one, we can oscillate from profoundly-moving, deeply-penetrating, positive spiritual experiences, to black, ego-ridden, negative states, whilst, in just one day, we can behave like an irritable child, a confused adolescent, a nagging spouse, a domineering parent, a beneficent friend and a wise adult.

Such mixed, dualistic responses are manifestations of inner conflict and may remain so throughout our lives, governing our attitudes and causing emotional upheaval. But, they can be transformed, in the same way as the fluctuations and opposites in Nature are transformed through the immense order of the universe, manifesting as it does in the visible changing patterns of the days, nights and seasons and in the opposites of raging storms and tranquil skies. By, therefore, observing our own nature and deepening our understanding of our own contradictory responses; by allowing their existence and accepting them without condemnation, and by the subtle transformation that this self-knowledge process creates, we can achieve some degree of balance in our lives. Moreover, when released from the blockages of internal suppression, accurate inner perceptions can arise spontaneously, enabling us to flow with life's circumstances as they occur – thereby yielding – and to take appropriate ego-less action, which is *wu-wei*. Moreover, by allowing our emotional and mental responses to have their rightful place within our psyche and by not attaching undue importance to either our positive or our negative attitudes, we can move nearer to living the fundamental meaning of the Chinese words "T'ai Chi" – the Supreme Ultimate – where the inner pendulum swing of opposites can arrive at a state nearer to equilibrium.

The aim of this book is to take the reader closer to that state and to present Taoism and its allied subjects in such a way that more of our varying needs and responses may be made accessible and the resulting increase in self-knowledge be of psychological and spiritual benefit.

Some features of this Allegory should be noted, however. Firstly, as only T'ai Chi's titles are used as a symbolic framework for the Journey's spiritual development, the reader will understand that the psychological and spiritual aspects offered herein are fewer than the many examples that human nature can supply. Secondly, this book is not meant to be read as one might read a novel, since, although it can be read sequentially, its implications are there to be considered according to the varying landmarks in the reader's personal journey. Thirdly, chapters can be chosen at random, or in response to the sub-titles given, since a particular meaning might be of interest. Finally, if the reader be a T'ai Chi teacher, the sub-title or basis of the book could be used – and then expanded upon - in whatever way were deemed appropriate to the Form or Style being taught. Teacher and pupil then could bring their own unique experience of life to what is being shared - thereby increasing the possibilities for insights – as well as deepening the bond in their already-privileged relationship.

This Allegory was offered in a condensed form to my pupils sequentially, however, with many visual illustrations to accompany it. They also absorbed its many meanings slowly, over a long period of time, since, from the outset, they had understood that, apart from the joy of teaching the Form, I was using the Titles as a symbolic vehicle for promoting philosophical and psychological insights and for an increase in self-knowledge. As a result, I was able to receive a clear-cut response as to whether this had meaning for them and found that its philosophical foundations often confirmed the reasons why, apart from wanting to keep physically fit in a meditational setting, they had been drawn to the teachings. Many had already felt that, to live and work more harmoniously within themselves and with others, was more important than, for example, fame, status, power, or the acquisition of more money than their lives actually required, and so the Allegory's various signposts towards spiritual liberation from these, sometimes, crippling ambitions, offered deeper meaning into their own lives.

Needless to say, the Allegory was not given (nor accepted!) in the expectation that 'enlightenment' would be reached simply by relating the titles and sub-titles to an inner spiritual journey, but significant insights undoubtedly emerged, and my hope in offering this book is that it may continue the process which so enriched my pupils' life-journey, as well as that of my own.

"...There is the mighty axis of Earth,
The never-resting pole of Heaven;
Let us grasp their clue,
And with them be blended in One,
Beyond the bounds of thought,
Circling forever in the great Void,
Yes, this is the key to my theme,"[1]

PART ONE

CHILDHOOD

1 COMMENCEMENT

The Stillness

It is pre-dawn and primeval-still
and we align ourselves to the North,
to that one fixed lode-star,
to that one fixed pole-star,
by which we shall navigate
to the Seven Stars of the night,
to the sacred centre of the heavens,
to the home of the Immortals,
in order that we may
return to the Source.

The head is poised,
the feet are firm,
the face is soft, and so are the eyes.
No tensions exist,
no thoughts intrude,
to mar this moment in time,
this moment before movement begins.

Buddha-like, tree-like,
well-rooted and strong, yet pliant within,
as secure as a babe, as yet unborn,
at-one with the womb of life.
Whole, unified, and wholly-safe,
in that mystical place of no separation,
between you and me, it and other:
seamless.

Released from yes and no,
from liking and not-liking,
from yin and yang,
the dualities of life,
we stand, expanded in space,
merged with the universe,
amid the circles of life,
immersed in the Stillness,
the Stillness before the Change,
which produces Form, Breath and Substance.
Relaxed and at peace,
we just stand…

In the Stillness

Traditionally, the T'ai Chi Ch'üan starts from Stillness, moves into Form and returns to Stillness and the Chinese say it is the same for all human beings on their spiritual journey. So we commence our Allegorical Journey standing quite still.

Our feet are shoulder-width apart for balance and are parallel, forming two sides of the 'square' which the Chinese saw as the symbol of our earthly existence. We face North to align ourselves to the home of the Chinese Immortals, the sacred centre of the heavens and, thus, to the Pole star, the one fixed lode-star, which will remain our constant compass point of reference. We face North out of respect for the ancient Chinese Emperors, the spiritual mediators between heaven and earth and conveyors of our prayers to the Taoist Immortals, and we face North so that our opening movement – which turns us to the right – will rotate us to the rising sun, since, traditionally, T'ai Chi is practised at dawn.

The head is poised, as if suspended at the crown by an invisible silken thread, drawing us upwards towards the heavens and connecting us to the stars from which we came. The 'pull' of the thread releases the neck and lengthens the spine and we feel taller, lighter, emptier, more open and receptive. The tensions are eased from around eyes, mouth and jaw, and the eyes themselves are soft and still. The tip of the tongue rests lightly on the palate behind the top teeth, forming a link from the crown of the head through to the mouth and down to the rest of the body, and the mouth is lightly closed.

The base of the spine is slightly adjusted, so that the three circles of head, rib-cage and pelvis are vertically in alignment. The shoulders are dropped and the chest and hips are eased away from the spine, releasing the body from tension and allowing the inner organs to be in their rightful places, relaxed and without restriction.

Our consciousness is focused on the most important energy-centre of the body, the *tan t'ien.** Sometimes described as the Storehouse of Power or The Sea of *Ch'i*, it is located just below the navel and we allow this area to be fully rounded, soft yet strong, as curved and relaxed as a Buddha's. Our thighs are firm and supportive and our knees eased-out to align with our feet. The feet are fully spread, with arches made higher and stronger by the widening of the knees. Grounded and anchored to the deepest layers of the earth by gravity, and by the strong currents of what the Chinese call the Dragon's Veins of the earth's energies, our knees lower a little with the pull.

Light above and weighted below, we stand like deeply-rooted trees, the branches of which can move in any direction that wind and rain dictate, because their basis is firm. Relaxed in the Stillness, empty of conflicting thought, we are released from the burdens of the mind and are united in both the inner spirit and the external form of our body. That which is hidden and that which is visible, the infinite and the finite, are – for the time being – at one, and we symbolise a state said

*The *tan t'ien* is a psychic field of energy and is regarded as the centre of the body. In mathematical terms, the central point between head and feet is roughly in line with the tops of the thighs, but when we lower our knees, as in the T'ai Chi Ch'üan, the *tan t'ien* becomes our physical, as well as our psychic-energy centre.

to have existed long before the world as we know it began: that of the *wu-chi,* or the Great Void.

The Chinese say we come from the Void and to the Void we return and thus this stance is not only our beginning, but is also our ending. Symbolising a state of emptiness as well as wholeness and unity where nothing is separated, nothing is differentiated, it represents the seamlessness of existence.

Modern physicists describe this seamlessness as Primary Reality, stating that all that the brain chooses to recall, and the conclusions it draws from its subjective, limited, differentiating perceptions, is a reality which is secondary to the underlying, inter-connected and primary condition of existence. They say it is as if we look at something and then bring the 'picture' into resolution, wanting it to 'sit still' for a moment (or as if we were wearing special lenses so that everything had an outline), but its true nature is in another dimension, where there are no *things* and that, without those lenses, the *blur* would be the basic, more accurate, reality.[1] Thus, Primary Reality is not what we see with our eyes or record with our brain and if it were not for those (essential to us) lenses, we would know those transcendental states of oneness experienced by the mystics.[2]

To the mystics, such a state of non-duality is experienced by the open mind, the mind without prejudice, the 'mind' of a mirror, which reflects but does not choose. No likes nor dislikes ripple its calm, no differentiation takes place, no comparisons of one thing with another. The brain functions and thoughts emerge, but neither judgement nor adverse criticism is attached to them. The mind is choicelessly-aware, flowing freely without inhibition or hindrance, moving spontaneously without the thickness of a hair between impulse and action, whilst observation occurs from a place that is ego-free, with no separation between the 'you' and the 'me'. Thus, the mystical mind is calm, empty of concepts and conditioned reactions, and such clear, unclouded vision reveals that *yin* and *yang*, the negative and positive polarities of life, are merged in the *wu-chi* - and that out of such stillness, balance and harmony can arise.

Stillness, or the Emptiness of the Great Void, is traditionally symbolised by a circle and, as we stand poised in the Stillness, we imagine our own circle, the circumference of which is made when we fully extend one arm out to the side and turn ourselves around to shape our own auric boundary, the boundary within which we soon will move. Not anticipating life by leaning forward to take a step before its time, nor leaning back from fear of failure, we are balanced and connected with the centre of the true self, secure in our own field of energy.

Thus we stand. At-one, held in the circle before creation, before the change which produces form, breath and substance, we are choice-lessly-aware, free from the burdens of the mind.

We just stand… in the Stillness.

2 PREPARATION

The emergence of yin and yang

As we stand, suspended in Stillness, the Tao, or the Way of Life, is unfolding and we emerge out of non-duality into the realisation that Stillness is not only wholeness, it is also a state of potential, for physical and spiritual completion cannot lie dormant and movement towards its fulfilment is not only necessary, but inevitable.

So, we prepare ourselves by standing with a more focused observation, a more detailed consciousness of our breath, of the flow of life within us, of the many sounds around us, of the circle of energy around us, of the earth beneath our feet and of the width of sky above - and of our deep connection to all of it. We sense the elements that we share with the earth and also with the stars and become aware of how the stars play their part, are born, live, die and fall and become one with the earth, and of how they shape our lives in seamless continuity.

A child encircled in its mother's womb experiences that same seamless state, the place of no-separation. Enfolded, contained, responding to its environment without self-consciousness, unconditioned by thought, yet 'knowing' when and how to move and grow and when to keep still, the child in the womb is almost in the state of non-duality. But, not quite. *Yin* and *yang* are there, in the child before birth. Physically male (*yang*) or female (*yin*), it has preferences and reacts to its environment and the changing conditions within it with responses that are not without their negative and positive aspects. And, although its consciousness is diffuse at this stage (for it is only later that thought crystallises sensation), it responds in a *yin* or *yang* way to the mother's thoughts and emotions, to her intake of food and liquid, to music, to other sounds both soft and loud, and to voices – especially those of its parents. Sensations of comfort and discomfort, of 'liking' and 'not-liking', are taking place which form the basis for some later attitudes, whilst pre-natal stresses – especially if as severe as attempted abortion, maternal suffering or self-abuse, or long-term nutritional deprivation – can foreshadow and influence later anxieties. Initially blurred and physically-located, such stresses become emotions which, in turn, translate into thoughts and memories, the most initially-traumatic of which can be birth itself and the physical separation from the mother.

Once born, the child's sense of seamlessness gradually fades in proportion to the degree of duality experienced, and the slowly-diminishing sense of oneness is accompanied by an ever-increasing string of memories which, as conditioned thoughts, later take over and dominate much of the child's emotional and mental responses. Thus, the initial, isolated, purely spontaneous reactions of the very young child become the multitude of conditioned, remembered, mechanical responses that are enmeshed in consciousness, whilst memory – physical in its early stages, emotional and mental as well as physical, later on – forms part of ego-development and, if significantly painful, produces the damaged ego.

At this stage of the Allegorical Journey, however, the sense of oneness which the unborn child experiences is the significant one, representing a paradisal state of spontaneous response and unity with its environment, and which, perhaps, at the same time – since we have all experienced such unity – may form part of that ineffable 'something' for which we later yearn, weaving itself into the spiritual urge and guiding us towards a re-union with that state of wholeness and stillness which we sensed at the beginning of our Journey.

Continuing in our stance, we deepen the breathing and learn that the out-breath is the active, creative breath which is required for all *yang* movements of outward-flowing strength and power. But, before we breathe out, we have, of course, to breathe in, and find that our quiet, *yin* intake of air relates to the child receiving all that is being given, not only by the physical mother, but by the breath of life itself.

"The breath of life moves through a deathless valley
Of mysterious motherhood
Which conceives and bears the universal seed,
The seeming of a world never to end,
Breath for men to draw from as they will:
And the more they take of it, the more remains." [1]

We draw the deep *yin* in-breath into our receptive bodies and then breathe out, preparing ourselves for our Journey away from the Source, as – with its first breath – does the new-born child in separating from its mother. We then breathe in again and, harmonising that breath with action, we slowly lift up our hands to shoulder-height, just as if a Grand Puppeteer in the sky were lifting them up from wrists and finger-tips, before, equally slowly, we breathe out and the hands move down again.

These simple movements then symbolise the beginning of our individual, separate lives which, from now on, will follow Nature's *yin-yang* pattern of opposites in action, whilst – as Stillness always precedes Action – we move out of the Stillness of the Great Void, out of the emptying circle of the womb, into all the conditions of life.

> *"From emptiness comes the unconditioned.*
> *From this, the conditioned, the individual things.*
> *So, from the sage's emptiness, stillness arises:*
> *From stillness, action. From action, attainment."* [2]

3a GRASPING THE SPARROW'S TAIL

The circular nature of our environment and
the awakening of consciousness

"Before creation a presence existed,
Self-contained, complete,
Formless, voiceless, mateless,
Changeless,
Which yet pervaded itself
With unending motherhood.
Though there can be no name for it,
I have called it 'the way of life'.
Perhaps I should have called it 'the fullness of life',
Since fullness implies widening into space,
Implies still further widening,
Implies widening until the circle is whole.
In this sense
The way of life is fulfilled,
Heaven is fulfilled,
Earth fulfilled
And a fit man also is fulfilled:
These are the four amplitudes of the universe
And a fit man is one of them:

Man rounding the way of earth,
Earth rounding the way of heaven,
Heaven rounding the way of life,
Till the circle is full." [1]

Now we sink further down into the bend and feel like small children do who are about to take their first steps: testing themselves, attentive, alert. One hand 'rests on air' like a canopy over the earth whilst, turning to the Eastern dawn to receive the rays of the world's largest source of energy, the other hand lifts up as if to form part of the circle of that rising sun itself.

Circles are essential to life and, looking at our universe and its myriad shapes, we see why. Not only are there countless orbs in the

skies, but our circular earth has trees with rings from which we gauge their age; birds' nests are round; animals curl themselves into a perfect circle before they sleep; flowers form circles at their circumference and each of their leaves contains circular cells; pebbles dropped into ponds make rippling circles, whilst snowflakes, hailstones, raindrops and rainbows all conform, as do millions of other forms, to the circular nature of our environment and exemplify the perfection of Nature - for straight lines cannot create wholeness.

Our bodies, too, reflect Nature's circular patterns, from the corona of the head down to the smallest toe; in all the ring-like shapes and cells found in bone, flesh, tissue, muscle and vein, and in the countless circular shapes that are invisible, except to the microscope. So, on this Journey, we follow Nature's patterns, from the beginning to the final Grand Terminus, shaping the air with portions of circles, curves and arcs, half-moons and full-suns, until, having come full circle in our ultimate Return to the Source, we dis-

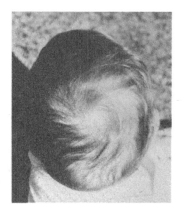

cover that we are the link between the circles of heaven and earth and, thus, have enacted the Chinese Triad of heaven, earth, and ourselves between.

We also begin to understand why the circular shape of what is known as the *yin-yang* symbol is so significant and why the Chinese use it to convey the origin of all creation.

Firstly, there is the empty circle of the Void which, when divided by a curved line into two equal portions and given relevant shading, is reduced to its primary opposites of dark and light, or the female and male principles respectively (a replica of which is popularly believed in China to be on the placenta at birth). The dark area is *yin* and the light area is *yang* and both symbolise all the opposites in existence. But, since nothing is static, nothing is stationary, its central flowing line conveys other aspects of Nature's contrasts, such as the flow of energy which draws the middle of the *yang* day to the middle of the *yin* night and then ebbs-away, by what we call 'time', towards mid-day again. Thus, the symbol as a whole is composed of circles or S-shaped flowing lines which have neither beginning nor end, and, by containing within each dark and light portion a smaller circle which represents the opposite of the portion containing it: the dark *yin* area having a *yang*, light circle, the light *yang* segment holding a dark, *yin* one, it conveys that there is every shade of grey from black to white and that, within each and every thing, each and every person, there is the germ of the opposite which links them together and brings balance and fruition to Nature.

The circle also represents psychological wholeness and unity and this is of major significance in our Journey. A small child is content to have others nearby, but, as adults, we sometimes feel that someone has moved too precipitately into our circle, has either come too close, physically, or needs to be kept at a 'safe' psychological distance away from us because they may not be allowing us sufficient inner space. Alternatively, when feeling rejected, psychological fragmentation can occur from lack of contact with both our true nature and that of other people and we then can lose ourselves and need to access the cause of our unrest, before allowing others into our space. Uncritical self-ob-servation then becomes the aid by which we can further a journey towards our own wholeness, as well as draw nearer to the wholeness in others.

Taoism teaches that there are as many ways to inner truth, and to that sense of wholeness, as there are people and that any study which emphasises self-awareness, slowness and silence, can create the opportunities to further whatever self-knowledge path has been chosen. T'ai Chi Ch'üan is only one of the ways, but, being the path we now are on, we find that its physical interplay of *yin* and *yang*, its slow, silent movements and its ebb and flow of contrasting rhythms, offers a degree of balance - both physically and psychologically - that can, for example, enable a too-yielding nature to become firmer and a too-dominant person to be more yielding. Basic to all spiritual teachings, however, is the need to 'know thyself' and, if the desire for this is strong-enough, an inner journey now can take place which can draw us nearer to each other and, eventually, closer to the inter-connectedness of Primary Reality again.

As has been indicated, our deeper sinking into the bend enables the *tan t'ien* to be our centre and, like the hub of a wheel or the central axis of the earth, that centre becomes the leader and pivot of all our future movements and promotes the physical balance we need. The lowering of our knees also allows our thigh muscles to take more of the torso's weight, thus alleviating lower back stress, whilst it straightens-out the only curve we do not want – that of the spine - which contains all the nerve fibres which mediate movement and which may even contain our earliest history, since it has been suggested by the late Dr. David Tansey of the Metamorphic Technique that the spine holds every 'memory' of our prenatal period within it. Thus, whilst easing-out and lengthening this most important part of our anatomy, we are not only strengthening the central nervous system, but the 'memory' held within it may even give access to our life in the womb.

Having established ourselves in this posture and turned to the East, we now take our first step. We have been told that a lightly-lifting 'empty' leg is *yin* and that a weighted *yang* leg is 'full' and that each step we take should be a sensitive, balanced shifting between one and the other. At this stage, however, we soon discover that we are often unstable and not unlike a very young child who either wobbles on legs that are too *yin*, or whose legs are too *yang* and rigidly held – and we may also be unaware of what we are actually doing. Our hands and arms give us some security, however, and as they start making shapes in space, sometimes waving 'blindly' about, or sometimes following our teacher's movements, repeated application comes to our aid and, with more confidence, we start exploring the space around us.

Like a small child, sensing that space, touching that air, not yet aware of being a separate entity and still deeply involved within the aura of the mother, we sense how much a child responds to life on a highly instinctive level and of how this arises from its unselfconscious simplicity and innate curiosity. These unfolding, immensely sensitive, seeking movements then symbolise both the known place of the womb which the child has just left and the shape of the world into which we are moving. They also convey that exquisite time of uncluttered awareness, before others have given the child its conscious identity and self-conscious ego, and thus represent those aspects which we love so much in a child, those times of openness, vulnerability, spontaneity and trust, those times when there is no mask and the child's true face is there for all to see.

On the purely physical level, there is very little, so far, that has been accomplished. On the mental level, however, much more has taken place, for, whilst brain development starts in the womb and continues until middle-age, by an early age the brain has given its instructions to the body for the intention to move and so the processes of *thought* have come into play. Previously, in the Stillness of the Great Void, there had been contact with Primary Reality and with the peace of a non-dualistic, non-differentiating state of being. Now, with thought having entered that empty space, we have the brain's interpretations of what is taking place. Comparisons occur of one thing with another, of one person with another, of ourselves with another and with a seeing that separates us from everything else. Thought itself has moved us away from the Stillness and we need to be aware of this if we are ever to retrace our way back, through the process of self-realisation, to the empty circle again.

On the emotional level, the feelings and reactions of the child are becoming embedded. The responses to its environment whilst still in the womb formed tentative emotional bonding, and the important first nine months after birth formed stronger ties. Now, the continued bonding with parents and others – or the possible lack of it - forms the foundation for its emotional conditioning and these first opening movements thus are symbolic of the child's emotional development, whilst still contained within the safety of its mother's circle.

Known, sometimes, as: "Grasping the Sparrow's Tail", the movement represents one of our deepest desires: the wish to know and understand what is happening to and around us and, thus, the desire for consciousness in its fullest meaning. The young child wants to make contact with that little bird, wants to grasp it and see how it works, wants to comprehend it and be fully-awake to the reality being presented to it. In the same way, we, as adults, now become conscious of each and every move we make, as attentive to each circle we form as to every step we take. Physical awareness then leads to mental and emotional awareness, and when we later add to this a consciousness of the breath – the *Ch'i, K'i* (Jap.) or *Prana (Ind.)* – which moves through the form and substance of our body, we can, very slowly, travel forwards into the realms of the universal, spiritual quest.

3b Ward Off – Slantingly Upwards; Pull Back; Press Forward and Push

Yielding and flowing with the Bamboos; the Tiger's Kitten and the first Gateway to Wisdom

The ancient Taoists deeply understood Nature and, from their gentle yet penetrating observation, saw how its fundamental attributes relate to areas of our spiritual development. They saw that the circular nature of our environment reveals the ability to circle-intuitively around a difficult situation, as a stream flows around an obstacle. They perceived the wisdom of being as strongly-grounded as the roots of a tree, yet as free-flowing as its branches in the breeze, and that to follow Nature's patterns and cycles of balancing opposites, was to live in harmony. Furthermore, if we interfered with the environment and the natural growth of living things in the belief that we could improve upon already-established natural laws, this would inevitably be followed by disruption, disease and disaster.

They also spoke of the need to 'yield' and, without implying weakness or compliancy, advocated the way of the 'soft', rather than the death-like rigidity of the fixed and unbending mind:

> *"Man, born tender and yielding,*
> *Stiffens and hardens in death.*
> *All living growth is pliant,*
> *Until death transfixes it.*
> *Thus men who have hardened are 'kin of death'*
> *And men who stay gentle are 'kin of life'..."* [1]

Symbols of such yielding frequently were used in Taoist philosophy, but bamboos became the best-known example of this soft yet strong characteristic, their unending pliability epitomising the highest order of ego-less activity and offering a degree of psychological significance that is virtually unlimited. Thus, said one Taoist: *"When the wind blows, the bamboos creak; when it dies away, they grow silent without giving a moment's thought to the relative virtues of creaking and silence. Bamboos just respond to circumstances. If the wind becomes a gale, they readily bow their heads and thus avoid being broken...* [whilst] *the bamboo, green even in old age, very strong and yet pliant, soft within and unashamed of bending, is symbolic of Taoist wisdom..."*. [2]

The next few movements – which technically are known as Ward Off – Slantingly Upwards, Pull Back, Press Forward and Push - still come under the general heading of Grasping the Sparrow's Tail and, herein, are called the "Bamboos", because they so-well exemplify such 'yielding to life' and because, when performing them, we enter into one of the most significant and frequently repeated series of movements in the whole of the Long Form, each repetition giving us more insight into, and a deeper understanding of their spiritual significance, whilst, through the softness of their flow, they allow us to enter into a realm of peaceful simplicity and contact with the Tao.*

Like bamboos in the wake of a breeze, well-rooted in our feet yet pliable within, we shift and flow both forwards and back and repeat that flow as our arms sway up and then go down and our body slides in curves like gentle waves in running waters. Stable in body, quiet in spirit, we move through the air like the breath of the Tao, each contrasting movement exemplifying the softness of *yin* and the strength of *yang*, the sweet harmony of a peaceful mind in a balanced body, one movement reaching its fulfilment and then flowing into its opposite with barely a pause between. Lifting and lowering the arms, swirling and swaying, spreading our arms and retreating, we take no active step yet, silently and with simplicity, "*respond to circumstances*", following the winds of change and the leadership of the *tan t'ien* as we flow in space and move with simplicity to the energies and rhythms of the ever-changing Tao.

A small child whose basis is firm has the innate ability of the bamboo

*In T'ai Chi Martial Art training, these movements are practised separately from the Form, and are known as "Sticking" or "Pushing Hands". To acquire this skill, two practitioners face each other, connect wrist to wrist and flow in the manner of this Bamboos movement, sticking, adhering, connecting to each other's energy and following each other's every move, without breaking the wrist connection. Once this is mastered and an awareness of each other's *Ch'i* is strong, their consciousness can progress to interpreting energy as a whole, and this can lead to spiritual illumination and, eventually, to the final realm of absolute transcendence. In the Long Form, this movement occurs eight times, with each Bamboos flow of energy linking us to the Tao, but it is only on the final Bamboos that we are closest to the Source.

to adapt to change, to respond here and to follow there, to be empty of judgements and thus be free from a mind over-burdened with the negatives of our adult 'oughts' and 'shoulds'. And, when so open to life, a young child is immensely pliant and resilient, unselfconscious and "*unashamed of bending*" because, as yet, it has no knowledge that such 'bending' can be perceived as a weakness of character. Nor is the child concerned with the need to be doing other than what is being done at a particular moment. The inner flexibility which we have lost, through letting our thoughts take us to an imaginary future, or to a remembered past, has not yet been impeded and the unhampered child lives spontaneously with the moment as it is, retaining direct contact with the uncluttered space within. As a result, *yin* and *yang* comparisons are almost absent, the "lens of differentiation" is blissfully undeveloped and the child can experience the many joys of its boundless energy in freedom.

Yin and *yang* have to unfold, however. For every joy there is its opposite, and this is symbolised now as we move our hands from the centre of our being into that of a "Push". And this is significant, for, whilst the Bamboos movements had enacted the measure of innocence and freedom within the psyche of the child; the joys of physical movement unhampered by self-conscious inhibitions, and the reaching-out for more conscious understanding through the senses of sight and touch, this final movement has the child come up against its first barrier, its first closed door. Wishing to move forward, something blocks its way. Wishing to be free, freedom is denied. Duality sets in, contrariness arises, and the ego starts a small but far-reaching process of domination. The young child is in conflict and, like any hampered and restricted creature, reacts with frustration and impatience. Now, the "Tiger's Kitten" has arrived on the scene.

It causes such trouble, this little cub, but, if there is to be enlightenment, so there must be its opposite. Ego-domination is part of the human condition, part of our identity, part of our strength, but, because of the psychological wounds suffered by many, a balanced or 'healthy' ego is rare. Having been frustrated or hurt, we want to hurt back; having been argued with, we argue in return. Causing childhood tantrums, family tensions, quarrels with friends and neighbours, friction at work, political self-seeking, greed, and large-scale wars, we barely realise that any conflict, of whatever nature, is based on the domination of a damaged ego, which says: "I come first", "I know best", "I want that now", "That is mine" – and means it. The child, of course, is unaware of this facet of its nature and, no longer childlike but childish, turns away from the barrier and goes in the opposite direction, sensing how unpleasant it was to feel so restricted and how lovely it was to flow so easily and effortlessly with life. A predominant 'dislike' thus comes into existence and the child simply does not want to know about it and wishes only to move away from the conflict, whilst ego, in the guise of 'rational thought', then says there was no good reason to go in that direction anyway and that it was someone else's fault that the obstruction was there in the first place.

A significant barrier to wisdom thus is erected in the shape of the rationalisation process which, defensively, has us paying closer attention to our self-protective thoughts and less to the promptings of our inner knowing, and has truth receding in proportion to its usefulness to the ego. But, whilst Taoism wisely advocates that, for ego to lose its power over us and for us to respect it in others, we have to acknowledge and know its damaging nature in ourselves first, this wisdom is what we resist.

Thus, the 'human condition' determines the Journey, and the young child who, so naturally, pushes against life, little-knows that to set up what you like against what you dislike is the disease of the mind and that ego's 'rationalisations' sever a vital connection with the 'Perfect Way' of Primary Reality. This, of course, may seem a loss, because it has been gained at the expense of innocence, but its arrival, in the shape of the Tiger's Kitten, not only indicates conflict, but also its spiritual opposite. For, whilst the rebellious nature of the Push revealed how the child responded in comparison with its previous – and opposite – quality of 'yielding', it is, in fact, an early harbinger of ultimate serenity which, in reality, has opened an inner "Gateway to Wisdom": the first of many in this Journey.

4 THE SINGLE WHIP

The Bird's Beak or the Phoenix Stance: balance and re-birth after conflict, and the dual sensations of self-consciousness and self-awareness

The opening movement and the flow of the Bamboos had us facing East. Now, conditioned responses are becoming embedded (*"Give me a child to the age of seven, and I'll show you the man"*, say the Jesuits), and the familiar, age-old human response of 'contrariness' has us turning to the West - the West which is symbolic of the way that is known and the conditioned patterns of human behaviour. Thus, with this second new direction, we are laying the foundations of the future, Western, life, as well as following-upon the same Journey that we all have travelled: the Way of the duality within the human psyche and in the world as a whole.

As has been said, Taoist wisdom is concerned with the balance of these opposites and, given that we have now turned into the opposite direction from where we were, it is not surprising that the movement we now make is an example of such contrasts, as *yin* and *yang*, empty and solid, left and right, are held in perfect harmony.

The weighted, left leg is solid (*yang*) and its energy links through to the right, outstretched *yang* arm. The right, dropped, empty leg is *yin* and relates through to the relaxed left, *yin* arm. Their central hub is the *tan t'ien*, the cauldron of *Ch'i* power, for the *yin* and *yang* energies which stream through the limbs, cross and meet there. The central vertical line in the body is clearly indicated and the whole stance expresses the meaning of the words "T'ai Chi Ch'üan" – the Supreme Ultimate Use of Energy. Nothing is wasted, nothing is fragmented, and the whole of the body, centred and still, gives an impression of energy held in suspension, as well as equilibrium.

Technically, this movement is known as the "Single Whip", but, due to the shape made by the right hand, it is often referred to as the "Bird's Beak". It is also the most repeated of all the movements and, in this Allegory, will always 'sum-up' and, thereby, define the inner development that occurred during the preceding movements. This first Bird's Beak thus depicts the renewal of the human spirit as it emerges out of conflict, since, to the Chinese, every opportunity that life gives of crisis or contention offers the opportunity to rise up again, clearer in mind and stronger in spirit. And so the 'bird' of the movement is synonymous with the one most renowned for its renewal, the Phoenix, the mythical bird of creation which, regarded as the most honourable among the feathered tribe, has symbolised re-birth and a spiritual uprising out of the ashes of despair for many centuries and throughout many cultures.

The much-loved Chinese poet, *Tu Fu* (AD 712-770), was only a child when he first heard of the phoenix, or the Bird of Inspiration, the creature, par excellence, of the Yang, the creative[1] and, later choosing it as his symbol, it is clear that some of its extensive meaning was important to him at an early age, since his first attempt at a poem went like this:

"Now I am six
I feel very strong
And open my mouth
With a Phoenix Song!" [2]

The young child in our Journey also is gaining in strength and this first Bird's Beak marks the first significant turning point in its spiritual growth. Moving away in frustration from the 'closed door' and turning into the opposite direction has revealed a strong reaction which will have long-term psychological repercussions. Finding itself in a difficult situation and retreating from the conflict has introduced the process of rationalisation and this has resulted in the uncomfortable sensations of self-consciousness - for the child now has become aware of its behaviour in terms of how it thinks it looks to others. Acutely sensing others' appraising eyes, she or he has begun to realise how significant it feels when on the receiving end of approval or disapproval, praise or blame, and this brings changes in the functions of the nerves in relation to the brain and thus in behaviour. Anxiety arises, together with inhibition, shame is introduced and then guilt, and these combine to create a sense of inadequacy. The child becomes more circumspect, more restrained, more cautious and, since it now seems necessary to avoid adverse comment, psychological self-defence is employed.

A different kind of awareness is also present, however, an awareness of 'how things really are'. It is the opposite of self-consciousness and has nothing to do with how the child imagines it is viewed by others. It is non-judgemental and is the sense we have of ourselves as we know ourselves to be in essence, the self that lies below the surface, beneath the interference of society's conditioning and ego's self-protectiveness. It is self-awareness at its purest, and, however diffuse it may be at this early age, it is the counter-balancing factor in the psyche, for if the child were predominantly self-conscious, there would be mainly defensive, reflex action in its behaviour, with very few of those vitally important, joyous and spontaneous responses which arise from its essence. Self-awareness is, therefore, the blessing which forms the other half of our dualistic nature for, beneath the layers of desire for approval and fear of reprimand, we do know what is actually taking place.

With great clarity of outline, this first Bird's Beak of the Phoenix Stance thus depicts this new duality in the child's life: self-consciousness and the uncomfortable ego on the one, closed hand; truth inherent in self-awareness on the other, open hand. Significantly, however, head, heart, and centre are turned towards the hand that is open, for the inner spirit knows full-well that which it seeks.

5 STEP UP AND RAISE HANDS

*The image-maker, and the blending of
self-consciousness and self-awareness*

Carl Gustav Jung, one of the world's great explorers of the human mind, used the word 'individuation' to describe the process whereby the true self could be realised and the individual made whole. His life was dedicated to the study of the various layers of conscious and unconscious responses and his deepest belief was that the fulfilment of the true self, with its vitality, its joys, its great powers of intuitive wisdom, was the most important goal in life.

He also perceived that, whilst such 'individuation' derives from the process of unifying the unconscious and conscious forces, the ego thrives only in consciousness and that, as: *"... the self comprises infinitely more than a mere ego..."* his deep concern was because: *"...again and again I note that the individuation process is confused with the coming of the ego into consciousness and that the ego is in consequence identified with the self... Individuation is then nothing but ego-centredness..."* [1] Moreover, since ego resists so much of the, sometimes, 'uncomfortable' information which stems from the deeper realms, such denial of our inner truths furthers psychological fragmentation and encourages a self-protective belief in ego omniscience, whilst this, in turn, becomes the problem in the human condition which relentlessly disturbs the smooth-running of the mind. Thus, from a very early age we identify with the responses made by the self-protective ego, rather than with those of the true self, because the ego's demands are so clear-cut and easily identified. They are also satisfyingly-emotional and, as a result, we believe that the ego is the essence of the whole being, rather than just the centre of consciousness, whilst, at the same time, such ego-centredness separates us from our intuitive, inner 'knowing', as well as from other people – and causes much conflict and suffering.

So the child in our Allegory now begins to identify itself with its likes and dislikes to such a degree that it believes that it is the sum-total of these opposites, whilst the areas which govern the underlying responses become less significant, for they neither gain enough attention from others, nor give the child sufficient clarity of definition concerning itself. Spontaneous insights – and, for those children who have it, the invaluable gift of extra-sensory perception – are sometimes frowned-upon, laughed at or brushed aside and, when thus demeaned, they frequently are replaced in the child's mind by the "image-maker".

The image-maker is the result of self-consciousness and its accompanying lack of self-confidence, and is the product of the degree of acceptance or rejection by those people with whom the child is in contact. The image-maker then forms a mental picture of how 'good' or 'bad' children behave and then reasons that: "I need to behave like a good child should, if I'm to stay out of trouble, even if I don't think or feel like one". Such dichotomy then produces the opposite result from that desired, as well as an even stronger ego-defence mechanism in the psyche.

Further – and severe – psychological damage can also occur due to the number of 'negatives' which the young child now receives as a result of his or her ability to move around independently, for our houses hold many things that can be broken or cause harm; situations arise for which society demands specific behaviour, and the world outside holds many (sometimes genuine) dangers. So many 'don'ts' then ensue (maybe twenty given for every half-dozen needed) that the child begins to feel inadequate, clumsy and sometimes unloved, and this is a shock with far-reaching implications, since the baby and very-young child hardly received a single 'don't' in its little life and felt very-much loved indeed! So, the child then feels 'wrong' and confused, whilst the self-conscious parent, well-trained in the art of the image-maker and of what others might think, begins monitoring the child's thoughts and actions until its developing ego becomes so bruised and shaken that it sometimes has difficulty in locating any true sense of self. The Tiger's Kitten then emerges more fully (and starts sharpening its claws on the best furniture) and the young child, no longer vulnerable and trusting, slowly forms a self-protective ego-shell as she or he grows more alert to psychological warnings and loses that haunting innocence we love so much.

Thus, from birth onwards, the sensory self-awareness of the baby flows into the larger self-consciousness of the growing child, and this, in turn, moves into the stream of the image-maker and the damaged ego. Fortunately, there still are many sufficiently-buoyant times of clarifying awareness and spontaneous expression, however, and the blending of these two facets of our development now is portrayed in the movement called "Step Up and Raise Hands".

When an open movement is made in the T'ai Chi Chüan, it is always followed by one that is closed. After the outstretched arms of the Phoenix Stance, we now draw our hands towards each other until they are almost in line - as if we were "folding in our wings" - and have one foot ahead of us.

Once more facing North, as we did at the beginning of the Journey, the fusion of left and right and of East and West takes place. With North representing the central point between the ancient spiritual wisdom of the East and the modern, ego-driven materialism of the West, we find that the true-self with its helpmate, self-awareness, interweaves with ego and its partner, self-consciousness. We also find that there is a residue of psychological balance in this, for, although the image-maker in the child's view predominates when with others, when left to itself or with people whom he or she can trust, the image is dropped and the child can respond in freedom, for, as the ancient Taoists knew:

> *"If the sign of life is in your face*
> *He who responds to it*
> *Will feel secure and fit..."* [2]

6 THE WHITE CRANE
SPREADS ITS WINGS

Wordless love from pure attention and trust; contact with higher spiritual sources, and further duality

As has already been indicated, a child's psychological formation is virtually complete between the ages of five to seven and, from then on, its responses will relate back to many of the basic themes which have been indelibly-stamped upon its psyche. The brain ceases its physical growth at approximately the same time and, although its billions of nerve cells will continue to develop and link up with each other, enabling innumerable cellular changes to occur, new skills to be learned and old ones reinforced, much of our adult psychological attitudes will relate to all that was imprinted upon those cells in those early years. Thus, they form the blueprint from which we can assess our later behaviour and at which, if we wish to pursue the path of self-knowledge, we need to look with some degree of penetration.

Just as a deep, silent river nourishes the earth, consistent loving care in those formative years will stabilise the child and enable it to mature more easily, share joys and interests and to respond to love with more love, and – even if emotional damage or physical deprivation have occurred in early life – later on-going, dependable love and security can alleviate some of the damage and, if the genetic inheritance predisposes it, can even transcend deep trauma.

Before such love can be experienced, however, something special has to occur through what the Buddhists call "pure attention", or "mindfulness". It is the attention we give when holding a new-born child; when watching-over a loved-one who is seriously ill, or – most rapturously - when newly in love, and it is pure because, at those times, both mind and heart are open and the being is extraordinarily alert. Thus, it is present at those times when we are deeply absorbed and the ego-self is absent.

Such pure attention is particularly significant in the spiritual quest, because it promotes the vital *connection* which creates clarity of mind and right-action and also awakens trust, that essential ingredient in any meaningful relationship, and because it can foster psychological healing. When fear and self-doubt enter into consciousness, however, and ego is present, pure attention becomes blurred. The images, anxieties and uncertainties concerning the ego's lack of confidence then interfere with the information being received, and this confuses direct perception and gives us the sometimes-less-kindly 'second thoughts' which negate the initially pure response. Such confusion also affects how others respond to us, for when the messages we give are muddled by ego's disturbances, the recipients of our words become confused in return.

Most young children's eyes are not yet overcast with permanent self-doubt or fear, however, since their inborn self-regulating optimism is not absent for long and, when this combines with rapt attention and unclouded observation, they connect with what they see in a very different way from how we do. Life is still fresh and, if we watch young children at play without interfering with their responses, we can see how effortlessly they unite with what they observe:

"Everywhere the spring birds are singing their new songs
and delicate flowers celebrate the soft air.
I explore each corner of the winding path,
making sure not to waste a single step." [1]

Our life-long conditioning and our swift habitual responses preclude perceiving with such focused attention and, on the whole, we are
unaware of the underlying connections in the world and of our relationship with our environment. We see an object or person subjectively,
asking: "how does that affect me?" or "what do I think of that?" and turn
our thoughts inwardly, rather than towards the observed, or heard. Yet,
as has been said, descriptions of the seamlessness of mystical experience
– and quantum physics and the microscope – reveal much of the mutu-
ally reinforcing and interacting facets of our environment and of how
apparently separate things and people actually are linked into a unified
whole. And a child, even though unaware of this on a conscious level,
can sense it and is less concerned with *how* it views relationships, than
with the relationships themselves: with their parents and siblings, with
friends, a much-loved book, pets, dolls and toys, with the room and bed
it sleeps in, with plants, trees, flowers, animals and birds, insects and
worms, stones and pebbles, water and earth – for, to a child, all things
have a life of their own and, in an almost-animistic way, the child feels
naturally 'at one' with them.

It is also during those tranquil times when a child is free from the
hindrances of self-consciousness and is most truly in relationship with
what is being observed, that imagination develops, contact is made with
the subconscious levels of response and joy in creativity occurs. And the
more the young mind can relate to new sights, sounds and sensations,
the more the awakening intelligence can flower. Love then flows from
the heart and inner promptings wander in peace, with the mind observing without another's (however well-intentioned) guidance.

Lao Tzu said: *"He who is open-eyed is open-minded, he who is open-
minded is open-hearted"* [2] and such openness of eye, mind and heart
enables the child (and ourselves), to be guided by one of the greatest of
fundamental urges, the spiritual hunger which draws us like a magnet

towards goodness or wholeness, regardless of our early conditioning. And, if we can remain alive to that, a tremendous bond can be forged between adult and child, and adults and each other.

The link between the Allegorical Journey and these qualities of pure attention, trust, unselfconscious response and love, now occurs with the next movement: "The White Crane Spreads its Wings". It is a beautiful movement, and the Crane, which represents many things in Chinese symbolism, is significant here, since 'protective motherhood', as well as 'joy', represent two of them.

The child is now of an age to feel protective towards, and to identify with others, especially if the other be small, vulnerable or damaged. She or he wishes to care for an ailing pet, mend a broken toy, comfort a crying friend, and this 'wanting to put things right again' marks an important shift in the child's consciousness, for it is part of the spiritual awakening which brings joy in relationships and indicates a clear transition from the purely sensory and emotional to the stirrings of a more spiritual nature.

The White Crane Spreads its Wings thus portrays this emergence of spirit and, physically, is the opposite of the movement preceding it. Having just 'folded in our wings', we now 'spread them out', as if in preparation for flight – and, symbolically, we *are* about to 'fly'. Before doing so, however, our hands form the shape of the symbol which already has had such significance in our Journey: that of the circle which depicts the wholeness and unity which the child experienced when close to the mother and also – in this case - the nests made by all birds from which, some day, they must fly. So now, having gathered together our powers for flight, one arm curves upwards in a bird's-wing shape  with its palm turned to the skies – as if in a salute to the heavens above - while the other hand moves down to face the protection of mother-earth.

The whole body links those two domains and this appearance of the White Crane indicates that the child is still relatively uncluttered; feels protective love for another; and portrays his or her *relationship* with all things - not least with those in the animal kingdom.

There is also much meaning in the placing of the hands, for, with the upturned hand linking us to the heavens, and the downward hand connecting us to earth, we are made aware that the greatest gifts we can give a child are spiritual joy and the stability of trust. For a child needs to know that we are not going to diminish or demean them, that we will be honest, that we will be there when needed, that we can see how life is for *them* – and that we like them as they are. If they have such trust in us, they will have trust in life and, even when life deals its inevitable blows, the growing child or later adult will not see those blows as a confirmation of how they feel about life as a whole, but as a variation on a theme. A truly *yin* and *yang* consciousness then can manifest in the psyche, forming the foundation for psychological balance in maturity, whilst our spiritual development is dependent upon this balance of opposites for, without it, there would be no altruistic reciprocity and we would be unable to experience the necessary integrity and compassion which enables us to care for others.

Such opportunities for trust may, so far, have been few, but the child's concepts of right and wrong (which the Taoists, in their non-judgemental way, simply refer to as balance and imbalance) have been developing from quite an early age.* Despite the many evasions of the adult world, the child recognises what is known as 'truth' and, whether that truth has been received from its earliest contact with others and then consolidated over time; whether it has been received through genetic inheritance, or whether it permeates all things at all times and is accessed intuitively, it is the fact of its existence that matters - and this the child senses.

Meanwhile, another process is being reinforced: that of the ability of the brain to classify. The child is taught to label what is presented to it and its brain then 'disposes' of the information into the appropriate cellular areas. It is also taught to admire the brain and its seemingly endless capacities, even though its classification and analytical abilities can sometimes preclude intuitive, wordless perception. Such 'labelling' is both important, as well as inevitable, however, and the thoughts and the words used by those thoughts are multiplying rapidly in the life of the growing child. This enriches the mind, but can lead to further psychological conflict. The child may be prompted by the stirrings of love and wishes to give and share without distinction, but is told (overtly or by more subtle means) to discriminate and love only those approved of by its elders. The child then learns that adult words, such as 'suitable' and 'unsuitable' (rather than 'good' and 'bad'), may appear well-intentioned, but can actually be unkind. Adult guidance as to acceptable social attitudes and emotional behaviour, and a double standard of ethics, are then added to those already-established dualities in the child's mind and, although she or he now is moved by love and curiosity to relate to people outside the immediate circle, these further dualities create emotional ambivalence. The child's sense of what is good, honest, and open is flowering, but is hampered by the repeated admonitions of elders - and even peer groups - to feel about certain things in a specific way or, even more confusingly, not at all. Then all the accumulating 'negatives' concerning its behaviour

*Child studies have indicated that a moral sense (as a 'moral molecule') can already exist in a child by the age of one, due to the trust that is engendered by the 'touching' between mother and child when breast-feeding.

so outweigh the far fewer 'positives', that deeper self-consciousness and even-more defensiveness becomes embedded in the psyche and duality becomes such an increasing factor in the daily life of the growing child that it often dare not heed, nor voice, its intuitive or spiritually-based insights. As a result, the attitudes of family and society towards people who are unacceptably 'different' – and towards competition, comparison, fame, prestige, property, ownership, success and status, money and ego-fulfilling rewards – are so intensely conditioning the child, that he or she rarely can relax into the joys of love. Nor was it any different when, more than two thousand years ago, Lao Tzu asked:

> "…Can you, with the simple stature
> of a child, breathing nature,
> Become, notwithstanding,
> A man?
> Can you continue befriending
> with no prejudice, no ban?...
> Can your learned head take leaven
> From the wisdom of your heart…?" [3]

The appearance of the White Crane thus symbolises the duality of the spiritual connection with heaven and the materialistic realms of earth. It connects the two spheres and gives us the opportunity to journey into both our heavenly as well as our earthly aspects and - by uniting these contrasts - fulfils the Way of the Tao. Movement towards and movement away, confusion and clarity, love and joy – all must be entered into. But, the lesson of The White Crane is, primarily, that of joy, as pure, wordless attention promotes trust, which, in turn, generates love. True relationship is impossible without it. It also teaches us that, despite all pain and suffering, the spirit *can* soar with the White Crane to the uppermost heavens, before swooping down to earth again as swiftly as it rose.

7 Brush Knee and Twist Step

A firm Bear Step* in the new direction and clarity of action through co-ordination of body, mind and spirit

One of the many legends associated with the T'ai Chi Ch'üan tells of a famous Chinese physician, *Hua Tuo*, who was known as "The Father of Chinese Medicine". He lived around 136-208 AD and, during that time, devised and taught various health-promoting exercises called *wu-qin-xi*, which were based on the postures and movements of five creatures: the crane, bear, tiger, deer and monkey. Each movement was said to be beneficial for specific ailments, and all were later incorporated into the health-giving T'ai Chi Ch'üan.[1]

Following on from the flight of the White Crane, the first of the five creatures mentioned above (the movement of which helps facilitate breathing through the stretching of the arms[2]), we now come down to earth again and take a firm, wide and powerful step which closely resembles that of the bear and which takes us, equally firmly, straight into the Western world.

As mentioned earlier, the West is symbolic of the conditioned patterns of thought and of the more physical and materialistic aspects of human nature. Our Journey thus has us facing that direction now (and for many movements to come) since, inevitably, much of the daily life of the growing child is taken-up with the deep reinforcement of the mental conditioning which occurs at home and in school; with physical games and growth in the playground and with the many emotional reactions which, though frequently linked to those experienced in earlier years, are becoming far more complex.

How this complexity is dealt-with is now portrayed by the upper hand which clearly depicts the child's self-regulating ability and ego's swift capacity to forget its own 'shortcomings', for, it cuts-down in front of the

---

*In China, some 'swinging arm' exercises are known as the 'Bear' movements, but this is the author's choice for this movement

body and thereby slices-through any possible anxiety or self-doubt. The *tan t'ien* then leads the body and both hands to the right before, simultaneously, all four limbs move in co-ordinated harmony as a firm, forward step is taken; the lower hand gives a strong "brush" from one side of the body to the other (as if continuing the sense of "brushing aside" any misgivings) and the other hand moves forward. And - as with any healthy, energetic child - there is much power in the movement, for the forward, energy-filled *yang* leg is balanced by the equally-forward, equally energy-filled opposite, *yang* arm, whilst –

as in the Phoenix Stance – health is promoted throughout the body as the cross-wise energies meet at the central axis of the *tan t'ien*. Total physical strength and balance thus result from the movement.

It is entitled: "Brush Knee and Twist Step", and indicates that an innate degree of strong physical and mental co-ordination can occur when a child – any child – applies that pure and focused attention which was described in the previous chapter, and of how clarity can result from any unfolding of the spiritual nature through contact with the White Crane. Moreover, as it is the *tan t'ien* which is leading the movements – first swinging right and then left in the way a bear slowly swings into action – it is clear that, at those joyous times of true physical and mental co-ordination, the child is well-centred and in accord with the pivot of the Tao.

If this were not enough, the movement also illustrates a new sense of psychological freedom as the brain produces the mental images which are necessary for the processes of clear and concise thought. This combination of clear mind and active body is then so exhilarating that it produces a great need for independence and change, and the degree to which the child has 'flown away' from the circle of the mother and her immediate protection becomes apparent.

The Bear Step is, therefore, immensely powerful, and the child's positive progress, and the capacity to take a step forward independently and without fear, is indicated by its balance, openness and movement ahead. More than that, however, the child is experiencing the clarity and inner strength which is motivated by one of the strongest of forces - that of the life-force which dictates that all growth should fulfil its greatest potential.

8 Play the P'i P'a: Strum the Lute

*Stepping aside for relaxation, merriment, music
and play, and the music of the spheres*

As has been said, *yang* and *yin* are as much in evidence within the framework of the T'ai Chi's physical movements, as they are in life's ever-changing, but consistent patterns. *Yang* is generated by motion and *yin* by rest, and these two modes of activity and passivity are the polarities which, through the natural cycles of life, underlie all growth and change. As the movement of the Brush Knee and Twist Step was essentially strong and *yang*, generating the energy needed for the child to move forward and make progress, so its opposite is experienced now as the child has that most necessary fallow-time of rest. 'Rest', however, does not only mean relaxing into conversation after school or going onto a computer for entertainment or getting a good night's sleep, it means psychological rest and that means physical 'play' – having fun and ball-games and making merry, especially in a garden or a park, on the sand or in water, for in these places there are far fewer 'things' to be damaged, far fewer 'negatives' to restrict and restrain and, most importantly, the mind can 'rest' as well, for being outside sets us free. It can also mean making music and so we now choose the latter, and 'step aside' and "Play the *P'i p'a*" [pron. *pee-baa*], an ancient, sweet-sounding Chinese musical instrument, and remind our adult selves that we, too, need those precious times of relaxation and play.

The Chinese word *p'i p'a* translates as 'balloon guitar', but, as it strongly resembles the lute (the word 'lute' having evolved from the Egyptian '*oud*', to the Spanish '*el oud*', to the '*lute*' of today), we choose to "Strum the Lute" now.

Historically-interesting, because it had to be made of the wood of the Chinese *dryandra* tree, "… *the only tree on which the Phoenix, that bird of happy augury, would alight*" (thereby making it of happy augury for us), to the Chinese the lute is the most revered of musical instruments, credited with the Eight Qualities of: happiness, sweetness, elegance, subtlety, sadness, softness, resonance, and strength[1], thus having the potential to fulfil all possible moods. And, since: *"… music has power to ease tension within the heart and to loosen the grip of obscure emotions"*, Emperors and Rulers encouraged this natural response to music, and elevated and regulated it to such a degree that music was regarded as both serious and holy, as well as *"designed to purify the feelings…"*[2]

Soothing the spirit, allowing time to pass without feeling that we should be engaged upon some 'useful occupation', we can benefit from its many virtues and use music as an antidote to the restless, anxiety-filled world we inhabit, and - if we listen with pure attention – we can also be released from the ego. Moreover, if we are highly-blessed in our hearing, we can alight upon something else, something which is quite profound: the chords, harmonics and rhythms which are known as the music of the spheres, the singing of the stars and the music of the currents of the earth, all of which – most delicately – are conveyed by the 'mathematics of the universe' and which are clarified for us when we perceive how music – and the lute - are further regarded in China.

To the Chinese mind, music is governed by the Laws of the Universe and, in its purest form, conveys an image of the relationship between the influences and forces of heaven and earth. For example, the five notes of the pentatonic scale which we consider in the West to be the most characteristic sound in Chinese music (and which, delightfully, can be heard if we use only the black keys on a piano), originally were associated with the five major planets of the heavens: Mercury, Venus, Mars, Jupiter, and Saturn, whilst these, in turn, were linked with the five elements (or activities) of: wood, fire, earth, metal, and water. These five notes also related to the colours of blue, red, yellow, white and black, and to the points of the compass: East, South, Centre, West, and North, respectively, whilst the Chinese twelve-note system was linked to the twelve months of the year, the twelve hours of the Chinese calculations of time, and the twelve allegorical animals of the twelve signs of the zodiac. Thus, the rat, buffalo, tiger, hare (or cat), the dragon, snake, horse, goat and monkey, the rooster, dog and pig, all gave meaning to universal harmonics. If we then add to all this, the fact that the wood of the lute: *"…was soaked in pure water for 72 days in order to correspond with the 72 divisions of the solar terms of the year. The length represented the 361 degrees of the circle made by the sun in its course round the earth. Its upper end was eight inches wide to agree with the Eight Annual Festivals. The lower end was four inches wide to conform with the Four Seasons. It was two inches deep to connote the two divisions of the Mundane Egg. There were 12 primary notes, male and female, or positive and negative alternatively, but some of them were lost. It originally had five strings to represent the Five Elements…"* [3] we can understand why the lute was considered such a remarkable instrument and why, for centuries, the Chinese Office of Music was closely associated with the Office of Weights and Measures!

A deep respect for, and a profound understanding of the mathematics of the universe was, therefore, of the highest importance to Chinese composers, musicians and makers of musical instruments and, due to the strong spiritual influence which music can exert over people, a proficient and high degree of the knowledge of harmony was considered an essential component of a cultural education. But, there was more. In order to understand the fundamental Laws of the Universe (and to what extent music was governed by them), a student of harmony was obliged to learn that certain instruments should never be played during the "Six Adverse Occasions", which were: the times of intense cold, great heat, high wind, heavy rain, loud thunder, or during a snowstorm. There were also "Seven Unfavourable Conditions" for the playing of music: when within the sound of mourning or of other music; when occupied with prosaic affairs; if the body and the clothing were unclean; without burning incense; and in the absence of an intelligent listener![4] Thus, the purest sounds of music were those which evoked the influences of heaven and earth and, as the Chinese character for 'music' shares the same graphic symbol as the word for 'serenity', it is clear why an inspiring piece of music, well-played and in accordance with Universal Laws, allows the body to rest from anxious activity and the spirit to align-itself to the heavenly influences.

So, now we step-aside and Strum the Lute and listen to music of universal harmony and can experience that rare gift, that of being able to 'lose ourselves' in the same way as a child can when in that most precious state: that of being 'lost in play'.

> *"Alone I am sitting under close bamboos,*
> *Playing on my lute, singing without words.*
> *Who can hear me in this thicket?...*
> *Bright and friendly comes the moon."* [5]

9 Three Brush Knee and Twist Steps

The Three Treasures of Ching: The Spirit of Form and Body;
Ch'i: The Spirit of Breath,
and Shên: The Spirit of Heart and Mind

The child now moves ahead with an abundance of energy as three more powerful, bear-like Brush Knee and Twist Steps occur. The physical movement is, overall, the same as in the previous Bear Step, as is the balance derived from performing the movement, but there is an addition now - and it is an important one - for, after each forward step, we then shift back, change direction, shift into it and – only then – return to moving forwards again. And this shift and change is significant because, although the child *is* moving ahead and these three steps indicate (however unlikely this may appear to others) that developments such as inner discipline, strength of character and endurance are emerging, the progress made is not straight-forward: there are always the many side-turnings of distraction and interruption, as well as life's own changes of pattern and direction. So these steps indicate that rarely is there visible, tangible or straight-forward progress, either in our own lives or in the growth of a child, and that, by shifting back and turning into a different direction, as well as moving on, we can learn how to flow *with* events (all the by-ways, which can sometimes be a guide to a direction of later importance), as well as how to move forwards with strength.

Another feature of these Bear Steps is their repetitiveness. Occurring three times over, their power is vastly-apparent to both onlooker and performer, as is the physical build-up of energy which results from such repetition. And, it is energy which is the key word here, for, almost more than anything, energy is what we associate with a child. Before we dwell-upon its significance in relation to this, however, we need to understand how it relates to us in the West, as well as to the Chinese mind.

In the West, we tend to look upon energy from various perspectives and, initially, somewhat subjectively. We say we either 'have' energy or not, and review the energy of our life-style according to our food-intake, exercise, sleep, mental attitudes, stimuli and emotional state, thereby regarding our energy as being the product of something we have or have not done or experienced. If this is not enough to explain our bursts of energy, or lack of it, we become a little more objective and look at the weather, the seasonal changes and cycles, or our (sometimes polluted) environment. More impersonally still, we might ponder upon the link between energy and a seed growing into a plant, or a child into an adult. We may recall the energy of water in tidal waves, in wind, electricity, fire and volcanoes, in landslides, earthquakes, comets and falling stars. Such thoughts then might lead us to dwell upon the pulses or energies which throb through the whole of our known existence and which influence not only the earth on which we live and the motion of the other planets, but everything upon which we have been pondering. If we then connect all that 'outer' activity with the inner beat of our heart and the pulses throbbing through our veins, and link all those 'external' energies with those of our thoughts and the activity in the central nervous system, we then might recognise the connection between the universal energies and the energies of the mind and spirit which move us to action. And we might also see that 'energy' is neither subjective nor objective, but is 'just there'. We may divide it into separate categories and give it specific labels, naming 'each' of our 'own' energies in accordance with the areas in which it manifests: mental, physical, sexual, emotional, nervous, or spiritual, but energy itself cannot be contained or made separate. It is everywhere, moving in abundance throughout the universe and our-selves as part of that universe and, although, of course, we do receive energy from good food and sleep, relaxation and exercise - and the quality of our thoughts - we also hinder its pathway through the body according to the degree with which we perceive ourselves as contained, separate and lacking in contact with others and the universe around us.

The Chinese also variously categorise and personalise energy, but they stress a fundamental difference, perceiving three main catego-ries from a predominantly spiritual viewpoint. Thus, there are Three

Spiritual Energies which are known as the Three Treasures of: *Ching*, *Ch'i*, and *Shên* and, although, of course, they manifest physically, they are basically spiritual and have great meaning, each of them, through their essence, action, and spiritual inter-action, contributing towards the fulfilment of the Laws which govern our universe and, therefore, the Way of the Tao.

The Way of the Tao means the Way of Life, and the Chinese ideograph for Tao uses two radicals or characters to convey a journey through the use of a Leader (the Universal Laws of Nature) and the Feet (which allow us to move forward), the two together indicating intelligent movement, as well as of a pupil following a master.[1]

The Tao is thus both the all-pervading principle of the whole of the universe, as well as the myriad things in Nature which follow that principle's leadership and fulfil its purpose. Energy is still a key word here, however, for it is energy which is a fundamental requisite for the fulfilment of the Universal Laws, whether it furthers the course of the stars, the tides in the oceans, the passage of the winds, or the creation, changes and growth of all life on earth. Moreover, the energies which empower these aspects of Nature are the same as those which enable us (as just a few of the myriad creatures) to breathe and feel and make love, to think, and to aspire towards a more spiritual dimension. And if we are able to sense and perceive the significance of that, we are nearer to understanding the depth of the Chinese concept of the Three Treasures and of how they relate to us – and to the child.

Our Journey now has the child nearing adolescence and, with the 'different kinds' of energy crystallising into a tremendous need for movement, we use the first of these Bear Steps to symbolise the first of the Three Treasures: *Ching*.

Ching is the first because it creates the unique and specific shape and form which is us, the arrangement of our appearance and the manner of our particular presentation. Physically, it is flesh and blood, hormonal activity, all the essential fluids, enzymes and neuro-transmitters, the D.N.A. and the generative essence of the energy which creates a child in the first place. Manifesting in powerful urges, a child who is sensuous, a jealous or resentful child, a warm-bodied or physically-affectionate child, a deeply male or very feminine child, or one with strongly maternal or paternal instincts, all are experiencing and expressing the energy of *Ching*.

In its cosmic or spiritual dimension, *Ching* is "The Spirit of Form and Body". It moves us to seek unity in friendship and partnership, and provides the vitality which enables us to obey our more 'positive' promptings which, when acted upon, give such a sense of buoyancy and joy. When, however, our 'movement-towards' or warmth is rejected, repressed or unrequited, when our affection is unexpressed (or we are ambivalent), the spirit becomes depressed and such 'negative' *Ching* can be felt as a sickness in the stomach, as a weight in the chest or a constriction in the throat. When emotionally-threatened, we experience discomfort in the solar plexus, our legs weaken, our hands sweat, and the mouth goes dry. Conversely, when moved by love or gratitude, its presence is felt by warmth and 'expansion' in the heart region, by an openness of being and by an arousal of the body, and its duality is indicated by the sensations of love and lust, jealousy and trust, which we all know so well.

But, how do such energies and urges link with the fulfilment of a Universal Law? The Chinese never viewed life on earth as functioning through laws which were separate from those governing the heavens and so they equate the intercourse of heaven and earth with that between the opposite sexes, whether human or otherwise, saying: *"Heaven and earth come together, and all things take shape and find form. Male and female mix their seed, and all creatures take shape and are born"* [2] The male of the species (as the *yang* element) and the female (as the *yin*), thus are as indispensable to each other if creation is to take place, as is the union of heaven (*yang*) and earth (*yin*), since it is through the heat of the *yang* sun and the influences of the *yin* moon, as well as wind and water, that life exists on earth. It is therefore due to the energy of *Ching*, as both Nature's sexual essence and the universal, invisible generative force, that such union occurs and creation results – and one of Nature's Universal Laws is fulfilled.

Now the child takes a deep breath, and *Ch'i* – the second of the Three Treasures – fills its lungs with one of life's great miracles: the breath of life itself. To the Chinese, there is more to it than that, however, since the energy which fills the lungs is the same energy that billows out the clouds. When the child shouts, the energy used is from the same source as that which makes a winter-wind blast through an open door. When the child cries with vexation at not being allowed to go out in bad weather, the tears have the same *Ch'i* as the rain which kept the child indoors in the first place, and when the child swallows in anticipation of joy, *Ch'i* in the saliva is as the *Ch'i* in the dew on the petal of a rose. The plaintive child who sighs has the same *Ch'i* essence as that which moves the wind to softly sough through the aftermath of rain, whilst the merry child who laughs and sings (and talks a lot!) uses the same energy of *Ch'i* as does the breeze which rustles through and makes to dance a grove of young bamboos. The independent but friendly child, the child who likes to help others (but does not get involved), the easy-going and adaptable child – and the child who is content to be alone – all are moving through life with an inner air of quiet certitude and calm which resembles the soft, yet still crisp air of a fresh, spring day. And the children who sneeze and snuffle and weep and wail and snore and snort and whine and moan, all are *Ch'i*-filled children, too (albeit *Ch'i* in its more 'impure' form!).

The essence of *Ch'i* does not only work on the visible, physical levels of vapour, steam, mist or breath, however, nor as the activator of vital functions through bodily cells and tissues. It has its cosmic form. When the mind and emotions are serene, it becomes *Ming* or "bright spirit", and then the child is high-spirited and gay, alive with laughter and skipping with fun, swift in movement and light of foot. And when we walk by a *Ch'i*-filled stream through air that is fresh and pure, or swim in a lake that is crystal-clean, thereby moving with the winds of heaven and flowing with the waters of the earth, we absorb pure *Ch'i* into ourselves and become as "bright spirits", also.

Ch'i is the second of the Three Treasures because, although it is the first breath of life, it arrives after conception, and also because, in Taoist meditation practices, *Ching* is the source of *Ch'i* and can be transformed into it. It is of particular significance to ourselves when adult, however, because the more we practise T'ai Chi (or yoga or other exercises which incorporate breathing techniques), the more we relax, constrictions are unblocked and its energy is released. *Ch'i* then can be sensitively experienced as an electric, prickling or magnetic sensation as our hands tingle with it; different parts of the body are warmed by it, and we become aware of this vital energy more acutely than we could have imagined. Thus, we can experience it when we have mastered the breaths of the T'ai Chi (or other techniques) and can yield more fully to the flow of life in and around us.

Deeply breathing in (*yin*) and out (*yang*), whilst in harmony with each *yin* and *yang* movement, we experience this invigorating vital spirit of Nature's manifestations, and are enriched by the sheer joy of it, not least when practising it outside, in the early morning, when the *Ch'i* energy in the trees, plants and grass is at its highest. Describing its cosmic form, John Blofeld wrote that, whilst its vehicle in man is breath, the real nature of *Ch'i* is cosmic vitality, and that it flows in freedom through sky and earth, but we restrict its passage in our own body by incorrect breathing, by smoking and by the intake of pollutants in the air which not only enter our body through the nostrils, but through the pores of the skin. Mental anxieties and emotional constraints also inhibit its natural circulation through what are known as the "dragon veins" of the psychic channels, which have long been recognised by yoga adepts but are "... *invisible to the most powerful microscope, although their existence has now been firmly established even in the West by the science of acupuncture...*". He also said that: "...*unlike ching, it cannot be frittered away because, even in its coarse form, it is not one's own property but a boon freely showered upon all...*".[3] Thus *Ch'i* flows freely throughout our universe and freely – if we do not block it - through ourselves as well.

As has been indicated, however, *Ch'i* has its duality. When impure (and although not as heavy as *Ching*), the body can feel as lethargic and unresponsive as the air on a humid and polluted summer's day, the result, for example, of attempting to force life into different directions, or through the hardening of our heart, or because we insist that things should be other than they are. We then create our own blockages and by not flowing with life's "by-ways", we lose our serenity – and our body responds accordingly. Then the *Ch'i* of life, which is stored in the liver (i.e. in that which sustains life) but manifests in the lungs, has to find its way through our body's meridians, either sluggishly or by bypassing blockages as best it may, whilst asthma, lung congestions, respiratory tract disturbances and skin irritations indicate how blocked can be its passage throughout the pathways. And why do we so insist that things should be different from how they are, and why do we try to force things so? asked Lao Tzu, since:

> *"Nature does not have to insist,*
> *Can blow for only half a morning,*
> *Rain for only half a day,*
> *And what are these winds and these rains but natural?*
> *If nature does not have to insist,*
> *Why should man...?"* [4]

Duality clearly is present also through *Chï's* opposites of 'in' and 'out', even to the point of new life occurring on its first in-take at birth, and death on its final exhalation and, since no movement would be possible without "The Spirit of Breath", *Chï's* existence fulfils another of the Universal Laws.

We then come to the third of the Three Treasures, that of the energy of *Shên* (or *shin*). On the physical level, it acts through the processes of thought and is the vitality which runs through the central nervous system, thereby connecting the heart's emotions with the mind. A child with a *Shên*-dominating energy is a serious child, a child who reads a lot and is stimulated by ideas – a cerebral or imaginative child. Or the child may be very sensitive, perceptive or psychic, be wise and compassionate of heart, idealistically 'high-minded' or more spiritual than most. A *Shên*-dominated child is also the child who is nervous, a worrier, hyper-sensitive and highly-strung, a child who retreats from life and desires to be alone from necessity, rather than from any contentment such solitude may bring.

Shên thus has its opposites. As adults, we can recognise the existence of a 'negative' *Shên* by the palpitations caused by nervous stress, by the trembling from fear, by the tingling in the back of the neck when we are criticised or feel vulnerable, by headache and migraine (with their accompanying stomach ailments), by ulcers, imaginary pain and illness, and by nervous breakdowns. And we can know of its presence most frequently by the sensations of weakness in the body (especially in the legs), by frustration and even boredom.

"When _shin_ is _pure_," said Trevor Leggett, "_thoughts do not arise from selfishness or passion, and inspiration passes through it. When _impure_, it is distorted and dark: everything has to pass through filters of 'will this be good for me?', 'will this get me what I want?', 'how shall I look while I am doing it?', 'what shall I do if it does not come off?', 'how terrible that might be!' and so on_" - much of which the ego of the child in our Journey is now frequently considering. But, he continued : "_A pure shin is serene, not plagued by worries over what happened or what may happen. It is not that there is no planning. Shin does plan, but once the known facts have been considered and the plan made, it does not worry; nor is its plan deflected by fear or hope._" He qualified its 'purity', however, by saying: "_Shin is never absolutely pure any more than a body is ever absolutely healthy. What we call a healthy body is one which is seldom ill, and which when it becomes ill (from an accident, for example) recovers quickly. Similarly a pure shin is one which is very seldom dark or selfish, and which when it is on rare occasions clouded by such things, throws them off vigorously without much worry over them._"[5]

Shên, therefore, as the processes of thought and the heart's activities in relation to thought - is most closely related to ego and, if the thoughts are of the defensively-assertive kind or motivated by gain, _Shên_ is ego-bound and impure. However, if the restlessness of brain and nerves is stilled, and ego-activity is thereby reduced, _Shên_ emerges in its 'pure' or spiritual form and ego-induced thought gives way to a serene mind and a generous heart. On the simplest level, this would relate to those spiritual stirrings already-experienced by the growing child when wishing to share something precious or give away something much valued, whilst, on the highest level, _Shên_ would manifest as the spiritual energy in an adult who relinquishes all that is possessed and leads a selfless life, devoted to the well-being of others. Pure _Shên_ thereby contributes to the Universal Law of spiritual unfolding and fulfilment and to the selflessness of compassion.

All the manifestations of the Three Treasures are familiar to us because we all experience their energies interweaving through all parts of the body (albeit in differing degrees and at different times), but we become particularly conscious of them when they are intensified or predominantly localised. There also can be some special, magical moments when we are energised by all Three Treasures almost simultaneously as when, for example, we are inspired by profound beauty, by the sweet or unselfish action of another, by exquisite music, or by a passage in a book of pure wisdom, for then *Shên* is activated and "The Spirit of Heart and Mind" responds; we may gasp, because the beauty, or the action, is breath-taking, and thus take in *Ch'i*, "The Spirit of Breath", and we may also feel *Ching*, or "The Spirit of Form and Body", as the physical sensations of joy, release, gratitude and an increase in energy. Thus the spiritual manifestations of the combined Three Treasures can unify our often-fragmented psyche, integrate our psychological responses and deepen our spiritual nature, whilst – at the same time – physically-experiencing an uplifting buoyancy as if suffused with light, pure air and warmth.

A similar situation occurs when we see or hear something which disturbs or threatens us. A swift, sharp in-take of *Ch'i* can occur and, if the 'threat' is genuine as well as severe, *Shên*, as mental recognition of the danger, is activated as a necessity for our survival. Shên then combines with *Ch'i* as the vital breath, and together they galvanise *Ching* (which is linked to the adrenal glands) and all three energies are harnessed to deal with the danger. If the 'threat' is based on psychologically-imagined fears, however, the "darker" aspects of *Shên* emerge in mind and heart and promote the more-unpleasant physical sensations of *Ching* (mentioned above), as well as imaginary pains and illnesses and/or *Ch'i* constriction.

Some people are blessed with more energy than others, however, and, apart from those who are constitutionally energy-filled by inheritance, perhaps had fewer psychological traumas in early childhood. The Three Treasures then would be unhampered by too many blockages of emotional fear and self-defensive thought-patterns, and the person so-blessed can make valuable contributions to society. As very few escape early stress, however, we can be grateful, at least, for those rare occasions when the Three Treasures of *Ching, Ch'i,* and *Shên* combine in their purest forms, for then the body, breath, heart and mind can be tranquil; our actions can flow in harmony with the cosmic energies of the Tao, and the spiritual aspects of the Three Treasures can fulfil their ultimate and universal purpose.

The first of these three T'ai Chi Bear Steps, as *Ching,* thus now symbolises the child's sensual, gender-orientated, and fundamental responses. The second step conveys the child's intrinsic *Ch'i* energy; and the third, the Treasure of *Shên,* guides the mind and heart of the child towards mental and spiritual clarity. These steps then are seen as unifying and harmonising all our various energies as we flow and shift with rhythm and balance; as we synchronise our movements in harmony with the breath of life and as we yield to the *yin-yang* rhythms of the Tao. And, even though the child in our Journey might be unaware of the significance of its abundant energy and is unconscious of the meaning of the *yin* and *yang* of its existence, it not only is constantly experiencing such opposites, but - born out of the (however brief) union of male and female and filled with every aspect (however partial) of the Three Treasures - it carries within itself both the potential and the fulfilment of the inter-acting energies of all three of these Universal Laws.

> *"Life, when it came to be,*
> *Bore one, then two, then three*
> *Elements of things;*
> *And thus the three began*
> *- Heaven and earth and man –*
> *To balance happenings;…"* [6]

10 PLAY THE P'I P'A: STRUM THE LUTE

*Music as part of the universal order; its significance
as sacred sound, and as an antidote to suffering*

How wise – and fortunate – were the ancient Taoists! Walking with attentive awareness of their environment, watchful of the inner, as well as outer aspects of life, looking and listening with ease of mind and openness of heart and acutely conscious of the depth of meaning in all that they saw and experienced, they not only had the White Crane of the Immortals flying in and out of their lives, but they also made sure that a musical instrument was not far behind! Their perceptions were serious, their philosophy profound, but they also knew how to relax, to laugh, and: how to 'play the *p'i p'a*'.

The previous chapter indicated how each of us, when activated by pure *Ching, Ch'i,* and *Shên,* can contribute to the harmony of the Tao – and the responsibility implied thereby is serious indeed. But before that, we 'stepped aside' and relaxed with music and friends or strummed a lute with, perhaps, only the moon as recipient of our serenade. And this we do again now, for – after all the 'striving ahead' and 'moving forward with strength and clarity' – we need to relax and be merry again, laugh at how seriously we take life, accept the limitations of our perceptions, and mock a little at the self-importance with which we view the world. For it has been said of Taoism that *"no other religion has linked so closely art, mysticism, and laughter"* [1] and that, if we can laugh at ourselves, at life, and even at death - which, to the Taoist, enables our souls to return to the Source from whence they came – we are paying heed to one of the loveliest aspects of the Taoist philosophy: that of the wit and humour which so clearly comes through to us in a story from Chuang Tzu.

"There were three friends discussing life. One said: "Can men live together and know nothing of it? Work together and produce nothing? Can they fly around in space and forget to exist, world without end?" The three friends looked at each other and burst out laughing. They had no explanation. Thus they were better friends than before. Then one friend died. Confucius sent a disciple to help the other two chant his obsequies. The disciple found that one friend had composed a song, while the other played a lute. They sang:

> "Hey, Sung Hu!
> Where'd you go?
> Hey, Sung Hu!
> Where'd you go?
> You have gone
> Where you really were.
> And we are here —
> Damn it! We are here!"

Then the disciple of Confucius burst in on them and exclaimed: "May I inquire where you found this in the Rubrics for obsequies, this frivolous carolling in the presence of the departed?" The two friends looked at each other and laughed: "Poor fellow," they said, "he doesn't know the new liturgy!"[2]

Ruefully-contemplative – yet having lost a good friend – the two remaining friends could bemoan their own limited, earth-bound state with humour; strum a lute with a song of envy for their departed friend, and show the zealous Confucian disciple that a liturgy could not only be light and lyrical, but could indicate a different way of looking at death. The Three Treasures of pure *Ching, Ch'i* and *Shên* were in harmony as they contemplated the larger order in the universe and, undisturbed by fear of death or self-pity at their loss, had turned to music, to Taoist warmth and philosophical humour, instead of the traditional Confucian duties of mourning. They also wisely knew that: *"By fingering a lute a sage verified the harmony of his soul with Universal Order"*,[3] and so the two friends were able to step aside from their loss and play the *p'i p'a*, an instrument with a history of more than 2,000 years and one which - as has already been indicated - has the most delicate and enchanting of sounds.

Musical instruments convey many moods and, as with all things on earth, mankind has it that they follow the lines laid down by Nature. Their shape and size denote whether they are *yang* or *yin*, whilst their many sounds, each peculiar to itself, can be either male or female, or even both (as when, for example, evoking bird song which can embody *yang* clarity and power with poignant *yin* sweetness, delicacy and purity of tone). When, then, composers and musicians attempt to transpose and convey Nature's music into those instruments, they learn that – at its best - such sacred sound can send the un-distracted listener into a state of almost intoxicated bliss, or what, in Indian teachings, is called *"samadhi"*, where the ego-self of name, position, power or individuality dissolves in the world of spirit. Moreover, the degree of relationship between the musician, the instrument, the music being played, and the listener, also had great significance, for – whilst, in the Western world, the applause of the latter is the reward for the former - in the East, in order for an audience to convey that Nature's harmonies had been fully recognised, it was considered appropriate for the 'sounds of earth' to be followed by the 'silence of heaven'. Thus, not only was the tumult of a loud ovation not advocated, but the importance of such 'silence after sound' was a deeply-respected component in any performance. Equally, a pupil of music was taught that silence should also *precede* a performance, so that - out of stillness - a sound should arise and then another and then another, with each sound flowing into the next and the next until, ideally, both musician and listener were flowing with each note without the interference of wandering thought or intellectual analysis. Both were released from ego: the listener in that state of inner emptiness and stillness which connects to the seamlessness of Primary Reality and the performer offering the spiritual essence of her or his musical being. Individual problems and anxieties then were forgotten, and so was time, since each was immersed in the immediate awareness of the fluid sounds in the air around them. Then, when the sacred music ceased, the listener had no inclination to clap or shout, speak or move, fidget, get up or go away – or even for the performer to bow - for such silence, to the Eastern mind, was seen as the greatest of rewards, revealing, as it did, the depth of the sacred sound which had promoted it. Thus, the highest aim of music was to reveal the essence of the universe it reflected.

In ancient China, yet another important aspect of music related to complexity. Great technical skill was, of course, essential, but it was suggested that music which showed off dexterity, or inspired only intellectual recognition, should be avoided, as witness the cadenza, which was thought to have neither musical value nor even relevance, as it tended to give an impression of conveying an athletic performance, rather than one of emotional delicacy or sensitive virtuosity.[4]

This desire for simplicity thus now leads to another vital aspect of music: its importance in therapy, for music can act as a bridge to joy, enthralling the sometimes unreachable spirit of, for example, the disabled and/or mentally-disturbed recipient of its sounds. And, if this occurs, the one who is thus handicapped can be seen to respond with such an amazing intensity when even the most 'ordinary' music is heard, or if they can touch or play a musical instrument themselves, or if the music once had special meaning for them, that the visible joy and the awakening of the spirit that emerges can be deeply moving to the observer, as well as being of inestimable value in the spiritual, as well as psychological, healing process of the one so handicapped. Moreover, the inadequacy of verbal communication becomes apparent, since the wordless contact made between, say, the music-therapist or carer and the disabled person, or the parent and the handicapped child, gives far greater meaning to life for both of them than is available in their usual daily exchanges, and it is clear that - at those times - they not only are 'strumming the lute' together, but the chords, rhythms and harmonics of Nature are plucking at their heart-strings.

We in the West, however, (who appear to be more-judgementally Confucian than Taoist, as well as easily distracted), sometimes find it difficult to lose ourselves in music and, when conscious of this, feel we must 'concentrate' and try to 'be responsible' and 'do the right thing by the performer' in accordance with socially-prescribed guide-lines - and tend to clap and shout all the louder, because of it. And, although such concentrated effort and responsible concern is a requirement in the learning process generally, it can be a burden in the T'ai Chi situation, because the 'wanting to get it right' and the 'striving to please' both our inner mentors and our teachers, hinders the learning process and the student cannot relax sufficiently to let the body flow with ease. In China, however, they do not 'do' the T'ai Chi, or perform it, or even practise it in the Western, concentrated hard-work way. They 'play' it and, as a result, soon find it easier to be lighter in their being and softer in their movements, thereby revealing the balance between their internal tranquillity and external activity - a factor which is required in all the Chinese arts. Furthermore, the significance of thus 'playing' the movements is clarified, when we step aside from the noise and activity of daily life by 'playing' the T'ai Chi whenever and wherever we can, for, by regularly moving into the realms of silence, practitioners can become immersed in the rhythm of the movements, each one flowing into the next and the next, in the same way as a gifted musician and enraptured members of an audience can be encased in flowing sound. All participants then are 'lost in play' with no wish for approval or gain and the movements themselves allow the divine intent to manifest.

In our Journey, that most sensitive and difficult time of adolescence is, as yet, only on the horizon and the child still can relax and have fun with some of the innocence and joy experienced earlier, and - much to the amusement (or annoyance) of their elders - also can reveal a beautiful sense of irreverent humour, much as had the Two Taoist Friends.

Music, the crafts, singing - especially in a choir - reading and even writing (although the latter is more challenging, since mental writing skills have to be harnessed in tandem with creative intuition), all now form bridges between the psychological manoeuvring which results from the need to comply with adult reality, and the areas where the reality of the child's own truths can be accessed. And, if enjoyed with any depth in these early years, it will be in later life and at times of stress that such healing realms can arise through contact with the arts and Nature, philosophy, meditation and allied silent practices, and with the spiritual quest itself. For, all of these can restore sanity and inner truth and the all-important 'connectedness' with others, whilst giving us the greatest gifts which the harmony inherent in the universe can offer - the opportunity for the "tranquil repose" which:

> *"... dwells in quietude, speechless,*
> *Imperceptible in the cosmos,*
> *Watered by the eternal harmonies,*
> *Soaring with the lonely crane.*
> *It is like a gentle breeze in spring,*
> *Softly bellying the flowing robe;*
> *It is like the note of the bamboo flute,*
> *Whose sweetness we would fain make our own...."* [5]

11 Brush Knee and Twist Step

Further development from mental application and an important transition between childhood and adolescence

We now swing into the last of the Bear Steps in Part One. Again we step widely and roll deeply into the movement. Again the lower hand brushes away obstacles. Again we feel the power, strength and dynamism of the movement as the upper hand swoops forward with a strong, clean stroke. And, at all times – if advanced in our practise – we are poised, the head held high by the invisible silken thread which links us to the Northern Star, and with the nose kept in line with the navel, so that, by not anticipating any move with a turn of the head, we stay firmly rooted in the here and now of the movement we are making and the *tan t'ien* remains our leader. So, we keep the balance and synchronicity which form the T'ai Chi's bodily co-ordination and retain serenity by not anticipating what lies ahead.

During these early Bear Steps, however, the beginner frequently does turn his or her head before taking the next step – by looking first to see to where the body will move and only then following through with the *tan t'ien* and the hands - and this training in 'looking ahead', especially psychologically, starts very early in life, for it is part of society's need to try and control the future. But, wisdom teachings indicate that, although some planning is necessary in the mundane world (despite rarely turning out as anticipated), it can be a handicap in the spiritual realm, since anticipation can interfere with full awareness and expectation can distort reality. At this stage of the Journey, however, the child is aware that it is essential to plan for the future, and T'ai Chi practitioners who are still 'young' to Taoist wisdom teachings are only indicating that they, too, received the same conditioning.

Looking ahead - at new schools, her or his own 'potential', new friends and the possible loss of old ones, careers, the experience of sex, and the psychological shedding of the well-rooted identity of childhood

- there is much that is happening in the child's daily life. Examinations take a prominent place and, although they may not assess the child's true potential with accuracy, they do give opportunities for inner discipline and application which can stand the child in good stead later on – and they do make the child work. *"Serious interest is the beginning of capacity, and both are strengthened by application"*, said Krishnamurti,[1] and Chinese children are taught that water does not flow on until every indentation is filled and that a difference of a hair's breadth at the beginning of a journey can mean a deviation of a thousand miles at the end!* However, despite the portentousness of these wise maxims (or their equivalent), and the weight of the daily school-work with its accompanying groan of: "I've got to do my homework", there are many compensations. The child's special interests increase his or her motivation; opportunities for a wider range of activities and outlets present themselves and life becomes exciting, as well as complex and serious.

There also is a great advantage attached to this period of the child's life, since the child is not yet *actually* involved with what is appearing on the threshold and thus is comparatively free from the decision-making and responsibilities that lie ahead. This promotes some fine clarity of vision, and such wisdom-teachings as were mentioned above, are relatively easy to apply. Moreover, through seeing life from a broader perspective, this last Bear Step of forward growth marks a very special period of transition in the child's development. No longer a 'little' girl or boy, nor yet a developed adolescent, the child is in a unique position. Having learnt almost as much as will ever be required concerning social behaviour and not, as yet, enmeshed in the adolescent's emotional and physical upheaval, there are far fewer negatives and admonitions being administered and, although there are still times of 'childish' behaviour, those moments are regarded almost with affection as something soon to be lost forever. So, this stage of the child's life is often happier, brighter and more peaceful than during many of the earlier years - and for most of the years to come – whilst the child experiences more freedom and ease of spirit. Significantly, however, the pre-adolescent eyes which look upon the world can be remarkably sharp, and the results of those

*Meng-Tsu (Mencius), 372-289 B.C

moments of real insight and quality of perception can be invaluable to the educator, as well as giving great pleasure to both parent and child.

> *"Politics and argument,*
> *Greedy, money, vote,*
> *Govern, punish, parliament,*
> *Briefing, world-tour, note.*
> *Lying, speeches, microphones,*
> *Army, Cabinet,*
> *Secretaries, telephones,*
> *Money-pinching, debt."* [2]

wrote one twelve-year-old, awake to both Haiku poetry* and the political scene, and yet, anachronistic as it may seem, this interval of such 'adult' clarity of vision, whilst still in childhood, may well mark the last time the child really is a child, internally, ever again. Meanwhile, for us, whilst portraying this very significant period of transition with yet-another strong Brush Knee and Twist Step, we can enjoy a movement which is especially lovely to perform, since, in its calm and clear power, in its strength and simplicity, it symbolises so much that is both young and old, both innocent and all-seeing.

*In this case, seven syllables, then five

12 Fist Downwards; Twisted Step, Deflect Downwards, Strike and Punch

The Tiger's Mouth and the fully-developed ego in command

In later years, the child in our Journey might-well look back upon that lovely last Bear Step as: *"Knees bent, I would swing into the slow, measured 'square step', the powerful walk into battle!"* [1], since that most painful, delicate and difficult time of adolescence has arrived and all its physical imbalances, emotional upheavals and mental strains are causing intervals of war-like chaos and misery.

Now the serious interest mentioned earlier is essential for success at school, but is difficult to sustain. The Chinese injunction to flow like water and fill in every indentation before proceeding to the next is even more difficult (since the adolescent often feels more like a lump of wood than smooth, running water), whilst the maxim that a hair's breadth difference at the beginning of a journey would make such a huge difference at the end! - well, in psychological terms, the child feels that 'all that' was so long ago that they may-as-well give up - and the emerging, more-critical ego starts growling with a rumbling sense of injustice.

Another 'injustice' occurs when the child is told that all the disruptive influences of adolescence are consistent with normal human development and that he or she is 'just going through a phase', when, at this most exacting time, the child is expected to try and behave like a young adult, just as if 'the phase' were over. Moreover, even if there is a capacity for serious interest or a genuine desire to be responsible and mature, such endeavour is undermined by hormonal changes and the accompanying emotional see-sawing; by the profound adjustments needed to cope with their newly-experienced aggressions and hostilities; by the need to develop autonomy and a personal value system; by the shedding of the old identity and explorations of the new; by sexual inexperience or new intimacies, and by an inner need to maintain a sense of adequacy and competence. So, the demands that they should be different from how they *are* seem utterly ludicrous, and what appears to be such paradoxical mendaciousness on the part of adults about the so-called "golden hours of youth" is viewed as an anachronism at a time when so much anguish is being experienced.

Thus, for as long as an adolescent experiences difficulty with adults and needs to identify with like-minded members in a peer-group – for there is special unity between those who are sharing a battlefield – there will be a wish to defy authority. And yet, with an irony which is not unnoticed in our current society, we now are re-discovering (that which our ancestors knew) that parental authority can be accepted by a child when the reasons for it are lovingly and fully-explained; that a lack of boundaries can be seen by a child as parental neglect, and that if discipline is denied, the results can cause deep frustration and friction between adult and child. Moreover, if the type of 'war' that can now occur were not enough for Tiger to work on, children's swift perception that adult attempts to impose discipline are sometimes based on 'role-playing' authoritarianism or self-fulfilling egoism, can produce even-less respect for the adult and place more pressure on all concerned.

Despite this morass of suffering, however, there are compensations. Not, as in some communities, having painful initiation rites to symbolise the upheaval which adolescents experience when severing themselves from parental spheres of influence, they frequently can be eased through this poignant period by expressing their new individuality in the outlandish dress, language, slogans and mannerisms used within their peer group and by various methods of 'showing-off' to their chosen friends. Moreover, the friendships now made can last a lifetime, and the sense of being stretched intellectually can be exhilarating and rewarding, enabling the adolescent's discussions to be both exciting and interesting and marking a time when the growing teenager's questions can be of the highest import. Further involvement in extra-curricular activities also can be enjoyed and, if these include the martial arts, the latter can be helpful in handling aggression and in teaching respectful attitudes to the 'opponent', whilst, on an academic level, one school that introduced the T'ai Chi Ch'üan as an exercise, found that: *"The 25 minute sessions have increased the reading age of Year 7 pupils by an average of a year".** Whether well-placed in life or otherwise, however, the adolescent still suffers, and, by making such a tremendous effort to define her- or himself as an individual, may also be indicating that this is a last stand against all the years of perceived conformity to come.

So, the ever-increasing dilemma of the duality between what the adolescent is really thinking and what is expected by others with regard to behaviour and thought - together with the realisation that society's doctrines are often based on contradiction and hypocrisy – requires more urgent resolution. Now the father or father-figure becomes important since he represents the results of his own attempts at reconciling the 'outside world's' demands for success and conformity with those of the inner life – and the young adolescent needs to know how he coped with such problems. But, since such a role-modelling parent may also have received a multitude of similar psychological wounds and may still retain many of his own doubts and uncertainties, he may be as hard-put to resolve his own conflicts as is the young seeker, and rarely can offer more than the usual conventional, superficial responses to the child's burningly-important questions. If he could speak his own truth, however, and simply say that adults often know little better than their children and that, maybe, they can find an answer together, the child (and he) would be released from many of their burdens.

Sadly, the opposite so often occurs and the quarrelling (which can continue for several years), means that many of the 'negatives' from parents, older people, and teachers, return in abundance – and if counted, how many would there have been so far? At a (very) conservative estimate of three of the most needed 'negatives' given in a day, those, multiplied annually from around the ages of two to sixteen, become nearly sixteen thousand of the *necessary* admonitions in the child's young life. Not surprisingly, therefore, with the added weight of all the unnecessary rebukes

*Henbury School, Bristol, U.K. (2013)

already received, and those being given now ("Don't do that! Why can't you behave? Why did you..? Stop that! WHEN are you going to learn? If I've told you once, I've told you a hundred times... When will you grow up? Sometimes I wish you'd never been born! I don't approve of your doing that. Will you pay attention! You're impossible! No child of mine is going to... You're taking just after your... I'll never understand why you... Why can't you behave like..? Why don't you listen! You're too fat. You're too thin. I can't stand how you... Be quiet! SHUT UP!!!") - together with the cold, silent criticisms which are sometimes imposed - many children now do "shut up", internally, and, sometimes, forever.

"Will they ever forget their hurts and their sorrows" asked Krishnamurti, *"or will they gradually build for themselves escapes and resistances? To keep these hurts seems to be the nature of human beings and from this their actions become twisted. Can the human mind never be hurt or wounded? Not to be hurt is to be innocent. If you are not hurt you will naturally not hurt another. Is this possible? The culture in which we live does deeply wound the mind and heart. The noise and the pollution, the aggression and competition, the violence and the education – all these and more contribute to the agony. Yet we have to live in this world of brutality and resistance: we are the world and the world is us."* [2]

Each generation tries to find answers to those burning questions and many studies have been made of adolescent behaviour. For example, it has been discovered that, in the areas of purely chemical change, teenagers lose 30,000 connections per second in the so-called 'grey matter' of the brain and that their thinking is being 'pruned' and coated in a substance which 'speeds up the super highways'. The last area of the brain to develop is the frontal lobe, which is highly relevant in terms of human behaviour* whilst, in puberty, many impulses are guided by the

---

*The frontal lobe relates to the area of the "3rd Eye" of mystical teachings and thus to the awakening of empathy and compassion. When undeveloped, and in combination with a childhood lacking in love and trust and a genetic inheritance which contains the MAOA gene (known as the warrior gene), the result will be the sadistic killer or psychopath, who, without a conscience, is most 'useful' in times of war. A lack of frontal lobe development will also manifest in those who lack high cognitive skills; who cannot discriminate between right and wrong; in the domestic or national tyrant, and in many who wield power in high office.

hormonal levels, when the creative levels are high, but when maximum risk-taking takes place. This goes on until the mid-twenties, with the majority of people in prison being aged between 18 and 25 – a factor often due to the risks being taken. These statistics are borne out by other studies which show that 40% of 17-year-old males have had a car accident within the first six months of driving; that 1 in 3 road-death victims in the UK are under 25, making road accidents the single biggest cause of accidental deaths for young people in the U.K., and that it is 3 times more likely for an 18-year-old to have a road accident, compared with a 48-year old.[3]

Hopefully, such statistical information has promoted action which protects the welfare of all concerned, but, despite a deeper understanding of young people's problems and risk-taking propensities, it seems inevitable that the psychological hurt, the pain, the wounding and the resistance will continue for as long as the adolescent continues to receive such a multitude of unnecessary admonitions and for as long as adults continue to impose their own unnecessary limitations. For the criticisms which have been repeated since the child first started moving around independently; the image-maker in the psyche which controls the ego-responses of how she or he looks to others, and the psychological rejections which may even have started in the womb, have the most significance in terms of ego development. Such unsettling accumulations then remain as a powerful residue in the troubled adolescent mind and the child believes that, fundamentally, he or she is inadequate, unlovable, unwanted and unworthy, and the behavioural responses based on such anxieties and fears now predominate.

These responses fall mainly into the categories of: apathy and/or compliance in order to conform or please; angry or manipulative control over others, which can be both obvious and subtle; power through acquisition, sometimes to the point of theft; and/or the creation of an idealised self-image - all of which (according to circumstances) can manifest in just one person. But, whether any one of these self-protective mechanisms predominates, or whether they combine, they create a split in the human psyche and, in consequence, the ever-deepening schism between the true self and the self demanded by others brings deceit, which may be quickly suppressed; guilt, which may be rationalised; prevarication and contestation, which can become habitual, and varying degrees of paranoia. Such disruption and imbalance then produce severe fluctuations in energy and can also disturb the curiosity which had been such a tremendous force in the younger child, producing even further periods of anger, depression, inertia and apathy.

So, the very young child who was vulnerable, intuitive and deeply linked with the mother, grows into the older child who slowly loses contact with her or his dependable inner world. The desire to learn about life is still there; the excitement generated by new discoveries is not lost, and still there are the energies of the Three Treasures. As the adolescent consciously or unconsciously looks to an uncertain future, however, the spiritual aspects of *Ching, Ch'i*, and *Shên* are lessening and their more physical manifestations, especially in the emotional and sexual areas, are taking over. Moreover, to add to the difficulties, some quick-sands of forbidden territories are becoming increasingly attractive.

With these very significant changes in the adolescent's life, an equally significant change occurs in the T'ai Chi Ch'üan. Now the open, forward-moving hand of the last Brush Knee and Twist Step becomes its opposite – and turns into a fist. Now, the martial-art applications of the movements become apparent and the battle is clearly depicted. Now with a fist, we draw it down across our body, lift it (and the other hand) high above the head, turn our body in a wide-angled step, strike forcibly downwards with the side of the higher hand and, with the fist now lowered to the hip, take a long step forward. And then, as our weight slowly moves into the forward leg, we *punch*.

It often feels so good, this punch. Time and time again, pupils (especially women) say: "Gosh, that felt good!", or: "I feel as though I've wanted to do that all my life!", or (both men and women): "I feel so much better, now. I feel I'm all right again", indicating how few times they have been allowed to express their anger in safety, and how healing the *yang* movements of the T'ai Chi can be for those who have over-repressed their damaged ego, or become too compliant. Equally revealing in the self-knowledge quest is the fact that many pupils cannot make a fist at all, or – even-more significantly and sadly - turn the fist inwardly towards themselves. But, for the adolescent, the battle now beginning is not so soothing. Not because battling itself is new, since this clash of wills between the child and others – and between its inner and outer selves – has been going on since the child was small, but because now, in the shape of the fist, the fully-developed, dominant ego has arrived. Now

the Tiger's voice cries out with a loud "NO!" at all the "NOs" which have been levelled at it, at all the rejections, lack of understanding and acceptance, lack of trust and non-judgmental love. Now all the pent-up emotions, all the times of unshed tears and of those which were shed but condemned, burst forth with the loudest of loud cries. Now the adolescent becomes unbearable – to him- or herself, or as often to others. Yet, at this time of acute mental reorganisation and physical upheaval and when the most supreme bid for attention is ever made, there is often so little heed paid to the underlying reasons for such outpourings, that the child's inner sense of truth is pushed back and down into sub-conscious and unconscious layers, and the conscious mind twists and turns in an agony of self-doubt and torment. So the young teenager fights – physically, with a twisting body, strikes and punches - and/or psychologically, with sullen, moody resistance, criticism, angry words or silent withdrawal. Now, the "Tiger's Mouth", as symbolised by the fist, is in command and, being the title of this book, needs some explanation.

The Chinese written character for 'tiger' consists of the radical character *hu*, representing tiger stripes, plus the character *jen*, for 'man' - implying that the tiger can stand on its rear legs like a man – or that man is like a tiger. Moreover, in Chinese acupuncture, there is a highly-important meridian point called '*Hegu*', which means 'mouth' and which is near the web of skin between the thumb and the forefinger. It is so-named because the configuration of lines around this point (especially when the fingers are drawn in towards the palm) gives an impression of a mouth, and because the Taoists, who frequently used visual imagery to convey meaning, knew that one picture was worth a thousand words. Thus, the Chinese pictogram for *Hegu* not only means 'mouth' but, because of the importance of the acupuncture point and its appearance, translates as: the "Tiger's Mouth". Also, as everything exists in two balanced and mutually-inclusive states, the passive and the active, the *yin* and the *yang* respectively, the Tiger's Mouth is no exception, having both an open and a closed phase. Thus, when the ego is dominant, the hand fists, the Tiger's Mouth is in its closed phase, and the aggression is trapped. When we surrender the ego, when we let go, the hand opens and the tension is released. But, why do we 'make a fist' when angry and the destructive ego is in control (for people rarely argue with open hands and we "can't shake hands with a fist"…)? It is as if Nature helps us 'come to grips' with the anger for, when we fist with strength, the tip of the forefinger exerts pressure on the *Hegu* acupuncture point, stimulating it into its complementary state of (eventual) relaxation, in the same way as the acupuncture needle draws off rage at the *Hegu* point and induces its opposite condition of quiescence.

The Tiger's Mouth area of the fist (which is also called the "Unification Valley") is, therefore, a significant feature of our physical as well as psychological make-up. When 'needled' by others and angry, we make a fist. By fisting hard and long, we therapeutically 'needle' ourselves and bring about the opposite condition of yielding, and thus the balance and harmony inherent in Nature is restored. Moreover, as a useful exercise, the Chinese say that, at times of stress, it is helpful to fist both hands and then release them – and to repeat this several times – as a form of self-help and healing.

In allegorical terms, the usefulness of *Hegu* is clearly significant, since a tiger is such a very *yang* and powerful creature and thus is synonymous with wild aggression and primitive rage. The clenched fist then symbolises the damaged ego in its mightiest form, and its appearance, at this stage of our Journey, indicates that, no longer kittenish and tolerable, the Tiger is now in full throat.

The Tiger may not always be so obvious, however, even though it is *always* part of the human psyche. In the over-compliant wishing-to

-please child, it is quickly suppressed, no matter how many times it tries to raise its voice. In a subtly-aggressive person it can manifest as the epitome of goodness and kindness. In a power-hungry and controlling nature, it can reveal itself as tyranny over those who are too compliant, or - having 'rescued' another from such tyranny - the self-admiring, 'kindly', 'image-making' Tiger might firstly befriend, then criticise and then manipulate the one who has been rescued. In the emotionally-insecure child, Tiger might be used to ensure that things and even people are 'captured' (often by charm) for its own enhancement; and in the child who believes in her or his own 'perfection', Tiger's very existence is denied, resulting in acute psychological imbalance. The Tiger is also all the paranoid aspects of ourselves which make us believe that we are rejected, persecuted, used and abused and yet really are much better than anybody else.

In our Allegorical Journey, future appearances of the fisted hand will nearly always herald, and then portray, inner stress and ego-dominated activity and will indicate that, although few people have occasion to physically pull-at or punch another in the normal course of their days, we, with our quarrels, resistance and antagonism (silent or otherwise), do punch and pull a great deal psychologically. The Tiger's Mouth then becomes symbolic of our conflicts and inner turmoil, the unease, anger or aggression we feel when thwarted, rejected, criticised or rebuked. But, the Journey of the T'ai Chi Ch'üan (or, as those words translate: the '"Supreme Ultimate use of Energy" with *Ch'üan*, to the Chinese, meaning 'fist' or 'energy') is one of both ego-damage as well as spiritual discovery, since, if the controlling Tiger were not there, we would not know its opposite.

Thus, we learn to regard the Tiger with gratitude and sometimes even affection, recognising that it can be a blessing, which, if used wisely for self-knowledge, can offer us some measure of truth and peace. But the process is usually slow, the fight itself can be painful, and with every blow and punch we make we tend to believe that we are fighting a battle with an 'external' opponent – or 'life' is seen as the adversary which is causing us such pain. But, the T'ai Chi teaches us that our opponent is not someone else, nor 'life' nor 'fate', but something which inhabits exactly our size, weight, and colouring, our height and build, our facial characteristics, genetic and astrological inheritance, our thought-processes and psychological responses, our personality and character – and is deeply rooted in the past, whether ancestral or recent. We perceive that it is with our own damaged ego that we have to make peace and for which we need compassion. It is we who are causing the conflict, it is our own unclear, egoistic and confused thinking that is causing the pain; and, if we can yield to this wisdom, we can release our fist and flow with love into the next movement.

13 WITHDRAW (YIELDING) AND PUSH

The withdrawal of ego; the Push, and the second Gateway to Wisdom

War is *yang*. Peace is *yin*. War creates a momentum of energy which must reach its peak, before it can become its opposite. By the same token, we cannot continue our aggression or self-assertiveness indefinitely. We cannot even go on being proud or strong for very long (in the, sometimes, tight-lipped, high-*ch'i*-chested, chin-pushed forward and always-being right-and-blaming-others way), since such an attitude inevitably results in a multitude of problems. We have to learn how to yield, to be soft of eye, kind of heart and gentle in spirit - and when to allow the opposites in life to have their natural fulfilment. And we symbolise this now.

After all the psychological pain which produced the forceful, *yang* movements of the Twisted Step, Strike and Punch, we now withdraw with a yield of body in a beautiful movement of flowing retreat. The fisted hand unfolds like a flower, the other hand slides towards that open palm as in a caress, and the whole body flows in a sinuous S-shaped curve. And, although the previous movement may well-have-been psychologically fulfilling (because it expressed the truth of our torment), the softness in this *yin* movement heals and soothes a very troubled spirit. So, *yin* yielding follows in the wake of *yang* force and we realise that, even though (at the time) it seemed impossible not to fight, there is tremendous relief in letting-go.

"As the soft yield of water cleaves obstinate stone, so to yield with life solves the insoluble..." [1] said Lao Tzu, ever-observant of the natural world and compassionate of human nature. And yet, in the realms of ego, the deepest lessons of yielding are not so easy, for - no matter how pliable or non-assertive we may have become as adults; no matter how many well-skilled methods we have learnt to imply to others that Tiger is absent; no matter how genuine is the yielding of the moment - ego rarely is far away and continues to bruise. Only when

we are sufficiently shattered by the behaviour of our own Tiger, or hurt beyond measure by its action in another, can we – perhaps - manage to withdraw our ego for longer periods of time and, thus, "*solve the insoluble*" by yielding to life – for only then is it possible to find peace from the conflict of personal strife and war. But, Tiger rarely allows such a message – even as a concept – to have any validity, and so Lao Tzu's message frequently is lost upon us.

Yielding-up our ego does more than release us from a very heavy burden, however, for when so opened, the mind can retreat from a favourite point of view and allow another's to take up its space. It can enquire more deeply and discover new avenues of thought, can explore, travel and question and be free from attachment, all of which brings great relief to the spirit. 'My way' is no longer 'the only way', or, as Krishnamurti put it: "*Truth is a pathless land*" [2] and, if we can be open to that, and receptive to the many other truths being offered, we can be eased into seeing – and speaking – the truth that is our own.

Thus this movement symbolises much softness of being and, in relation to the child, conveys some of those special and lovely moments in life when the troubled and ego-bound adolescent suddenly sees another, and very different, point of view. Then, out of all the 'certainties' of 'being right' or 'badly done by', a clarifying insight comes and, for those few precious moments, there is light in life. He or she then not only sees how a situation looks to another, but goes beyond that and sees how it looks as a whole. The growing teenager then might put an arm around her or his parent and say "I'm sorry, Mum" or "I've been wrong, haven't I, Dad?", and, if ego has dissolved in both parent and child, the space left behind is available for love.

More physical energy becomes available also, for, although we are often lethargic and unmotivated when silently locked in ego's bondage or depleted by Tiger's anger, beneficial changes occur in the body when we are deeply interested and released into the areas of truth, or when an insightful spiritual connection has been made. Thus, this immensely soft and flowing movement reveals that we can obtain a better perspective when so released from our Tiger and this then enables us to move-on again with greater clarity, as well as physical strength.

So, after the gentle movement of withdrawal, we gain from its strengthening revelations and, turning in the *tan t'ien*, shift our weight and repeat The Push we made so long ago, the Push that depicted the very young child's first contact with ego's demands and the significant arrival of the Tiger's Kitten. Experiencing its claws was not pleasant but, because it was just a kitten and the child was still within the realm of protective motherhood, it was bearable. More importantly, however, its arrival opened the first Gateway to Wisdom by offering the child an opportunity for later self-awareness and inner growth.

Now, however, our consciousness of the well-developed and painful Tiger has been so-frequently experienced that there have been ample opportunities for self-knowledge. Having recognised that Tiger's domination only can lead to conflict, and having discovered the peace which 'yielding' can bring, the older teenager is free to push ahead into a different realm of perception – and the second inner Gateway to Wisdom opens to the touch, revealing that, if we are to comprehend and live with our ego, we have to accept the turbulent Tiger, cradle it in our arms in a place of stillness and serenity and - both spiritually and psychologically - travel further by taking time to ponder upon it. Now we must turn and "Carry Tiger to the Mountain".

14 Carry Tiger to the Mountain

Reflection upon ego in a peaceful environment,
and the end of Part One

The more we practise the T'ai Chi Ch'üan, the more we become aware of an inner, still place which is accessible through its enchantingly slow, meditative movements. The lack of musical or verbal accompaniment, the absence of heavy footfall, the increased awareness of our place in space and the lucidity which results from this heightened awareness, all contribute to the sense of stillness which we experience at the end of a prolonged and deep practise. The peace this stillness offers enables the conscious mind to connect with the mind's sub-conscious layers as well as the body, and to make contact on a deeper level with other people and the environment surrounding us. The unconscious levels, however, are not so accessible, and often require symbolism, sounds, dreams and imagery to evoke the important information they sometimes can reveal.

The symbolism in the Titles of this Allegory - when seen in this light – can help us discern some of the many levels of meaning behind our patterns of behaviour and, if we observe these with non-judgmental awareness, there is much to learn. So, now – at the end of Part One - we are given an opportunity to ponder upon the Tiger and its place in our lives by exploring the symbolism in the movement called: "Carry Tiger to the Mountain" or "Embrace Tiger, Return to Mountain".

We already know that the Chinese written word for 'tiger' consists of the two radicals: *hu*, as tiger stripes, and *jen*, as 'man', implying that the tiger has human attributes. Given the human condition, however, and how tigerish we can become, we can justifiably reverse this and regard ourselves as 'humans with tiger stripes'. And, although the Tiger, as representative of the ego, may not be the most subtle of symbols (since its obvious and diverse effects are both powerful and vastly wide-ranging), we have seen how some of its manifestations most decidedly are. So now, from the insight which we received when we pushed open the second Gateway to Wisdom, we understand that there is even-more to assimilate than the vital and important spiritual lesson of 'yielding'. We see that, in order to understand its subtleties, Tiger not only must be recognised, its dominance acknowledged, its presence accepted, and its existence made welcome, but it must be 'embraced', as well.

As children we are given guide-lines on how to look after the physical body with food, hygiene, rest and exercise, but rarely are we given guidance as to the care of mind and spirit, since the peace and solitude we need for this are rare in a child's life. Moreover, as adults, we cannot begin to understand our trouble-making ego when involved in any situation which causes it to start roaring, since the inner spirit has difficulty in manifesting itself when surrounded by loud noise, mental and physical pollution, every-day anxieties, fatigue or any other disruptive

interference. So, we need to retreat in order to view it objectively and we now turn to the North, towards the sacred home of the Immortals and the direction we faced at the beginning of our Journey. Having circled our arms outwards to both East and West in an embrace of opposites and, at the same time, looked to right and left in an acknowledgement of both, we now place equal weight into each leg, cross our hands in front of the chest and thus cradle the Tiger so that we may be gentle towards it, kinder to the damaged ego in others and accept it in ourselves, as well. We then rise up out of the bend to signify a movement towards a higher place of spirituality and Carry Tiger to the Mountain to find the necessary place of refuge which can give ease to the troubled spirit and peace to the unquiet mind.

Mountains are sacred to the Chinese and, through their symbolism of stability, enduring strength and towering presence, give a sense of perspective which enables us to view ourselves in greater depth. Nearer to the skies and closer to the heavens, with air that is pure and clean, there is no noise from the world below and less 'noise' in the mind, and so we can access our inner turmoil with more clarity than when down on the plains. The 'mountain' need not be an actual, geographical location, however, since a specific place for meditation, or a silent forest in which to walk, can provide sufficient spiritual recuperation, nor need we seek it far, for it can be located within. Through sitting quietly, or moving meditatively, or perhaps with help from a trained therapist or spiritual teacher, we can begin the process of stilling the mind. Regular contact with such an internal state then helps us lead our external lives with more balance, whilst daily practise swiftly-provides the inner refuge which can be entered into whenever needed. So, in the same way as a child might retreat to a room to recover from stress, we can go to our own 'inner mountain' whenever we can find a quiet place in which to ponder upon our Tiger.

"True quiet means keeping still when the time has come to keep still, and going forward when the time has come to go forward", states the *I Ching* hexagram: 'Keeping Still, Mountain'. *"In this way rest and movement are in agreement with the demands of the time, and thus there is light in life."* Stillness (the Mountain) represents the end and beginning of all movement, as now - at the end of Part One and the beginning of Part Two - it does for us. The hexagram then suggests that we must concentrate on the back, because: *"... in the back are located all the nerve fibers that mediate movement. If the movement of these spinal nerves is brought to a standstill, the ego, with its restlessness, disappears.... When a man has thus become calm, he may turn to the outside world. He no longer sees in it the struggle and tumult of individual beings, and therefore he has that true peace of mind which is needed for understanding the great laws of the universe and for acting in harmony with them. Whoever acts from these deep levels, makes no mistakes."* [1]

Thus, ego *"disappears"* when the spinal nerve fibres are brought to rest and, by now, through the slowness of the T'ai Chi, we have begun to appreciate this process. We have become more aware of ourselves, of what we are actually doing in space, of our reactions to others in the group, and to the T'ai Chi itself. We notice sooner when the neck stiffens, when the body slants forward or back, when the spine (especially in the lumbar region) becomes rigid, when our legs are too *yin* or too *yang* - and we are also more conscious of our thoughts. Moreover, when thus relaxed, we perceive that the Tiger, which was so noticeable when we first began our Journey, is not clawing at us, or others, nearly so often!

As did the Taoists when pondering upon nature as a whole, so do we now find a quiet place and ponder upon those words from the *I Ching* and on the relationship between ourselves and animals. We then perceive that there is a very important difference between animals and ourselves for, although they have their bodily functions in the same areas as we do, they are noted for the sensitive use of their spine and back-of-neck. This, of course, is with good reason, since the nerves in those parts are used to detect the information which is essential to their survival. But, when their 'hackles rise', their responses are visible, whereas – despite our awareness of our nervous reactions – our responses rarely are, so determined are we to inhibit our nerves and/or hide their reactions from others. Moreover, since we have become upright, we tend to think of *all* our important functions as being in the front of the body and, more often than not, are only aware of the face, with its eyes, nose and mouth; of the manly chest with its muscles and/or hairiness; of the female's fuller or smaller breasts; of the flatness or otherwise of the stomach, and of the genitals. We pay little attention to the spine except to rectify bad posture, even though we use words which indicate how pejoratively we regard the back (e.g. 'turn-tail', 'back-sliding', 'spineless', 'unbending', 'stiff-necked', 'back-biting', 'backward', or 'she/he's a heel') and thus regard the back in terms of unacceptable psychological behaviour, rather than for its usefulness (as in animals) in the areas of inner-sensing and outward-sending of informative messages. But, we can have a more heightened awareness of the spine and have more of its use available in terms of health and serenity, by becoming even-more aware when the back of the neck tingles from self-consciousness, or when it stiffens at criticism, stress or aversion. We can notice how we curve the spine sideways into an 'S' shape, when trying to appease or seek approval, or of how we push the coccyx and sacrum forward when wishing to dominate another, especially sexually. We can sense how the spine stiffens when someone is looking at, or touching us, when we think that they should not. We can become more alerted to the degree we lean back, when too fearful or compliant, or forward when over-ambitious or aggressive; of how we hunch the shoulders defensively when attacked, or tighten them backwards, when aggressively assertive, thus sticking out our chest. We can be more sensitive as to how we raise the shoulders and tighten the upper back when doing even relatively un-stressful activities like vacuuming or pushing a super-market trolley, and can pay more attention to *when* the back goes into spasm, by tracing back the thoughts and emotions relating to the circumstances that occurred, prior to the appearance of the physical reaction. And, in general, we can ponder upon, and have insight into, the reasons why we immobilise or incapacitate ourselves so much, and in which areas the problems manifest.

Much research has been done concerning psychological cause-and-effect with regard to illness, and to the importance of self-knowledge in relation to this, but, if we could regain more *use* of the spine through being more alert to ego's interference - and to the psychological defence mechanisms which result in physical and mental ill-health - we might get closer to achieving higher fulfilment in evolutionary terms. Such an increase in awareness of the spinal nerves - and of the organs and other areas of the body that relate to each vertebra – then could lead to a relaxation in the central nervous system, so that the damaged ego, with its restlessness, could finally find some measure of peace. And - if that could occur - we would be a little closer to what the Chinese call: "the State of the Immortals".

The Chinese ideogram for 'immortal' comprises two characters: that of 'man' and that of 'mountain' and, by now 'going to the mountain' (as, metaphorically or otherwise, hermits, monks and mystics have done since the human spiritual quest began), we are a little nearer to understanding that ultimate State, for – once we have settled-into our own place of stillness - the spirit is purified, the nerves relaxed and the ego rests.

So, the end of the first of the three Parts of this Allegory has us making contact with that inner place. Childhood is past, adolescence is over. The 'young adult' has emerged and, as we pause, relaxed and at peace, we return to a similar place of stillness to that from whence we first came, and - for just a little while - the Tiger sleeps in our arms.

PART TWO

ADULTHOOD

15a ELBOW STROKE, BRUSH KNEE
AND FORWARD STEP

Coming down from the Mountain of Stillness

At the beginning of our Journey, we turned to the East, since, for those who have been influenced by Eastern teachings: *"The East in a man is symbolical of all in him that is awakening: the West is his old life, his past, which he must eventually leave"*[1] and, in those early stages, our T'ai Chi movements symbolised the awakening of consciousness and the flowing in harmony with the Bamboos, before the Tiger's Kitten arrived and requisitioned many aspects of our lives. Then, together with the inevitable conditioning of childhood and all its variety of experiences, we moved into - and faced - the West, for the majority of movements which followed.

Now at the beginning of Part Two, and with Tiger still resting in our arms, we turn to the East again before moving down from the spiritual mountain to the temporal life of the plains. We have been replenished in spirit and released from restless thought, and so the mind is calm. Much appears to have happened, but as we are still innocent of life as a whole, and still are seeking, we are eager to return to daily life and to share our experiences.

We feel different. We seem to have a sharper sense of perspective, a deeper understanding of life and some clarifying insights into our ego – and Tiger wakes up with a start! We experience a sense of achievement and a buoyancy of mind, which leads us to believe that we have arrived at a place of great psychological and spiritual liberation – and Tiger starts purring. We feel we have 'seen the light' and are uplifted and excited by this new dimension - and Tiger beams with satisfaction. We start praising ourselves for our newly-discovered insights, tell others about them and wish to convert them to our new way of seeing and, so certain are we of what we have learnt and so convinced are we of our 'arrival' at a new and better place of understanding, that torrents of words pour out to convince others of the one truth, the *only* truth of our perceptions: "new insights, new seeing, new person, quite different now, so happy, so sure, so clear, I've *really* learnt something now", and: "you must have it, too, you must know it, too!". Fortunately on these occasions, life (in the shape of other people) comes to our aid and knocks our blind certainties on the head, hits us with the impact of laughter, scorn, argument or anger - or the potency of assumed interest or polite silence - and then: "What?" says Tiger, "resistance to my ideas and inspired insights? Why, surely, what has now been perceived, and is being shared with you, could change your lives forever!"

Unwilling to acknowledge ego's swift return and of how active Tiger has become, we are puzzled as to why others seem unable to value all that we offer and why life has become so much more complex and difficult as a young adult than it had been as a child. And this confusion can equate with what can happen at the beginning of Part Two in the T'ai Chi Form. We could see the necessity for a Retreat to our Mountain and had found it fulfilling to have arrived at this more-adult stage of our Journey (for, surely, says Tiger, arriving at the end of a Part, represents 'progress' and 'moving on'?) - and we *did* feel so different. 'Climbing down' again is not so easy, however, and we are not accustomed to the degree of focus required. As a result, we sometimes wobble or unexpectedly stumble, and then find that we are elbowing something away and brushing something else aside and that, whilst trying to clear a way through the unexpected 'opposition', we are pushing forward with the flat of a hand, too eager to arrive at a new place and too lacking in experience to see what novices we are and with what inflated egos we are viewing ourselves and the world. And the more we try to convince ourselves as to our importance, the more we fail; the more external opposition we experience, the more defensive and irritated does our Tiger become. This resistance is useful, however, since it shows how un-stable we are and we are given another opportunity to learn an important lesson.

15b Ward Off – Slantingly Downwards

A Zen lesson for the novice's inflated ego

There is a Zen story of a young novice who had finally and 'successfully' meditated. Tiger's temporary absence had brought serenity of mind, and, with peace flooding his being, the body had become amorphous and floating like a cotton-wool cloud, released from stress-induced discomfort. The novice is so new to this experience and to the contemplative life as a whole - and so thrilled by this first, apparently-egoless state of freedom from the domination of thought - that he rushes up to the Master and describes his state of detachment from the ego-self, pouring out all his spiritual discoveries: "The Self is gone, All is One, there is only Unity and Wholeness, separation is over, One is all, everything is Light, there is no duality, there is only Being, I have been at-One with the Universe!" and further describing his liberation from all material and sensory hindrances, he tells of his certainty that he is free from the ego-self - forever. The Master listens carefully to these excited outpourings and waits patiently for them to end, but then, contrary to the novice's expected approval, he imparts a sharp 'whack' with a stick across the novice's shoulders, causing Tiger to throw a tantrum and the novice to cry out with self-righteous indignation at the seeming injustice of the blow. The Master then knows how far from egolessness is that young soul and that, without the blow from the stick, the novice's attachment to the new state of (momentary) liberation, and his sensory enjoyment of the experience, would not only lead him to further attachment to his 'egoless' state, but to a craving for the sensation to be repeated.

It is the same for us in our Journey. As novices, we are so lacking in experience and yet so certain that we have arrived at a place that is 'right', that it is fortunate that others can be as insightful as a Zen monk, recognising intuitively that we are not where we think we are and releasing us from our illusions with a psychological blow. And we have to 'duck' as best we may and learn what we can from the experience.

Thus, while the empty state which we experienced on the Mountain undoubtedly brought genuine peace, it soon disappeared when we filled it up again with self-praise and an egoistic desire to change others, and the sharp but necessary awakening – which made us let go of our certainties – enabled us to regain our balance and move once more into the joy of relating to others.

15c Pull Back, Press Forward and Push

The Bamboos and the third Gateway to Wisdom

Having 'ducked our heads' in an attempt to ward off the down-coming blow, we now straighten up and flow into the second of the lovely Bamboos. Once more, as in early childhood, we move as if led by a gentle breeze, shifting and blending with the rhythms of Nature and the currents of the Tao. Once more we flow with the *yin* and *yang* of left and right and down and up and forward and back and in and out, and sense again the balance which, this time, has been offered by experiencing some of life's more painful opposites.

Learning more about bamboos (of which there are over a thousand varieties), we discover that artisans who work with them, call them 'grateful', since they are both flexible yet tough; light but very strong[1] and that, known as "The Friend of China", their most striking characteristics are immense vitality and the ability to overcome almost any kind of hardship. Moreover, due to their far-ranging network of growth beneath the ground, all shoots are linked together and nourish each other,[2] and this is how it is with us now, as we practise the Bamboos together again. Linked as irrevocably as are bamboo roots, we give and receive of our energy and strength, of our gratitude and friendship and of our unity of mind and spirit, and all of this - as nourishment for the spirit - we offer each other as we weave through the network of beautiful shapes that we make in space. And, moreover, so absorbed in the movements are we, that we become like the Chinese painter Wen Yü-k'o, who, when he painted bamboo, saw bamboo only and became so rapt he 'became bamboo' and forgot even himself.[3]

Thus, 'becoming bamboo', we flow with the Tao, and, having learnt another somewhat daunting and unexpected lesson concerning our Tiger, we make a forward movement of another Push which, as it opens lightly to our touch, reveals a third inner Gateway to Wisdom.

16 Press Down and Stand on One Leg and Fist Under Elbow

The Deer Movements*: seeking an answer to the problem of Tiger's swift return and grasping a clue

The delicate deer, the fourth of the Five Animals, now arrives on the scene with alert sensitivity and lightness of foot. Symbolising 'meditation', which occurred on the Mountain of Stillness; 'meekness' which was the result of our Zen Novice's Lesson, and the 'gentleness' exemplified in the movements of bamboos, the deer is significant here.[1]

The young adult is seeking, sensing, exploring new avenues, trying to find the joy which life is meant to offer. But time is passing, and, as he or she follows the various paths which beckon, there remains a sense of unease which haunts the true seeker who, consciously or unconsciously, is asking the same questions as posed by Chuang Tzu over two thousand years' ago: *"Is there to be found on earth a fullness of joy, or is there no such thing? Is there some way to make life fully worth living, or is this impossible? If there is such a way, how do you go about finding it? What should you try to do? What should you seek to avoid? What should be the goal in which your activity comes to rest? What should you accept? What should you refuse to accept? What should you love? What should you hate?"*

Then, describing a world no different from our own, he added: *"What the world values is money, reputation, long life, achievement...*

What it considers misfortune is bodily discomfort and labor, no chance to get your fill of good food, not having good clothes to wear, having no way to amuse or delight the eye, no pleasant music to listen to. If people find that they are deprived of these things, they go into a panic or fall into despair. They are so concerned for their life that their anxiety makes life unbearable, even when they have the things they think they want. Their very concern for enjoyment makes them unhappy.

*As with the "Bear Steps", this is the author's choice of subtitle

93

The rich make life intolerable, driving themselves in order to get more and more money which they cannot really use. In so doing they are alienated from themselves, and exhaust themselves in their own service as though they were slaves of others.

The ambitious run day and night in pursuit of honors, constantly in anguish about the success of their plans, dreading the miscalculation that may wreck everything. Thus they are alienated from themselves, exhausting their real life in service of the shadow created by their insatiable hope." [2]

Thus it goes on. Human nature does not change. In essence, inner turmoil today is no different from when we lived in the days of the Taoist sages and it is only in life's outward manifestations that there are changes.

What that wise old sage, Chuang Tzu, omitted to mention, however, was: sex - that potent physical manifestation of *Ching*, running like a thread through our lives, creating its own excitements and problems, governing actions and responses with fantasies forming, needs arising, desires directing. Sometimes suppressed, camouflaged, covert; sometimes flamboyant, flagrant, overt. Flooding the mind with ideas and images, and the body with sensations – sweet, seductive, overwhelming sensations. Love-sick, craving, desiring, the need to procreate and the intensity of the pleasures obtained from its fulfilment, can be overwhelming. And the deer, symbolic also of the 'love-sickness' [3] which can make us mad and blind and bitterly unhappy and yet so astonishingly, radiantly-filled with buoyant energy, goes racing off in the direction of the new scent.

We yearn for union in partnership, for freedom from inner disquiet, release from the Tiger, freedom to "be ourselves" and to live a life which has more meaning, and the inner spirit continues to prod us into trying to locate the sources of our discomfort. And yet we are so fearful, so lacking in confidence (since the damage has been done, the wet cement of childhood has set, and all those 'negatives' and rejections have been embedded in so many cells of our being) that we continue to be split by our lack of certainties and - with always some underlying fear - the opposites continue their work in us and duality remains the constant factor.

We shift back, pondering upon what has taken place, conscious of the contrast between the peace on the Mountain of Stillness, and the restless malaise of the spirit after Tiger's swift return. We compare one state with the other and then recall the changes which overtook us when – oh, so eagerly - we spread the news of our discoveries. We go over all that happened: what we said, what they said, how we looked, how they responded, what we meant, what they misunderstood, what we should have said, what they could have said, and why we feel so diminished with certain people and so much more comfortable with others. And, if we are really honest with ourselves, what we really felt when we denied what we were feeling. Having been unable to establish any continuing resolution of the opposites in our nature, we see that our lives have such conflicting currents and contrasting situations that the actual experience of Tiger resting in our arms, and of our subsequent flow with the Tao, seems poignantly nebulous. But, we also sense that the beauty of the Bamboos was due to the merging of the *yin* and the *yang*, not from their

differences; we do know that, while Tiger was sleeping, the world seemed blessedly benign, and we do want to explore the reasons for Tiger's swift awakening.

So we turn into a different direction and press down our hands as if to calm the hyper-activities of the less-pure activities of *Ching, Ch'i,* and *Shên,* and then, sharply alert and as acutely sensitive as a light-footed deer, we mirror its movements, lift one knee lightly upward, turn our head and upper body in the opposite direction and point our hands towards that third Gateway to Wisdom, as if sensing that, perhaps, from there, some help may come.

We then turn around and sense the air and send out circling, yearning, probing movements of hands and arms. We seek to the left, we search to the right, we change directions as swiftly and as need-fully as a deer in flight, and yet, all the time, we know that soon we must pause and cease our attempts to rationalise our inner dis-quiet by seeking outside ourselves. Instead, we must ease our body and mind into a state of trust and try to 'come to grips' with the dilemma.

So, we ask ourselves: what actually happened on the Mountain? We can see that we distanced ourselves, had moved away from our problems and so had viewed them with more equanimity. The problems had not gone away, but we no longer anguished over them and, as when on holiday, the way we perceived them was more objective, different, detached. And there had been that sense of peace. So, was that the difference? Was it simply because we were 'elsewhere'? Surely, that cannot be the whole answer. Was it not also because, at those times of equanimity, we had had some flashes of insight into something that might contribute to the nature of our problems and then, later, after all our outpourings to others, had we not sensed that the outburst might not have occurred had we not thought too highly of ourselves and of the thoughts that had accompanied our experiences? We ponder on this and rather than thinking about it in the familiar, conditioned, relentless way, begin to wonder about thought itself. ("But, we've got to *think* about things," says Tiger swiftly, sensing trouble, "we can't change *that* - that's what makes us (ME!!) so special. If we didn't *think* about things, nothing would get *done*!"). Yet, we are not so sure (and are beginning to understand Tiger's ways) and we continue our quest, sensing that there *is* something here, there does seem to be a clue, there is something we can grasp. Is it, perhaps, the *way* the mind works - the distracted and distracting chatter of the mind that is the problem? Is it all those repetitive, conflicting, fear-ridden, anxiety-making, self-protecting, self-pitying Tiger-based *thoughts*, which go on and on, so relentlessly? Are they part of the problem? And - if so – is Tiger right? Could *all that* ever change? We ponder on this and sense Tiger's alarm but, having come so far, we feel we must continue.

Seeming to understand what path we must take, we feel a measure of peace again and, as if a guiding inner spirit had taken us gently by the hand, the T'ai Chi symbolises this as we reach out and clasp that hand, which then guides us towards the heart of the matter, as our other hand moves nearer to the head that is causing all the trouble. We have begun to 'come to grips' with the problem and after all the circling, searching, 'out-there' movements, we find a measure of comfort within again.

17 STEP BACK AND REPULSE THE MONKEY

The Monkey Thoughts and ways of dealing with them

The road to self-knowledge and liberation for the spirit can be the longest road in our lives and the arrival now of the fifth of the Five Animals, the chattering, cheeky, mischievous Monkey, proves to be a major landmark along the way. But the journey is not easy. The inner spirit can take us by the hand and point the way, but the actual work has to be done by ourselves.

Now we need to focus fully on what are called the "Monkey Thoughts", for they have a great deal of influence upon us, distracting us, removing our attention from the actions required or from the meaning in the moment being lived. Our consciousness, or 'mindfulness' as the Buddhists call it, does not want to pay attention, wants to do what it likes, when it likes. Seemingly innocuous, but vastly disruptive, the Monkey Thoughts hinder us from transcending onto higher levels of consciousness, deeper levels of meditative awareness, sharper insights into reality, and the Monkey's chatter in the head – and the relentless chatter between people – obliterates the underlying truth of what is actually going on.

To focus on this, the T'ai Chi now has us moving backwards, retreating as we retrace our steps, whilst, at the same time, guiding us towards various meditational practises. It also ensures that, by moving backwards, we cannot see ahead for, if we could, we might come to some conclusions about our Journey and that would mean that Monkey was distracting us.

So, we step back in order to focus on the life of the mind, and, although we are facing West - where our main conflicts occurred – our steps are back to the East again, to the source of light which, though not visible to our eyes, gives us insight into how to follow the promptings of the inner spirit, and, at the same time, grants us a heightened awareness of the spine.

Recollecting our childhood in relation to where we are now, we perceive how much we are the product of our past and of how (as Krishnamurti put it), *we are the content of our consciousness*. Needing to look at that content, we become more objective, and realise that we would do well to relinquish established attitudes and conventional ideas as to how we think we, and life, should be. We then sense that, perhaps, ultimately, *everything* we have come to value and accept has to be scrutinised with the question: "Is that *really* so?". Having accepted that advice and started to probe, however, we then find that such questioning leads to the arrival of the very thing that appears to have caused the unrest: Monkey immediately swings in on the scene and starts distracting us again.

So we step backwards again and probe further but, as soon as we start pondering on a deeper level, Monkey locates an itch, our attention wanders, the mind becomes fragmented and Monkey leaps to yet-another branch of yet-another tree. Then, just as we perceive how thought itself is hindering observation, Monkey dashes in again and says that all this probing is a waste of time and effort, that it's far too difficult, that it's much more fun to have fun and let's watch television. But, we step back a third time and we observe Monkey's antics and see how rarely it lets us focus fully on what we are doing, or tells us we 'have forgotten' when, in fact, we had not really listened, or had interfered so much that we had become blind to reality.

We refuse to let go of our quest, however, and, journeying further into the mind, recognise that the two 'states of being' mentioned in the early Bird's Beak movement: self-awareness and self-consciousness, are like twins who had been united in the womb and deeply connected in early childhood, but who later separated and now function in the adult world in different directions. The first twin, the serious one, is still linked to the womb of the Tao, has occasion to be deeply desirous of self-knowledge, wishes to look at life without that "lens of differentiation" (mentioned in Chapter 3), wants to see the true relationship between things, to observe in an uncluttered way, to be free of the past, and to think and act with clarity in the present. The other twin (to whom Monkey is *very* attached), focuses the lens of the past onto every situation and then draws upon social convention, tradition, conditioned fear, guilt, insecurity, resentment, past pain, competition, comparison, self-aggrandisement, self-protection, fame, pleasure, comfort, prestige and rewards, and indicates that what is being looked at should be viewed through whatever is appropriate to those lenses, and those lenses only. Virtually unhindered, the Monkey Thoughts go on the merry-go-round of the mind and move so swiftly and adroitly that they almost convince the serious twin that this way is the only way to think and respond. But not quite – for, having now stepped back and questioned anew - the self-aware twin gains in strength and clarity and recalls the many times when Monkey found a variety of reasons for making excuses (for Monkey loves making excuses) and for justifying its 'second thoughts' and self-interested Tiger-based rationalisations - and begins to perceive to what degree the Monkey is the tool of Tiger.

Then, given that this clearly is the way of much of human behaviour, the serious twin asks: how can we overcome it? How can we increase our consciousness of Monkey and lessen its power? John Blofeld, an English Buddhist who spent much time with Taoist monks, not only lucidly described this problem, but offered various mind-calming, 'one-pointed' meditational techniques to deal with it. He said that one makes a start by focussing on anything at all – the flame of a lighted candle or a steady point of light; a cross visualised in front of one's eyes; the area of the *tan t'ien* [or the *in* and *out* breaths that move it in and out]; the 3rd Eye, located between the eyebrows, or a glowing syllable,[1] or, as is done in T'ai Chi classes, we could repeatedly 'draw' the breath along the pathways allocated throughout the body in various Taoist breathing exercises.

He also said that, due to our limited functioning of sense perception (i.e. because of the 'lens of differentiation' mentioned previously), the mind is deluded by false concepts and that, until *"the waves of idle thought"* can be stilled by meditation, there can be little possibility of intuitively perceiving the *"objectless awareness"* [of Primary Reality], which the mystics experience. Thus, despite the many distractions that can occur and the lack of reward in the beginning of the meditational practise, unwavering contemplation, or sustained one-pointedness of any single object, is one of the ways of attaining inner stillness. He added, however, that it should not be imagined that true objectless awareness is ever possible, since *"awareness by its very nature has to be awareness of something"*, and also that, since these practises can lead to visions of bright lights and even sensations of *"joyous tranquillity sometimes amounting to bliss"*, these sensations should not be dwelt upon – nor sought - any more than any other distractions, for the importance of contemplation lies in maintaining silence for its own sake.[2]

These 'one-pointed' techniques are of inestimable value in directing us towards the cessation of Monkey's distractions, but there is another approach towards stilling the mind that is equally valuable. It was advocated by Krishnamurti and resembles Buddhism's Vipassana meditational technique in that, whilst meditating, we *allow* the thoughts and feelings to remain in consciousness in order that we may focus upon them. Initially, this means finding a quiet place and paying very sensitive attention to our every thought and feeling; becoming conscious of their source, and then accepting their presence in an uncritical and non-judgemental way. This, of course, is not easy and we may find that – as mentioned earlier - Monkey interferes or takes over completely, or that we cling to a thought and it gets stuck, but, by asking ourselves *why* we became blocked at just that point and then allowing the mind to delve more deeply, we can become aware of the cause of the blockage, which then releases it and it flows away. So, the more conscious we become of all our thoughts and feelings, and the reasons for them, the swifter is our awareness and subsequent understanding of them, and the more frequently this occurs, the more the Monkey Thoughts slip away like leaves on a stream, floating with the current until they reach the ocean and then disappear.

Such a method may imply that, although many thoughts and feelings will 'just slip away', they will be always be followed by more, and so the head will always be filled with useless, non-productive, disconnected, distracting words and sentences occasioned by having so many Monkey Thoughts. But, the converse happens. The more self-aware we become on a moment-to-moment basis and the more drawn we are towards a contemplative life-style, the fewer are the thoughts that distract us. As less and less is fed into the brain and fewer words are needed, the thoughts that do arise become those that are necessary to the action in hand and to the provision of a more direct and lucid response to life. Psychological integration then occurs because, whilst *all* thoughts are allowed to flow as naturally and as effortlessly as do impulses from the heart, the more one is aware of them, the more peace it brings, and the more peace it brings, the less conflict there is between the "what is" and

the "what should be". Distracting Monkey Thoughts thus are allowed to be a part of the brain's activity, without censure, and, by more closely observing them, they not only decrease in number, but disturb us less, whilst, significantly, it has been found that, if we try to 'catch' a thought by focusing on it totally, it completely disappears!

We have three, back-stepping, Monkey Steps to take, however, and there is a third, very helpful, method of mind-calming, also advocated by Krishnamurti, which is: writing down as many thoughts and feelings as we can manage to record in the moment, or recall later on. All should be put down, with utter honesty, and with no concern about our own or anyone else's opinion of what we are writing interfering with our integrity of purpose, for such writings are not intended to be judged by us, nor read by others. This may seem an arduous and time-consuming method, but it not only releases the thoughts from their hold over us - by helping us to be more aware of them as they emerge - but it eventually enables us to write down each "thought-feeling" with swiftness and ease, either as it occurs, or from memory later on.

As Krishnamurti explained it: *"This whirling machinery must slow itself down to be observed, so writing every thought-feeling may be of help. As in a slow motion picture, you are able to see every movement, so in slowing down the rapidity of the mind, you are then able to observe every thought, trivial and important. The trivial leads to the important, and do not brush it aside as being petty. Since it is there it is an indication of the pettiness of the mind, and to brush it aside does not make the mind any the less trivial, stupid. To brush it aside helps to keep the mind small, narrow, but to be aware of it, to understand it leads to great riches.*

If any of you have tried to write as I suggested..., you will know how difficult it is to put down every thought and feeling. You will not only use a lot of paper but you will not be able to write down all your thoughts-feelings, for your mind is too rapid in its distractions. But if you have the intention of putting down every thought-feeling, however trivial and stupid, the shame-ful and the pleasant, however little you may succeed at first, you will soon discover a peculiar thing happening. As you have not the time to write every thought-feeling, for you have to give your attention to other matters, you will find that one of the layers of consciousness is recording every thought-feeling. Though you do not give your attention directly to write down, nevertheless you are inwardly aware and when you have time to write again, you will find that the recordings of inward awareness will come to the surface. If you will look over what you have written, you will find yourself either con-demning or approving, justifying or comparing. This approbation or denial prevents the flowering of thought-feeling and so stops understanding. If you do not condemn, justify, or compare but ponder over, try to understand, then you will discover that these thoughts-feelings are indications of something much deeper. So you are beginning to develop that mirror which reflects your thoughts-feelings without any distortion. And by observing them, you are comprehending your actions and responses, and so self-knowledge becomes wider and deeper. You not only comprehend the present momentary action and reaction but also the past that has produced the present. And for this you must have quiet and solitude. But society does not allow you to have them. You must be with people, outwardly active at all costs. If you are alone you are considered anti-social or peculiar, or you are afraid of your own lone-liness. But in this process of self-awareness, you will discover many things about yourself and so of the world..." [3]

So, we step back and each of the three Monkey Steps can symbolize each of the three meditational methods described above: the first step leading to the various one-pointed meditational techniques; the second, the conscious "allowing" which, when integrated into daily living, can be utilised whether sitting on top of a bus or doing the washing-up, and the third, the process whereby an increase in self-awareness can be obtained from the writing-down of our thoughts and feelings. Since our individual learning processes vary, however, and there are other meditational techniques, the practitioner can decide how best to use these Steps.

Finally, we have three 'Monkey Stories'. Two are factual and tell of tragedy and of how seriously Monkey can interfere with what the Chinese call "*wu-wei*", or action that is ego-free, whilst all three have one factor in common.

1. In the 19th century, the Siamese Royal Queen was boating on a lake with her three children when the boat capsized. Servants were near and swam towards the boat, but the Queen and all her children drowned because a Crown ruling decreed that no servant, nor any person of inferior rank, could touch a member of the Royal Family without the severest of penalties.

2. In the 20th century, the famed film star, Rudolf Valentino, was rushed to hospital at mid.day with a burst gastric ulcer and a ruptured appendix. A 'desperate search' was then begun to find someone willing to 'disfigure' the world's most celebrated, not to say valuable, torso. But, no-one wanted to take the responsibility of operating on Valentino, said his brother, Alberto, and they all waited for "*some big, well-known surgeon to come along, and it took until six o'clock.*" The operation itself eventually took place, but its delay caused excessive weakness in the body and, two days before he was expected to be discharged, peritonitis, pleurisy and other complications set in, and he died at the age of 31.[4]

3. There was a monkey and there was a dolphin. Each was placed in a situation of *simulated* danger. The monkey looked, looked again, became agitated, started to scream and then ran away, still screaming. The dolphin looked, looked again, appeared to calmly assess the situation, showed no sign of stress, and quietly swam away.

In the first two stories, the reactions of the human participants were based on the desperate thinking prescribed by society's dictates and (understandably) by profound self-preservation. So tragically were they paralysed into non-action by fear of doing the wrong thing, however, they actually did do the wrong thing. In the third story, the monkey behaved as we so often do, its fear overcoming its ability to see that, in reality, there was nothing to fear. Thus, the one common denominator was 'fear' – which is the Monkey's most-frequently used emotion – and only the (Taoist) dolphin had the true seeing which enabled it to take the right action and peacefully swim away.

Thus, do we further our own destiny. By placing people on pedestals – or below us in rank - we remove them from direct relationship with ourselves and are unable to make the (sometimes life-saving) contact that the human condition essentially requires. By utilising fear-filled thinking to establish the rules of conduct which create distances between us and by 'allowing' it to forsake our humanity, we also lose the most important common denominator of all: that of the life-affirming connection between everything and everyone.

18 SLANTING (DIAGONAL) FLYING

Hearing with the Spirit and freedom for the creative gift

"Tell me," said Yen Hui, "what is fasting of the heart?"

Confucius replied: "The goal of fasting is inner unity. This means hearing, but not with the ear; hearing, but not with the understanding; hearing with the spirit, with your whole being. The hearing that is only in the ears is one thing. The hearing of the understanding is another. But the hearing of the spirit is not limited to any one faculty, to the ear, or to the mind. Hence it demands the emptiness of all the faculties. And when the faculties are empty, then the whole being listens. There is then a direct grasp of what is right there before you that can never be heard with the ear or understood with the mind. Fasting of the heart empties the faculties, frees you from limitation and from preoccupation. Fasting of the heart begets unity and freedom...

You know that one can fly with wings: you have not yet learned about flying without wings. You are familiar with the wisdom of those who know, but you have not yet learned the wisdom of those who know not.

Look at this window: it is nothing but a hole in the wall, but because of it the whole room is full of light. So when the faculties are empty, the heart is full of light. Being full of light it becomes an influence by which others are secretly transformed." [1]

In the first two Monkey Steps stories, 'hearing with the ear' and 'hearing with the mind' meant hearing the cries of the drowning and yet thinking: *"We are not allowed to touch any member of the Royal Family"* - even though it meant four people could lose their lives. It was hearing the name: *"Valentino!"*, and then mentally-agonising over so many of the implications of his fame and importance, that the necessity for urgent action was denied him. *'Hearing with the spirit, with your whole being'*, however: *"These people are DROWNING!"*, *"This person may DIE!"* and spontaneously taking the vital, urgent and essential action required, could have saved five lives. And yet there are other aspects concerning such events that in no way negate the vital human imperative to save life, nor lessen the importance of acting spontaneously from the orders of '*Hearing with the Spirit*': there are also the Universal Laws concerning life and death, over which we have no control. They are the *yin* and *yang* of the Tao as a whole and have such influence that the five deaths just recorded could have had profound, long-reaching effects on all concerned, to such a degree that their outlook on life could have been radically altered, whilst, in the case of Siam, its whole history *was* affected, since their barbarous laws were subsequently changed so that such tragedies could never occur again.

Conscious now that: *"when the faculties are empty, then the whole being listens"* and that various meditational practices can release us from the Monkey Thoughts, we now form the beautiful, circular symbol of unity, before rising up as if in the beauty of flight, to enact one of the loveliest of T'ai Chi movements: that of "Diagonal Flying".

Freed from the burden of fear-induced thought, we move as though borne upwards by the lightness and emptiness of our inner being, beyond self-consciousness or even self-awareness. With the head poised and the body balanced in a wonderful distribution of *yin* and *yang,* and with the central vertical axis in perfect alignment, the movement portrays to what extent the whole being can be in harmony.

Physically and spiritually, we sense the release from conventional, conditioned responses and, from this, the spirit is liberated and a fundamental aspect inherent in the insights of mystics is revealed, for: '*Hearing with the spirit*' empties the mind, and the freedom from the burden of fear-conditioned thought is so uplifting, and so clearly depicted in this movement, that we can well-imagine how the Taoist Immortals felt when they flew towards their celestial abode on their own, magical 'flight without wings'!

Photo used with permission of Cheng Man Ching Enterprises, LLC

19 STEP UP AND RAISE HANDS

The return of duality and the merging of opposites again

Following on from the upsurge of spiritual release, we experience three movements which, like refrains in a song or life's recurring themes, repeat those made earlier in our Journey, and – because they are repetitions – we feel relief on dealing with the 'known', as well as an urge to question whether any internal or physical changes have occurred since last we performed them.

The first of the three has us touching ground again and moving into a physically-opposite expression from the movement just experienced, since, after such a divine flight, we need to come down to earth and make contact with our normal, human state. After having travelled so far on our T'ai Chi Journey, however, and having had so many spiritual 'messages' to absorb, we ask ourselves: have we changed, and, if so, is our T'ai Chi any different? We ponder on this and sense that, perhaps, we do view ourselves in a somewhat-altered light and are no longer as clumsy and unsure in our lives - and in our T'ai Chi - as hitherto. We may not feel as softly-stepping and empty of anxiety as we would like to be and perhaps we could have practised more often and listened with more 'emptiness', but we are less stiff, we do have more balance and we do feel more relaxed. More importantly, we now see that, as with all things in Nature, growth must be organic and that if there are to be any lasting changes, they should be unforced. We are, therefore, not as impatient with ourselves for any continuing lack of co-ordination or stability and, having been given so many opportunities to improve our physical expertise and to grow psychologically and spiritually, we also feel more buoyant in spirit.

There are, of course, still many of the inevitable 'niggles' of conditioned 'oughts' and 'shoulds', but, as our outspread hands draw in towards each other and we "Step Up" and 'fold in our wings', our questioning reveals that, whilst the twins of self-consciousness and self-awareness are still in evidence and continue to form the fabric of our lives, their duality is less troublesome; we are clearer about their influence; we can observe them with acceptance and can recognise in what way they are manifesting. Moreover, we have discovered that self-consciousness can lead to greater sensitivity and that self-awareness is immensely enriching. These changes then guide us into a further – and deeper – outcome of the earlier meditation upon the Monkey Thoughts and, with greater freedom for the spirit, we move into the second of the repetitions.

20 THE WHITE CRANE
SPREADS ITS WINGS

*Another outcome from meditation upon the Monkey
Thoughts, and an increase in spiritual awareness*

> *"Old men speak of Li the Immortal,
> who once ascended to the outer limits of space.
> He took along no unnecessary baggage,
> only the crane he was riding on."* [1]

The next repetition brings us into contact with The Aerial Courser of
the Immortals, that lovely creature, the White Crane, which has arrived
and is gently spreading its wings upon us.

We recall that its first appearance in Part One arose out of an opening of the heart and was a significant turning point in the child's later
search for truth and peace of mind. Now its arrival relates to a different area of growth. We have been released in some degree from mental
turbulence by meditation on the Monkey Thoughts; have experienced
the spiritual uplifting which Hearing with the Spirit can convey; have
achieved balance from the Diagonal Flying movement and - having
been enriched by its connection with the realms of the Immortals - have
been offered much spiritual enhancement. Now, with the arrival of the
White Crane - which flies between the two spheres of heaven and earth
- we have had to come down to earth again to focus further on the 'twins
of duality' and, as we do so, it is as if we are poised between self-consciousness and self-awareness in order to decide which, currently, has the
greater influence.

As with the previous repetitions, this movement feels both familiar
and new - and again we are comforted by its familiarity. What is surprising, however, is that our understanding of 'time' has changed and that

this seems to be directly related to whether self-consciousness is upper-most, or self-awareness. It has taken a long time to learn little more than five minutes of the T'ai Chi, and we well-remember how self-conscious we were when first we started and how each new movement seemed such a challenge. And yet, since then, we have discovered that we can do a great deal in what used to be *"only"* five minutes, provided our attention were directed solely on what we were doing, *without the interference of self-consciousness* - and that the reverse is also true. This change in our perception of time, thus has brought forth a change in our sense of priorities, for it now is easier to recognise what we have to do, and when we have to do it, as well as what we cannot, or need not do, with the result that no time is wasted. The utter simplicity of T'ai Chi's 'one step after the other', with each step taken slowly and attentively (which, is exactly how Cranes appear to walk), has us extending this pure attention into other realms of life and this, in turn, enhances the quality of each moment we live. Thus, the scales are clearly on the side of self-awareness. But, there is more, for - as always with Chinese wisdom-teachings - the satisfaction which stems from this new perception of "time expanding" leads to another facet of the White Crane's symbolic meaning since, to the Chinese, the Crane is also linked with "life expanding" and, thus, long life itself!

Longevity has always been important to the Chinese, as it is to most people and, moreover, they have always recognised – as we do - that, if the body were regularly fed by a nourishing balance of *yin* and *yang* food, and if sufficient rest (*yin*) and exercise (*yang*) were adhered to, such cultivation of physical well-being would lead to a clearer and more stable mind. Then, if the mind were clearer and more stable, the spirit could flourish and, if the spirit flourished, long-life was virtually assured – hence the belief that, with age, came wisdom. Sages were never youngsters and people lived long if both their spiritual *and* physical capacities had been developed. More-importantly to the Chinese, however, if a person had lived healthily into old age and, thus, had had more time to acquire wisdom, death was not to be feared, since the ultimate, perfected wisdom of a sage would assure life with the Immortals, the spirits of whom, together with those of the ancestors, were deeply revered.

This second and potentially powerful appearance of the White Crane therefore indicates that 'time' can shift and change, lengthen and shorten, according to the degree of our focus upon what we are doing, and that it no longer need be seen as such an 'enemy', in our over-busy, Western world. Furthermore, if we combine spirituality with the cultivation of a balanced *yin* and *yang* life-style, there is – with due respect to the dictates of the Universal Laws of Life and Death - the promise of longevity as well.

21 Brush Knee and Twist Step

Cutting through projections; further co-ordination of body, mind, and spirit, and moving ahead with clarity and awareness

The third repetition now occurs with the 'slicing down' and Bear Step of the Brush Knee and Twist movement, giving us yet another opportunity for mindfulness.

Some of us may have become too spiritual, over-reaching ourselves in our imaginative flight with the gods, to the detriment of the necessary fulfilment of other, more earthly aspects of our human condition. Conversely, we may have reacted against the spiritual message of the White Crane and plummeted too wildly down to earth in the opposite direction. Perhaps our feminine, *yin*, yielding and receptive qualities have been overborne by our masculine, *yang*, and active components - or vice-versa. But the inter-play of opposites in the T'ai Chi can counteract such possible imbalances and show us how to avoid the dangers of what Carl Jung termed 'projections', projections which are based on illusion and which frequently cause much conflict.

As has been made clear, there is nothing – whether mental, physical, spiritual or emotional – which does not have its opposite. This not only applies to the more obvious conditions of night and day, black and white, love and hate, life and death, but includes the more subtle, sometimes less-definable attributes of fact and fantasy, truth and falsehood, reality and illusion, right and wrong. And although we try to give meaning to a life that is based on these complementary opposites, we seem unable to find both of them acceptable. We like one thing and dislike another, preferring (perhaps) day to night, morning to evening, summer to winter, white to black. We may be happy with facts, truth, or what we consider to be reality, or we may delight in fantasy, imagery, make-believe and illusion. Yet, how do we recognise one from the other or sift through our mental and emotional responses in order to establish what is true – or not - for us? How do we evaluate, and deal with, all the dualistic information we are offered?

Social and parental conditioning governs most of our basic attitudes, whether we like them or not, but, on the whole, we like what gives us psychological or physical ease, and dislike what make us feel uncomfortable – and make our judgements accordingly. There are times, however, when we feel uneasy about things that are seen to be 'right', or find that there are differing levels of truth about the same set of circumstances. This causes confusion and we find it difficult to come to a conclusion that is clearly defined-enough for us to feel comfortable. The emotions produce one reaction, reason another, conditioning a third, and a fourth may be provoked by someone else's entirely-different point of view. So, to find a solution, we suppress certain thoughts and feelings and promote others, condoning those we believe are acceptable to others, in order to appear 'normal', and disapprove of those of which others disapprove, turning our own reality into its opposite by wishing it away with rationalisation. But, we still can feel uncomfortable (and sometimes quite ill), since our rationalisations are based on our desire for what society sees as mental and emotional security and not upon the truth of things, with the result that our observations often place us in a state of psychological suspension. Still insecure, we then might project as valid for the present situation, accumulated information from a previous experience, or we listen only to other people's views and then, later, proffer, as our own, their (second-hand) opinions, projections and conclusions, whilst, at the same time, feeling an uneasy sense of inadequacy.

This familiar split in consciousness can cause depression, but also can result in a form of rebellion which, if not as pronounced as that in adolescence, is equally an attempt at the 'individuation' process. Because adult life has become so difficult and is not resolving itself as we had hoped, we are drawn towards others whom we think are freer, more psychologically secure or more spiritual than we are, or, out of contrariness, those whom we imagine our parents or society would not have approved of, or 'understood'. We try to think and act according to the new image, use new ways of speech, emulate different styles of clothing, copy the behaviour and adopt the belief-systems of our new-found friends and, in so doing, imagine that we are free of our past, our parents' influence, or from the standards of our society. What we have done, however, is taken on the mantle of other people's ideas about what inner freedom, or psychological security, or spirituality is supposed to be about, and then projected their beliefs onto our own, thereby conforming to just the same degree as before.

Whatever the circumstances – and they may vary considerably – we are familiar with most of the conditions in which projections ripen. Best known of all – and the most destructive to true seeing – are the projections of Monkey's fears which have already been mentioned, and which we impose upon so much of our thinking. But there are so many others. The person who had little conventional education, or who did badly at school, becomes passionate about literary exactitude, or projects those who teach, or who are in authority, onto a pedestal. Someone who had early difficulties in social situations may project 'ideals' onto those who appear to be more adept in handling political or social circumstances and form a belief that such people can further their own inadequacies. 'Do-gooders' who, from a spiritual concept or conceit, rarely behave out of line with specified spiritual precepts, then project virtues, which they often lack themselves, onto their 'leaders' or 'gods', as well as upon themselves. The psychologically-insecure project their mistakes, failings and guilts onto others, using the "it's your fault" response at times of discord. Parents project onto their children much of what they themselves wished for, or failed in. Those who have been rejected in childhood criticise those who appear to be rejecting them; and the swift 'falling in love' and attraction of opposites creates endless projections which can cause considerable conflict when early joys start to fade. Thus, we may think we feel respect or love, but are drawn to that which we lack or have been denied – and when the member of the political party, or the person in authority, or the teacher, or the newly-found loved one, becomes all-too-human and is seen to be without the virtues we had imagined, we are filled with resentment – and respect and love no longer.

Thus, our projections form some of our psychological burdens and, although they are fundamental to the human condition and may even, in one sense, contribute to 'making the world go around', they remove us even further from Primary Reality and we need to deal with the illusions they foster and the physical malaise the engender, with whatever help we can obtain.

Jung believed that we could learn from such projections and could work upon the areas we lack by, for example, acquiring further education without assuming that our teachers were superior to ourselves; by promoting the firmer, masculine sides of our nature, if too compliant and yielding; by nurturing the feminine within, if too aggressively assertive and dominant, and by being more-swiftly alerted in both mind and body to the physical and psychological reactions that relate to our disappointment in others. This means seeking spiritual growth without gullibility, idolatry or worship, and accepting the flaws and failings in others (and in ourselves), before committing ourselves to a cause, a belief-system, or to 'undying love'. And, although it might be necessary to recognise how rapidly (despite possibly long and conscientious 'work' on ourselves) we move to yet another person to idolise, or group to be attached to - and how, once again, we put more knowledgeable people onto new pedestals - our experience of these repetitions can help us recognise the patterns of our responses and be freer from the tyranny of our earlier needs. Life can then be perceived in such a way that there is simply 'observation', without a projecting 'observer', and we can act from the *wu-wei* or ego-free state, which contributes to the larger order of the universe.

Illustrating this in our T'ai Chi Journey, we have a choice. We can consciously cut through projection, by using the upper hand - which had been nearer to the heavens – to slice downwards towards the lower, earth-facing hand and then brush-away any remaining debris with the other hand, or we can allow those fluctuating and conflicting projections to remain in the mind without acting upon their impulses or re-acting to them emotionally. In either case, we can complete the movement with a strong, clear Bear Step forward, with an awareness that we *can* be released from projections and that the three repetitions have prepared us for the next - and fascinating - life-enhancing movement, for we now are ready for the search for our creative gift.

22 Looking for the Golden Needle

The search for our creative gift or talent for living

Now the time has come for us to seek "The Treasure of the Golden Needle at the Bottom of the Sea". The needle in the title refers to an acupuncture needle - which, in China, could be made of pure gold, since gold neither rusts nor erodes and is immensely strong - and the movement that we make of 'seeking and diving down' is towards the opponent's foot. Allegorically, however, we seek a *golden* needle because alchemists and philosophers alike not only respect the attributes just mentioned, but recognise gold's intangible and symbolic qualities - for it is the colour of the sun and, like the sun, has a powerful, *yang* effect upon our well-being, growth and creativity. It is also, at its finest, extremely malleable and so this Golden Needle movement is symbolically perceived as denoting the power of insightful creativity, which dives swiftly down towards a target, with intuition as its guide.

It is an exciting and entirely-different movement - as is its equivalent meaning in life - but, because it is said that: *"Contemplating the Tao releases unparalleled creative power, bestowing spontaneity and serenity – in a word, unbounded freedom – but it is something each must find in the silence of his heart"* [1], its meaning also suggests that, before we can experience and fulfil our true creativity, a peaceful inward state is required so that a measure of focus and *'contemplation of the Tao'* can be obtained. Thus, the movement not only follows upon the messages in the recent repetitions and in our ability to dispose of both Monkey and Tiger through meditation and allied practises, it also furthers an understanding that a calm mind can release the creative spirit, as well as engender psychological and spiritual clarity.

Such a search also requires a second component that is by no means of secondary importance: an external location that offers freedom from our daily concerns and is without noise and/or Monkey-chattering people. So, again, as we did when we Carried Tiger to the Mountain, we step aside from the materially-minded world and, in so doing, are reminded that the intrinsic value of any creative gift or action is lost, if it is expressed from a spirit of competition or with a motive for personal gain, for, as Chuang Tzu said:

> *"When an archer is shooting for nothing*
> *He has all his skill.*
> *If he shoots for a brass buckle*
> *He is already nervous.*
> *If he shoots for a prize of gold*
> *He goes blind*
> *Or sees two targets –*
> *He is out of his mind!*
>
> *His skill has not changed. But the prize*
> *Divides him. He cares.*
> *He thinks more of winning*
> *Than of shooting –*
> *And the need to win*
> *Drains him of power."* [2]

Eastern wisdom also teaches that the creative gift cannot be found by 'floating on the surface of things'. We have to dive – and deeply so – into what are known as the "Waters of Wisdom", where all is still and crystal clear and where, whilst still benefiting all things, water's exceptional qualities of neither striving, climbing nor clinging are made manifest. Thus, the Taoist seeker has no craving for recognition; no wish to rise to fame; is not attached to her or his gifts and does not cling to what has been created, for, when these desires arise, the world of the spirit is lost. In true Taoist fashion, the mind is allowed to flow like water into deep pools of meditation before creation is to take place; whatever talent arises is used to create that which the spirit directs, and the artist then can proceed to whatever comes next, like a stream to a river and a river to an ocean.

And we do the same. We do not look back to where we were, or ahead to where we imagine we might be going, and thus have time to pause in stillness, reflect, and let the mud settle, so that we can listen to *"the silence of the heart"*. We step aside and ponder on all this and, when ready, prepare for our search. Like birds that circle before they land, like artists that handle and mix the tools of their craft before preparing a canvas, our arms now form beautiful arcs outwardly and then gently draw inwards again. One hand brushes aside any remaining cobwebs in the mind before, fully-conscious of the wisdom teachings, we then send the other hand high towards the heavens to receive a blessing from the

gods of creation. And then, as we lean forward, the higher hand dives down. No lifting of shoulders nor of upper back takes place, no dropping of head occurs. The head remains poised, the spine remains straight and the *tan t'ien* and diaphragm are relaxed. All that is required is that the hip joints rotate the torso forward whilst the weight sinks into the opposite leg from that of the divining hand. And thus - as stream-lined and smooth of motion as a diving dolphin – we dive-down with focus and arrow-like precision.

Down we go, and down and down and, diving even deeper, we submerge ourselves in the depths. We know not what we will find and nothing will be revealed until we reach the "Bottom of the Sea". But we do know that we are seeking our Golden Needle of Creativity for its own sake and, having arrived at the ocean-bed of our being, we find that, by such seeking, we have also received. For the next movement reveals that, indeed, we *have* located the Golden Needle, and that this perfection of 'seeking and finding' has made the search a perfect balance of opposites, for, once the movement is fulfilled and our creation is complete, we can send its results out into the world.

23 FAN THROUGH THE BACK

The expression of our creative gift

Simplicity of design and economy of movement are so deeply engraved into the Chinese soul that they are taught that the *one* symbolizes the *whole,* as one 'branch with leaf' can portray a forest. As a result, a Chinese artist can take forty years of preparation, before painting a single 'branch with leaf' which satisfies his or her philosophical understanding and artistic training.

On a different, but just as meaningful scale, the discovery of the hologram has revealed that one cell exemplifies every cell in the body, but still we fill our canvases full, unwilling to leave an empty space, adding here, embellishing there and leading over-full lives, as well. And we find it difficult to accept that the whole of life might be expressed in a single stroke, or that one T'ai Chi movement – when studied over time and repeated many times - can convey the essence of the whole Form.

Thus we learn from the Chinese artist who, exploring the spiritual dimensions of her or his creative gift, takes a very long time to find the centre of stillness before applying the first stroke of the brush. Carefully and meditatively choosing the brushes and preparing the materials, slowly grinding the tablet of ink into powder and then mixing the powder with water, they sense the inner spirit through the tools of their art. As with the silence of the Quakers, which – when deeply experienced – can bring forth considered speech, such meditative attention allows the artist to become one with his or her vision, before making that first stroke, but they also are taught that it may only remain on the canvas as it was when first placed. As with the spoken word, it cannot be rubbed out, gone over, re-arranged or altered in any way and remains the one true expression of the artist's inner state, at that moment in time.

The relationship between the inner state and the creative process also applies to calligraphy and, before they apply their talents to any other area of creativity, many Chinese artists are trained in the skills of this highly-developed art form, because each character used is symbolically so meaningful. For example, the character for 'great' combines three strokes to convey a great person, with arms and legs that are spread wide-open, whilst the word for 't'ai' has these three strokes with one more added in the middle, to indicate a great person who is 'centred' in the *tan t'ien*, thereby - with just four strokes – depicting a supreme human being who is wide-open to the world. If, however, one more stroke is placed just above those, the ideogram for 'heaven' is created.

The analogy between Chinese painting, the performance of T'ai Chi, and Chinese calligraphy applies here also, for, as well as the shared components of Stillness and Preparation, the Chinese calligrapher must always paint the ideograms, or characters of the Chinese language, in the same order of stroke formation; the emphases of *yin* and *yang* must be indicated by variations of pressure and usage of brush, and continuity must be so maintained that, ideally, there should not be a hair's breadth pause between one stroke and the next. By the same token, T'ai Chi's movements are performed in exactly the same order and sequence; the expression of a hand or leg varies according to its *yin* or *yang* components; continuity of movement is an absolute requirement, and the flow should be as that of the supreme Yangtze River itself. Nor can any one person's handwriting or calligraphic skill ever be copied *exactly* by another, in the same way as any one person's expression of the T'ai Chi Ch'üan can ever be identical to that of any other practitioner. We may learn from and be influenced by the same teacher, but *how* we move our bodies or *how* we write does not only depend upon the teacher's methods, but upon our physical capacity, intrinsic nature, psychological responses, our perception of each movement, and on our comprehension of the subject as a whole.

The T'ai Chi's analogy with the best in other art forms, thus becomes clear: at the beginning of our Journey, at the time of The Stillness, we released ourselves from the day's activities, emptied ourselves of duality and allowed ourselves to be attentive, not only to each moment, but to the depth of silence in the timeless Void. The expression of that Stillness then streamed from the mind and activated the body and The Preparation took place. The dualities then manifested in physical and mental action and we continued through the many movements of the Form and with all the varieties of change, until the arrival of the 'now' – and that 'now' is hereby portrayed.

We have sought *and found* our creative power. We have plunged deeply into our inner being and now can use the Golden Needle to weave our particular blend of colours and shapes, designs and forms and our unique richness of pattern and individuality. And we can also send the result out into the world with no desire to shine like gold when making the offering, nor any wish to influence anything that may result from the giving, for it is enough that the creation has been accomplished for its own sake. And so, from those depths of meditative awareness, we now draw up the Golden Needle from the Waters of Wisdom and

convey it to the surface, slowly, strongly, cleanly. Then, with one hand rising in spiritual gratitude to the gods of the Tao who enabled us to divine our talent, the other moves forward to offer the gift out into the world.

The movement is called "Fan Through the Back" and the title refers to the fan-like shape made by the arc which curves up and over from the lower back to the lower hand, as well as to the shape made by the back-muscles (which are strengthened in the process), as they 'fan outwards'. In the T'ai Chi,

it might convey an actual fan that has been created for a Japanese Noh play or for use in a Chinese opera, or it might form the background for a beautiful painting or for some words of wisdom or poetry in exquisite calligraphy. It is immaterial in what realm the creative gift manifests, for, whilst it might be in the traditional areas of artistic expression, it can also be in cooking, weaving, or running a business without power or greed. It might be in the gift of relationship, knowing how to listen, how to care, how to heal. It may be in such diverse activities as making felt dolls for the poor, or becoming an actor. It does not matter as long as the gift has been divined in the silence of the heart and has been offered to others without wish for reward: for the giving of the gift is that which is pure in the gold.

* Translation: "I have heard the sounds of the pines since the beginning of time" (Pines are a symbol of Longevity)

24 TURN BODY AND CHOP WITH FIST

Fulfilling the creative process; pondering upon T'ai Chi's 'choreography', and the subtle re-appearance of the Tiger

The creative process is a form of therapy, integrating those elements in the psyche that have become separated and bringing the opposites into consciousness, and, although the process has its difficulties, it can give great joy. See the pleasure on a child's face as she or he produces (frequently circular) shapes on paper; put a paint-brush into the hands of an ape and watch the excitement as its paws involuntarily describe (frequently fan-shaped) curves onto a canvas – and see how justly proud are both children and apes of their achievement.

Notice, too, how, when drawing something as specific as a house, children often abstract only what has meaning for them by putting (like the 'branch with leaf' of the Chinese painter) just one window to signify the many.

As we grow older, the pleasure remains, but, with so much to synthesise internally, the ability to abstract what is important decreases and artists of every calibre are often hard-put to describe the roots of their inspiration, or why they are compelled to create. Moreover – in China – the inner urge of a true artist is not only to portray what is perceived without, or sensed within, but the results of their inspired vision should accord with truth as a whole, in the same way as the Chinese musician hopes to compose that which is in harmony with universal harmony and

125

the Chinese poet aspires to 'become the bamboo', before he pens its reality. But, the miracle is that there is access to those areas which the artist attempts to make tangible and that much inspired creation can occur, for, despite all the pains and hard labour which can form part of creative achievement and the frequent lack of recognition or reward which can accompany such a creative urge, most artists have little alternative: paint, write, compose, sculpt or design they must.

Did the originators of the T'ai Chi feel the same as such artists, with regard to the symbolic titles and the order in which they, and the movements, were arranged? Did they – from the depth of their monastic meditations – become 'choreographers' who were compelled to place the movements in such a way that, from an aesthetic point of view, their 'shapes in space' would combine beauty, art and Nature and thus be woven into what has been recognised as today's T'ai Chi meditative art form? Or, were the movements and their specific order devised solely through a wish to improve the health of body, mind and spirit? Historical accounts tell us that the movements emerged from the necessity for exercise after long hours of meditation; that the Forms emerged over many centuries as linked physical exercises (some of which, as has been said, were based on those of animals), and that the movements were also used as a method of self-defence. More than with any of the T'ai Chi's creators, however, T'ai Chi has been identified with two monks.

The first monk, an Indian called *Boddhidarma*, or *Ta-Mo* (who brought *Ch'an* (Zen) Buddhism to China in 527 A.D.), taught the monks of the now-famous Chinese *Shao-Lin* Buddhist monastery how to obtain physical fitness by exercising properly and then, later, incorporated his teachings into the still-famous classics: "The Change of Sinews" and "The Marrow-Washing", as well as into various Ch'i-Kung exercise systems. The second monk, *Chang San-feng*, who lived into the 2nd Century A.D., was said to have so focussed his mind on the Tao that he expressed, as it were, his own fulfilment of The Search for the Golden Needle with the *"supreme achievement of creating the art known as T'ai Chi Ch'üan"*, by re-working the developing martial artistry of the monks in the *Shao-Lin* monastery into what became known as: "The Thirteen

Postures". He also furthered Boddhidarma's emphasis on 'exercise after meditation', as well as incorporating even-deeper *Ch'i* promoting breathing techniques into the movements, thus following upon that which the sage, Chuang Tzu, (369 to 286 B.C.), had already handed down as the important system of combining inhalation and exhalation with each movement.

China then produced many T'ai Chi Masters over many centuries, all of whom taught in private and some of whom adapted its martial orientation into further varieties of Form and Style. The Form most practised, however, both in Asia and in the West, has been the Yang Style, Long Form, as given by Master *Yang Lu-chan*. Known as "*Yang* the Unsurpassed", he was the first to teach T'ai Chi *publicly* in Peking in the 19th Century and it is his grandson, *Yang Ching-pu* (1883-1936) who continued to teach this Form, the 88 movements and titles of which comprise the basis of this Journey.[1]

This brief outline of only one of China's splendid art forms, enables us to recognise how T'ai Chi's foundations were laid; why - from a physical viewpoint - the Order of movements of Master *Yang's* Long Form arose, and why so many of the movements are repeated. Firstly and most importantly, the body is not required to perform a difficult movement for which it has not been physically prepared and so the easier movements are placed in the first sections and the more-difficult ones much later. Secondly, the vital complementary opposites of *yang* and *yin* are incorporated into all the movements, so that there is a clear distinction between solid and empty and internal and external energy. Thirdly, there is the *tan t'ien* central leadership, and, fourthly, there is the vital, flowing continuity between one movement and the next. All these factors alone would thus ensure that no bodily stagnation would occur and that all attributes would combine to create the perfection of dualistic balance in a physical foundation. There are also the repetitions, however, which not only enable what has been learnt and experienced to be improved-upon and more-easily retained, but, simultaneously, offer a superb symbolic arrangement in Allegorical terms. And, it is this latter Allegorical component that is made even-more apparent when (apart from the other repetitions) one finds that ten of the thirteen sequences in the original, Long Form conclude with the same 'summing up' of the beautiful Single Whip (Bird's Beak/ Phoenix) movement, whilst the three remaining sequences conclude with the sublime and highly-symbolic Carry Tiger to the Mountain, which not only delineates the end of each of the three Parts, but, in the case of the 'finale', is followed by the grand fulfilment of the whole of the Form.

Then there is the breath. From observation of the *yin* and *yang* in relation to sickness and health, each movement incorporates the deep knowledge of *Ch'i* and its passage through the lungs, its effect upon the energy-meridians that run through the body, and the importance of various *Ch'i*-inducing exercises on all its parts. Thus, the T'ai Chi's rhythmic flow, its combination of breath with movement, and its *yin/ yang* balance in the arrangement of the movements, all unite to produce a Form which integrates the whole system and enables the body to function at its best.

We then have the significance of the great boon that comes with the titles themselves, for, from their inspiring and fascinating array, we have so many symbols allied to the movements: cranes, bears, music, mountains, monkeys, diagonal flying birds, golden needles, clouds, horses, a goddess, snakes, waters of wisdom, a golden rooster, the Seven Stars, a lotus and, of course, the tiger! The symbolism inherent in the naming of the movements is, thus, of great significance, whilst their order indicates a very-clearly defined 'story', which gives us many opportunities for self-knowledge and spiritual growth and offers the vital fact that the specified progression of their symbolic spiritual dimension could not have been by chance.

We therefore have a unique Allegorical story that combines: a) psychological and philosophical insight; b) the knowledge of human anatomy and the effect physical and breathing exercises have upon it; and c) movements that align themselves with how Nature's creatures move, all of which must surely answer the question concerning the T'ai Chi's symbolism and choreography in the affirmative, as well as clarify how, undoubtedly, they were motivated by awe-inspiring creative endeavour. Equally without doubt, they would have seen its spiritual potential in the slow, silent, rhythmic continuity of the movements, for, apart from the calming effect it has upon the performer, one need only watch an observer of T'ai Chi to see how much he or she is moved by its aesthetic beauty and is stilled into peace by the depth of its meditative qualities. Moreover, not only does it have these components of silence and continuity, but when a more advanced level has been reached, there is also the deep focus that accompanies each movement.

From all this, it is not hard to imagine how an exquisitely choreographed series of movements could have emerged out of the meditative practices of *Boddhidarma* and *Chang san Feng* and the other monks who later practised and taught the T'ai Chi Ch'üan; to what degree they understood the vital importance of symbolism in movement, and how all the factors mentioned above could not only provide the perfect vehicle for their own physical, mental and spiritual needs, but an Allegorical Journey.

So now we, too, have sought the Golden Needle of creativity and, having discovered it and sent it out into the world, pay tribute to those ancient monks by drawing our hands up and over our head in a beautiful completion of the fan-shaped movement, as if following the golden sun across the blue dome of the heavens, before bringing one hand down to face the earth to thereby complete another arc of creation. But, now, something else becomes apparent. Now something of a different order occurs, for, despite our understandable joy in the fruits of our talents, our gratitude for their fulfilment, and our happiness in having others appreciate our work, we see how true it is that the journey of the spirit is beset by pitfalls and that the most frequent accompaniment to the display of creative endeavour, or to success in any field, is pride in achievement. Now, our mortal, human frailty takes over again, for, no sooner do we receive praise, than we begin to praise ourselves. No sooner do we praise ourselves, than ego returns in the shape of a Tiger which, at this stage, barely reveals itself, hardly moves into the forefront of our consciousness. Symbolised by the almost unobtrusive re-appearance of the Ch'üan, the fist, the Tiger only appears at the end of the downward-hand movement and then almost disguises itself, and - because it so often arrives without our conscious awareness - we do not immediately register its subtle, soft, padded-paw arrival.

25 Lunge with Fist and Swoop Down; Twisted Step; Deflect Downwards, Strike and Punch

Striving to repeat the creative process;
anger at rejection, and Tiger in total control

We continue the movement, still barely conscious of Tiger's presence, and find ourselves caught up in a wave of new creative activity, sweeping the left, *un-fisted* hand back and down and forward and up in a clean, strong burst of artistic expression, fulfilling all that the right, creative side of the brain has produced and feeling very alive and filled with the energy generated by other peoples' (and our own!) recognition of our creative talents. But, whilst our consciousness is focused on the creative self, we are unaware that, in a dynamically-circling *fisted* right hand, the dictates of the left, worldly side of the brain are holding pride in our previous achievements; an increasing desire for further reward, and a deep need for recognition and fame.

Tiger has leaped out from behind its cover and, avid for validation, urges us to create more, and more, and even-more, so that we may repeat our successes and gain worldly recognition and respect. "But, what..? Oh!" (Tiger is shuddering), our new creations are not received nearly as well as our earlier, more modest, triumph and, worse, when our next 'masterpiece' is entirely rejected, we totally forget the lesson of Chuang Tzu's archer; dislike Life intensely; become irritable and quarrelsome; criticise other (more successful) works; decry the system which allows such mediocrities to be acclaimed; declaim (frequently): "it's always whom you know, not what you know"; lash out at our own work; flare up, fume, and fret, and before we know it, *all* the lessons of spiritual wisdom recede into the background, as if they had never been there at all.

This anger is now portrayed, and fiercely so. As the clenched fist lunges out and the Tiger roars and lashes its tail in a flashing torment of swishing and swirling and swooping and punching in a sea of red-hot rage, nothing and no-one could convince us that the loss of our innate sense of truth and unique talent is because we allowed ambition, vanity, fear and pride to influence our creative endeavours. But, it is so. The required Stillness before creation had been absent. No Preparation had taken place to link us with the Universal Laws. No inspiration had been drawn from a meditative dwelling-upon the tools of our endeavours and no quiet joy had been felt in the consciousness of creation for its own sake. Now, in turmoil, with no awareness that our opponent is still our bitterly-hostile and sorely-damaged self, all we know is that we have been thwarted and rejected, and our only wish is to lash out at anyone who dares repudiate our worth.

"Are artists so very different from other human beings?" asks Krishnamurti. *"Why do we divide life into the scientist, the artist, the housewife, the doctor? The artist may be a little more sensitive, may observe more, he may be more alive. But he also has his problems as a human being. He may produce marvellous pictures, or write lovely poems, or make things with his hands, but he is still a human being, anxious, frightened, jealous and ambitious. How can an 'artist' be ambitious? If he is, he is no longer an artist. The violinist or the pianist who uses his instrument to make money, to gain prestige – just think of it – is not a musician."* [1]

So, pride in achievement with conceit as its companion; competition; comparison, envy - all emerged out of the 'need to win' and, inevitably, resentment and anger followed in their wake. But, then, as is the way with all opposites, a change occurs. Due to our own suffering and the pain we are causing to others, we slowly recognise and accept how it was that Tiger had re-established its place in our lives and had been so completely in charge. Eventually, this perception moves us away from Tiger's influence, as *Hegu*, in the fist of The Tiger's Mouth, does its work. That acupuncture point was very-firmly pressed – and lengthily so - in those angrily-fisted movements and caused much pain, but such an extreme sensation forced us to let-go of the fist and re-learn something which is beyond the satisfaction

132

of creativity, something which is beyond the self, and which we had understood much earlier in our Journey. From *Hegu* we learn, yet again, that, by unfolding the fist and dissolving Tiger's bondage, joy can come flooding back and that this enables us to flow – with relief – into the next movement.

26a (Single) "Painting the Rainbow"*

*The re-emergence of creativity as ego is
relinquished and joy is released*

The fist has unfurled and we circle the hand in a beautiful movement of joy-filled inspiration and creative energy. We reach for a new canvas, another piece of wood or clay, place another blank page before us, connect again with love to the world around us. In tandem with the joy of open-handedness, we more-fully understand something which is not new, but which comforts us immensely. After all the pain of rejection and the suffering of the creative spirit, Nature's necessary and inevitable opposite follows as consistently as calm follows a storm - and an exquisite portent, a rainbow, appears.

With Tiger's withdrawal, the spirit is free and we 'paint' that rainbow. We use its seven colours of violet, indigo, blue, green, yellow, orange and red (although the Chinese acknowledge only five colours, due to the first three being almost indistinguishable) and, as our fingers trace each brilliant hue, the action integrates our fragmented emotions and allows the results of our re-found talent to flow out in ever-widening arcs of coloured light, thus utilising those highly-coloured emotions in the most creative of ways. And, we ponder upon colour in relationship to emotion and imagine what it would be like if such rainbow-coloured lights were visible to others *during* our various outbursts, with each colour depicting the seven sensations of joy and love, grief and desire, fear, anger and hatred. We would then be so much more tolerant of others (because we have a tendency to imagine other people to be more stable and secure than we are and would see that they are as vulnerable as we) and we would understand our own feelings so much better, because they would not be repressed and, thus, could not be hidden. And what rainbows we would make, and how much swifter and deeper might be our efforts to deal with our imbalances, and how much easier it would

*this title is the author's invention

134

be to recognise and then let go of Tiger...! But, we are usually opaque (and often dense) and it seems more-than enough now to flow creatively with all the colours of the rainbow for, as we proceed, we find that the emotional tensions disperse in their exquisite light and that the spirit is as open as the hand – and is listening.

We then recall the earlier message of *Hearing with the Spirit* and a deep spiritual awareness slowly descends which indicates that – although a little more probing is needed – we are soon to enter into the peace of the Tao again and the flow of the lovely Bamboos.

26b GRASPING THE SPARROW'S TAIL: WARD OFF – SLANTINGLY UPWARDS; PULL BACK, PRESS FORWARD AND PUSH

*The Bamboos: harmony restored,
and the fourth Gateway to Wisdom*

A more sensitive awareness now arises and we are asking questions which we had not considered before. "Why were we so proud of our achievements? Did we produce ourselves, design our brains, put in the intelligence, form the bones and the blood, create the central nervous system, install the organs, the pulse, the heartbeat, instil the energy, infuse the spirit, manufacture the talents? Did we make ourselves, that we should be so proud and arrogant of the creation that is us?"

We cannot say "Yes" to any of these questions and we see that any talent we have, whilst not of our making, can only be furthered with gratitude, and that the world's view of fame and importance is of little import. For our talents are the fruits of the Tao and fame is illusory and, through the acceptance that we know no more than that, we are delivered into the lovely flow and ease of the Bamboos, into the melodies of life's harmonies and into a place as open-hearted and peaceful as that which was experienced by the unselfconscious child in Part One - for again we are blending with the rhythms of the Tao.

Once more we ebb and flow and lift and sink and are carried along as if reclining on silken cushions in a beautiful bamboo swing, rising up and swinging back, advancing and returning. And again we learn why the bamboo is so significant in Taoist teachings and is one of the most revered and respected of all plants in the East.

Often the first choice of would-be artists, the bamboo is more-frequently depicted than the tree peony, the lotus, the chrysanthemum and the cherry blossom, even though these four symbolize the seasons of spring, summer, autumn, and winter, respectively. When the bamboo is painted with the crane, long life and happiness are symbolised, and when it is linked with the sparrow of awakening consciousness, it symbolises good and lasting friendship.[1] Moreover, with true parental unselfishness, the mother bamboo takes no sustenance for herself, but passes it all on to strengthen the young shoots that surround her[2] and, because of the emptiness of the stem and what the Chinese call the 'humility' of its pliability, all varieties of bamboo are symbolic of the supreme virtues inherent in the Perfect Man of Taoist wisdom, indicating that, if mind, body and spirit act as one, good for every living thing will come about of itself. Thus, if a person abides in her or his true nature and in the intuitive understanding of what and when action is needed, she or he would naturally be clear-sighted, kindly, and free from the burdens of self-centred activity - and would not lose sight of the way to live.

So, as the seasons flow, one into the other and we flow with them, sometimes practising our moving meditation indoors, sometimes outside on grass or heath, and frequently making good, supportive, and lasting friendships in the process, we become like bamboos again, empty, pliable, and humble. We then dwell upon the recognition that on this, our third contact with their virtues, our temporary egoless state has arisen from the understanding that we are not our own maker, and that pride in achievement stems from a spurious idea, not of our own superiority, but of a fear that we may be inferior.

With this insight, as offered by our small, in-dwelling sparrow of consciousness, we now joyfully release our burdens, and, as the beauty of the *yin-yang* flow of opposites in harmony engenders in us a deep and fulfilling contentment, another Gateway to Wisdom unfolds within.

27 THE SINGLE WHIP

The Bird's Beak or the Phoenix Stance: the duality between inspired creativity and ego-domination, and its summing up

We now move into the second Bird's Beak and recall that the arrival of the Phoenix indicates a summation of that which occurred during the previous movements, as well as the renewal and re-birth of the spirit after conflict.

The series of movements in question has been particularly long, commencing as it did when we came down from the Mountain of Stillness at the beginning of Part Two and, looking back, it would seem that some of the events along the way have not been so different from those on our earlier travels. Tiger is sometimes (and, occasionally, ferociously) in charge; a measure of calm returns after the fury it created, and duality is still in evidence. But, there have been many other important moments to consider. We are not as blindly enthusiastic as was the young Zen novice. We have absorbed the messages of the intrusive Monkey Thoughts, even if we cannot quite put them into practice. We have understood the meaning of *Hearing with the Spirit* and of how to fly again with the White Crane; and we have come to realise that, although society's demands and Tiger's fears are insistent - as are our psychological projections - there *are* ways of dealing with them. We have learnt that when a Tiger-based creative gift is held up to the light of other people's in-built truth detectors, it is fear of inferiority and illusory pride in achievement that damages our talent, and have re-discovered that when our Golden Needle of creativity is offered to others, with no motive for gain, there is a richness and fullness to life. And there have been four Gateways to Wisdom, indicating much spiritual growth. Most comforting of all, the quiet voice of the Tao has spoken to us again, for when we relinquished the ego, unfolded the fist, and yielded inwardly, we re-learnt something which is beyond the satisfactions of creativity, something which we had understood much earlier on in our Journey, but which had slipped away from our consciousness. We re-learnt that, just by opening the hand, we can be released from Tiger's

138

bondage; that joy *can* come flooding back and that – when we flow with the Bamboos - peace is restored.

So, now we turn to a poet and writer who - like *Tu-Fu* - used the phoenix as his symbol and who poignantly sums-up and describes what happens when the voices of the Tiger and our society take over and our inner knowing is crushed - and of how much pain this causes:

> *"The only reason for living is being fully alive;*
> *and you can't be fully alive if you are crushed by secret fear,*
> *and bullied with the threat: Get money, or eat dirt! –*
> *and forced to do a thousand mean things*
> *meaner than your nature,*
> *and forced to clutch on to possessions in the hope*
> *they'll make you feel safe,*
> *and forced to watch everyone that comes near you,*
> *lest they've come to do you down.*
>
> *Without a bit of common trust in one another, we can't live.*
> *In the end, we go insane.*
> *It is the penalty of fear and meanness, being meaner than*
> *our natures are."* [1]

So now we enact the Phoenix emblem in a physically-identical way to how we first depicted it in Part One, but with a different meaning. In this case, the closed, 'beaked' hand expresses the suffering we experienced when our creative offerings were rejected, and the pride and fear which injured our subsequent endeavours and genuine talent, while the open hand depicts the rebirth which can arise out of those ashes of despair. The head is turned towards the open hand, however - as it always will be - because the direction of our consciousness indicates that the enrichment of self-knowledge proves stronger that the fears inherent in rejection, and that the ever-abiding spirit of the Tao can continue to steer us away from the Tiger.

28 WAVE HANDS LIKE CLOUDS

The 'Dance of Transition' and contemplation,
and dispersing the transitory clouds of anxiety and doubt

A new and lovely movement called "Waving our Hands like Clouds" now has us peacefully floating, drifting and shifting in a dream-like sideways dance. We learn that clouds are symbolic of our doubts, fears and passions and of all the ordinary thoughts of our mind[1] and, conversely, of a celestial condition and life force[2] and so we contemplate the clouds and appreciate their strange duality because, due to the many repetitions of movements to come (which thereby shorten the learning process), this Cloud Arms movement marks the half-way point in our Journey. This, of course, offers some satisfaction, as an indication of the arrival of a major landmark, but it can also reveal the opposite, since - having already given so much time, thought and energy to learning the T'ai Chi Form - the discovery that we are only half-way-through can cause some restlessness.

So, in true Taoist fashion, we step aside and pause a while, restore ourselves with, perhaps, the enchanting song of blackbirds at the end of a lovely summer's day; a glass of wine with friends beside a lake; with the writing of a poem, or – as now - by contemplation upon nature and clouds in the ever-changing skies - and we only continue, when ready.

Replenished and at peace, we now recognise that the restlessness was beneficial, since it revealed both the wish to 'achieve' and the belief in the importance of 'arrival', and we find that the gentle dualistic meaning in the Cloud Arms movement symbolises an opportunity to ponder-upon both those aspects of our conditioning.

We have been taught to strive for excellence in sports, dance and other physical activities, with all the five senses functioning efficiently in as healthy, as well-regulated, and as co-ordinated a body as possible. We have also – and necessarily - been urged to work towards scholarly and intellectual achievement, since these further the self-discipline which enables us to function to our best capacity. And yet, as if there were no proof of our value without them, such accomplishments are often accompanied by prizes and diplomas, badges and certificates, degrees, titles, awards, crowns and jewels, ribbons and medals, robes of office or of spiritual status, and, of course, the acquisition of more solid, material 'proof' of our value in the shape of what we own.

In Taoism, however, it is considered that such acquisitions can set us apart from those who do not have them and that, because they take us into the realms of comparison, they can be a hindrance to the spiritual path by moving us further from the simplicity of the Tao. Moreover, by being 'better', someone else will be 'worse', inevitably there will be rivalry, and rivalry leads to struggle. Once famous, or wishing to be so, we are removed from a state of grace, trapped by the demands of the image-maker as to how we should feel, think, behave and lead our lives, and the more we follow the dictates of fashion or society, the more inwardly-fixed becomes the role we have assigned to ourselves.

Chuang Tzu said:

> *"If you wish to improve your wisdom*
> *And shame the ignorant,*
> *To cultivate your character*
> *And outshine others;*
> *A light will shine around you*
> *As if you had swallowed the sun and the moon:*
> *You will not avoid calamity."* [3]

and this gem of wisdom confirms that, if possible, it is inadvisable to seek situations where one might be conspicuous since, being unnoticed, there is more peace of mind than if one were aspiring-to, or had successfully arrived-at, a position of prominence. And yet it is difficult to remove ourselves from our conditioning and accept that we are just what and where we are, without competition or comparison, and it is equally difficult to stop ourselves from thinking that, by now, we should be some-where else and, even, 'there'. For achievement is bound-up with arrival as well as rivalry and, as this Cloud Arms movement is also sometimes known as "There is no beginning, there is no end", we learn that, apart from the one, certain arrival of physical death, we never psychologically *arrive* anywhere on a permanent basis, but carry our inner, changing responses with us wherever we go. We may have passed examinations, gained *entree* into 'higher' social circles, started a new job, risen in its hierarchy, moved to a different location, changed our name (and even – eventually - completed the whole of the T'ai Chi Form!), but, unless our errors have been serious-enough to shatter our habitual reactions, we still carry the past within us and have to live with what we actually are, even as we, and new circumstances, unfold. Thus, achievement and arrival are spurious in the world of spirit, and this Waving our Hands like Clouds offers an interlude for pondering upon these illusory goals.

Being Taoist-inspired, the interlude also has us meditating upon the nature of clouds in relation to our own nature and we realise that there is a connection between the ever-moving clouds in the heavens and our transitory, ever-changing moods on earth. We perceive that, if dark clouds appear, they are as reflections of our own dark moods and that, if we are wise enough to cry, the tears are as the rain, which clears away the darkness. We see that our doubts can be dispersed as inevitably as are those shifting clouds and that, as in the heavens after a storm, when the sun shines forth and the sky is like a pearl, or the translucent moon and the sparkling stars shed their light again, there is replenishment and renewal and space - and that it is the same for us. It may take hours, days, weeks, sometimes longer for such space and light to appear inwardly again, but, if we listen carefully to the promptings of the unconscious and to the relevant information it wishes to convey, those clouds will dissolve as surely as the sun will return. For our black moods do not represent finite places of psychological arrival, but are infinitely transitory.

Describing this in a different context, the meta-physicist, David Bohm, wrote that the important thing was the flow between the two opposites of the finite and the infinite, for *"each has its role to play"* - but that, although there is an infinite that contains all the finite, the infinite has to be seen in all its finite ways. He also looked at metaphysical thought: *"... as a series of movements in a dance – movements that we make in which we are able to see our errors and so move on"* and said that, whilst carrying out this dance, we not only bring order into the whole universe, but to ourselves as well, for it is *"through the errors we make that we are able to learn, to change ourselves and to change everything."* [4]

Thus, *any* resolution of our neuroses, doubts and uncertainties, any resolution of Tiger's destructiveness, contributes not only to our inner development, but also to universal folding and unfolding and, thereby, signifies a great transition. When, then, we look upwards and ponder upon the clouds in their journey across the heavens, we can be aware, in the most moving of ways, of the celestial life force of the *Ch'i* which fills the skies with such nourishment, and of how it offers such unequivocal proof of the beneficence of the very breath of the Tao.

So we enact the gathering and dispersing of clouds, their layers of light and shade and shape and their shift in slow-motion, whilst these few movements also have us gently reflecting on how to move, unresistingly, with inner change and how to let-go to our expectations. Repeating circular, rolling movements of the arms and legs in three complete cycles, we accompany the three widely-placed sideways-steps and circular arm movements with a gentle rising and a sinking of the legs, which promotes a cloud-like, rhythmic, circular motion. And, in order to incorporate balance, the three circles made by the upper and lower limbs include three *yang* and three *yin* hand movements, the *yin* upper hand symbolising the clouds as they

float across the sky and the lower *yang* hand generating the 'celestial life' force itself as it passes across the area in front of the *tan t'ien,* the storehouse of *Ch'i* power and psychic energy. All this then furthers the strong *Ch'i* energy which, by the powerful tingling in our hands, reveals itself as one of the notable features of healing which these delicate and unusual Cloud Arms movements provide, offering even-further proof of the celestial life force inherent in Nature.

Thus, by using these gentle, swaying, soft movements as a time of transition, an interlude, a resting place, we increase our understanding of the Universal Laws and – with the delightful increase in our physical, tingling energy – we can disperse the clouds of anxiety and doubt and enter into our third Phoenix Stance of renewal and rebirth.

29 THE SINGLE WHIP

The Bird's Beak or the Phoenix Stance: the duality between spiritual contemplation and inner darkness

We have dispersed the clouds and used their gentle, softly-swaying movements as a 'space-between'. We have dwelt upon the Universal Laws of folding and unfolding, of heavy-laden clouds and light-filled skies and, while the Cloud Arms had us moving in a dance, we were able to view our errors, gains and losses from a different perspective, from an understanding that they are as variable and acceptable as are dark clouds above, and that our own ever-changing moods, insights and understandings are but reflections of those ever-shifting cloud formations. Thus, as contemplation released us from the darkness of doubt into a lightness of being - in the same way as night is released by dawn - the Cloud Arms movement revealed the process of transition.

This is now portrayed in another Phoenix Stance, for, amongst its many attributes, the phoenix (or *Feng-huang*) is said by the Chinese to be a symbol of the interdependence of the *yin* and the *yang* in the universe,[1] thus imparting the inseparability and complementary nature of opposites. The first Phoenix in Part One portrayed this duality with the negative self-consciousness and the positive self-awareness that arise out of the difficulties inherent in the human psyche, but it also expressed the potential for spiritual renewal. The second Phoenix symbolised the dichotomy between ego-based activities and the endeavours which arise from spiritual sources. On this, the third Phoenix Stance, we portray contemplation upon the darkness occasioned by our doubts, fears and restlessness, together with the light which follows their resolution.

The movement itself is, of course, a repetition, but there is a difference in the way we flow into it, for we find that, as the last of the three, circling Cloud Arms movements is completed, the back of the right hand sinks down and then outlines a perfect, but small, circle of wholeness and unity, before floating up to make the now-familiar formation of the closed Bird's Beak hand. This small, circling hand-movement thus resembles a farewell, as if to indicate that the beautiful Dance of Transition, the interlude of contemplation, has enabled us to leave behind those doubts and fears which caused us to feel so restless at that 'half-way stage' in the Form, whilst the darkness of their moods is now encapsulated in the slowly-closing hand of the Bird's Beak itself. But then, having acknowledged that closed right hand by a turn of the head, we take the step which enables us to focus fully on the left hand of 'openness to renewal' and our awareness of the illusion relating to 'arrival'.

Facing West with head and centre, we realise, yet again (for it can never be repeated enough) that reflection upon the past enables us better to deal with our problematical present and that, by pondering upon the transitory nature of our black moods, as well as realising that they can be of service to us (and even to the universe), we can understand that, symbolically, our self-protective closed Bird's Beak hand has some distinct advantages. Moreover - if we are wise-enough to use its message well – it encourages us to accept the gift of our darkness and to value the beauty of its opposite, and this generates the essential balance which this movement so powerfully portrays.

30 HIGH PAT ON A HORSE

Pent-up, controlled energy, before strong, aggressive action

The next movement is a surprisingly swift one, swifter than any we have so far experienced, and has us, as it were, drawing back the reins of a horse with our left hand to bring it sharply to a halt, whilst, at the same time, rising up and moving the right hand forward to pat it high on its head.[1]

From the speed of the movement, it is clear that we have received a great deal of *Ch'i* power from the previous sequence of movements. What also is clear is the inevitability of this movement appearing now, for the previous Cloud Arms is also known as: "The Heavenly Horse-riding Steps" and so we are given the opportunity to thank the beautiful, high-stepping horse, which so rhythmically led us across the sky, for enriching us with such strength and energy.

Our left foot has, however, also drawn back in the manner of a colt impatiently 'pawing the ground', and - with the horse representing both speed and power to the Chinese - this pent-up disquiet indicates that our increase in energy may be something of a mixed-blessing. For, although the child and the adolescent had vast reserves of (very obvious) energy with which they conveyed their impatience or aggression, we, as young adults, may have too many suppressed and unresolved conflicts to contend with, which – if not resulting in the malaise of apathy, fatigue, or illness – can generate strong, nervous, ego-dominated energy. Thus, from the restlessness which has now returned, we sense a need for immediate and prolonged activity, as much as a happily-cantering horse might feel when, having suddenly been brought to a swift and unexpected halt, is then held-in-check for far too long.

But, why should we feel this so soon - and so swiftly? We seemed so serene in our contemplative acceptance of our dark clouds and so content with life as it was, and so we question why those insights have dissolved and such impatience returned? Does there have to be still-further evidence of the unease lying just below the surface of our dualistic nature, even-further awareness of our Tigerish under-belly? Do we feel constrained by our insights, restricted by the wisdom-teachings, uncomfortable with the floating serenity just experienced? Is it because we "know in our heart" that "we are not *really* like that", that our Tiger is very much alive, and that it retains an abundance of ego-energy? Or is this swift change yet-another indication that *yang* will always follow *yin*, as *yin* will follow *yang*, and that it is simply yet another example of the opposites in life?

Possibly all these factors are operating and the speed and energy of this swift, but forceful movement are indications that our apparent acceptance of ourselves has only served to make our Tiger more restless and impatient. For the movement is a telling one, and serves as a precursor to convey that, whilst the Cloud Arms undoubtedly gave us a beneficial pause for contemplation, the gentle, apparent 'farewell' to ego and aggression not only did not last long, but the interlude itself was in direct contrast to the high energy of the many assertive, combative and adult Tiger-based movements to come.

31-33 SEPARATION OF RIGHT FOOT; SEPARATION OF LEFT FOOT, TURN AND KICK WITH LEFT SOLE

Continuation of the sharp inner change, and the need for psychological and physical balance when 'kicking out' at life

Still imbued with a strong and pent-up energy, we continue to face the various challenges which life, in a supposedly adult society, presents to us, whilst, at the same time, hoping that we can face such challenges with equanimity. But, it is proving difficult, and we begin to experience swift anger at the frustrations and disappointments which now begin to beset us; an uneasy guilt at responding in this way, and shame because we thought we had become somewhat wiser.

Perhaps ambition is now directing us, acquisitiveness controlling our motives, pride dictating our attitudes again, or are all these contained in the strong drive for power and money and self-protectiveness which is so highly-regarded in our society and which might be influencing us? Whatever the cause of our malaise, it is undermining the spirit and - as is virtually inevitable in a world of hypocrisy, ambiguity and highly-active egos - we retaliate against those who are blocking our path and then are met with such resistance from other people's Tigers, that our own becomes even-fiercer in return. The frustrated or unhappy child, the rejected or rebellious adolescent or the angry young adult - all of whom remain within - rises to the surface in whatever guise, and, together with our strong retaliatory actions, expresses a deep grievance that has us rationalising with such questions as: how could our reactions be otherwise, when the gods of our society are those of rivalry, competition, envy and greed, and how else could we respond, except by a hardening of heart and attitude and the use of the same methods as those used by others? For, these basic instincts are upon us again and we find that they can manifest in a multitude of ways: by ice-cold silence or angry verbosity; swift shifts from friendship to hostility; supposedly-friendly words which subtly can cause the recipient to feel attacked or diminished; by devious and clever 'hair-splitting' when the meaning in the words being spoken can clearly be understood; by 'not listening' or 'forgetting'; by misrepresentation and prevarication; by betrayals; lack of humanity; self-pity and even mock illness; by mental cruelty, or by the terrible use of physical force which can maim and sometimes destroy. But, all who cause pain are in pain, and each, according to his or her nature, will wreak some form of suffering onto others in reaction to the pain he or she has already experienced.

In the T'ai Chi class, we discuss situations in which relatively-mild Tiger activity can occur and the example which comes up consistently is the well-recorded and excellent one of: when people drive, or are passengers in a car. Driving any vehicle is, of course, potentially dangerous to all, but we feel so psychologically-protected by the enclosing nature of a car's body that our Tiger emerges in a satisfying and seemingly acceptable way, and the reasons for this (which were vividly offered) are manifold. For, not only are we in charge of the car, but other people cannot easily 'get at' us. We can say what we like about other people's driving and they cannot hear us. If we anger another driver, there rarely are consequences (that we know of), because seldom are there subsequent face-to-face confrontations. Some car-owners feel superior if their car is newer, bigger, cleaner, faster or more expensive than another's, and hostile or embarrassed when it is not. Some feel justified in competitive overtaking, yet angry when overtaken, and, if a minor conflict of interest occurs, there is the advantage of a quick get-away. There are no factors of friendship, nor even acquaintanceship, to interfere with any hostile reactions (although the situation changes rapidly when we find the other driver is known to us and we think she or he has witnessed our hostility: then confusion, shame and Monkey's swift rationalisations flood the mind to justify such an 'unfortunate' situation, or we defensively 'laugh it off'). So, given all these circumstances, we are in the rare position of being supreme master of the situation, whilst the power invested in such master-ship is heady and immensely-fulfilling to Tiger's self-esteem.

These examples of competitive aggression only do relatively-mild damage to the aggressor, and it is not difficult to recognise the Tiger in our responses. But there are many other examples that can be more demanding of understanding, and in this, our first "Kicking Section", they are symbolised by three kicking movements which require great physical balance, deep grounding, stability of focus and an understanding of the nature of *yin* and *yang* in action. Most importantly, however, the movement must come from our centre and, initially, being unsure of how to kick effectively – and feeling far from balanced - we wobble and jerk, kick somewhat wildly, have no focus of mind over matter and no sense of our *tan t'ien*'s leadership, all of which is understandable, for although small children kick each other mechanically and remarkably often, few adults continue (or have been trained) to do so. So, although our arms give balance and can synchronise with the legs, it is clear that we are physically unstable and all we can do is learn how the movements are supposed to be accomplished and how they relate to their psychological symbolism with regard to our Tiger.

The first two are known as 'extension' or 'separation' kicks, their aim is in different directions and, for kicking purposes, they use only the top of the foot. In relation to aggression, they are relatively innocuous, but both demand focus and, since all the kicks require stability by connecting the energy in our heels up to the *tan t'ien*, it is – as has been said - from this centre that we need to direct all the movements. Thus we use these two, top-of-foot, separation kicks to equate with 'separating things out' and 'assessing the circumstances' so that, if we find we are in a Tigerish position in the external world, these two kicks can correspond to extensively preparing the ground and obtaining all the facts prior to facing a confrontational situation.

The next kick - which has us swing-ing around into a third direction as if an opponent had come up from behind - uses a stronger, fully-flexed heel-sole movement which, whilst also requiring strong focus and *tan tien* centredness, requires a mental 'intention' that is both calm and clear and results from any abil-ity we had to fulfil the two preparatory movements with some balance. Thus, this full kick at an opponent would be – in T'ai Chi terms - at its most effective if it had arisen from a firmly-established, rooted position; in-corporated a calm and balanced mind and body; a clear and poised head, and the use of energies which stream out from a balanced centre of judgement.

In the external world, however, we can see how badly, meanly, nastily, or (what, to Tiger, is infinitely worse) ineffectually, we are 'kicking out' and we wonder how can we achieve balance of mind and body when we feel so un-stabilised and vulnerable? For, all we are doing is furthering our own self-doubts and anxieties by expressing such mean-mindedness or impatience, irritation or rage, manipulation or fear, and the results of such ill-advised psychological 'kicks' are not only unproductive, but both parties are usually 'knocked-out' emotionally by the confrontation and its aftermath.

So, we have to learn that - if a psychological kick is to have real value - we must justify its necessity by obtaining as much information about the situation as possible, in advance, and then assessing the circum-stances with clarity, for only then, slowly and from a firm and balanced standpoint, can we take the appropriate action. We must be free from Tiger's self-defensive mechanisms, for a defensive ego interferes with clear perception and the resulting 'kick' will be disruptive and bring retaliation and difficulties in its wake. It will also serve to no purpose, because we are not allowing others their right to their own 'space', nor listening to their own ideas of freedom and individuality before taking action, since it is only from this foundation that we can speak our own truth with clarity and justice and, if circumstances require it, kick with any power.

These kicks, then, clearly represent what they obviously do – we are kicking-out: at others, at ourselves, sometimes on behalf of others, mostly for ourselves. But we need to be truly balanced, both physically and psychologically, before we can kick with any real effect, for otherwise we not only hurt others, we damage ourselves.

34 Brush Knee and Twist Steps

*Two more Bear Steps: moving ahead, but directed
by the 'lower' energies of Ching and Shên*

As practitioners of the T'ai Chi Ch'üan we are given Ten Essential Points which come from the T'ai Chi Classics of <u>Yang Ching-Pu</u>.* The 2nd of these: *"Suspend your head from above and keep it up straight"*, related to our stance at the Commencement, since, when this Point is applied, we are connecting with the heavens and the spirit of higher consciousness is released upwards, whilst, on the physical level, we find that the spinal column is lengthened and the energy of the central nervous system is strengthened (and that this also applies to yoga, sitting meditation, Chi Kung, the Alexander Technique, lessons in deportment, or when walking, etc.).

The 3rd Essential Point states: *"Loosen your waist"*. Thus, when we are not 'holding in', but are poised and relaxed and can focus on the *tan t'ien's* leadership and - as in the Kicking Section - draw our energy upwards from the feet and legs up to that 'Chinese Waist', our centre is strongly linked to the deep energies of the earth and we can remain secure and firm.

All the Essential Points are important, but it is by the continued application and ultimate mastery of these two, that pure *Shên* energy is released through the lightness and suspension of the upper body and pure *Ching* energy is strengthened in the lower. However, by now we are feeling so physically scattered and lacking in spiritual and psychological strength that, when attempting to apply these two Points to the next two Bear steps - in order to move forward in life and brush away obstacles - we find that the 'impure' energies of *Ching* and *Shên* are governing our actions.

As has been mentioned in the previous chapter, there are many causes for these imbalances and, in the case of our *Ching* energy, it might be that the body cannot so swiftly heal itself from the stresses of our kicking activities; sleep may be elusive and relaxation rare, or artificial tranquilisers may be being used. There may be an over-indulgence of our

*see Appendix B

154

sexual resources, or we are eating and drinking too much or too little of the wrong kinds of food and beverages. Perhaps we are smoking, taking 'recreation' or other drugs, using energy-boosters, or drinking too much alcohol. Perhaps we are chronically over-extending ourselves, working both late into the night and too-demandingly during the day. But, whether we are abusing our natural energies in all, or only a few of these ways, the result will be a depletion of *Ching;* longer periods of recuperation will be required to restore it to its former energy-producing state, and *Ching's* higher attributes of love and compassion, although not entirely absent, will require time to re-establish their full strength and application.

On the spiritual level, the aggression inherent in confrontation and in our kicking would undoubtedly have influenced us, and, as we try to move ahead and deal with obstacles, we find that the ego is still in charge, our *Shên* is governed by high nervous energy, rather than pure spirit, and (again) we are being ruled by ambition and/or fear of failure. So, although tremendous power can be generated from the drive for success, our nervous energy – which is too *yang*, too strong, too lacking in the *yin*, the intuitive and the soft – is causing the spiritual elements of *Shên* to be suppressed. Nervous breakdowns, depression, illness or deep fatigue, and even, at times, a confused sense of who we are or what we are doing, can follow, as well as physical depletion and a loss of contact with inner-knowing. The higher manifestations of *Shên* and any opportunities to lead spiritually-fulfilling lives then are rejected, whilst the pure energies which accompany spiritual fulfilment, and which are created spontaneously by the joy of following the mainstream in ourselves, are diminished.

The ancient Taoists, however, were more fortunate in some respects than we are. In their era (between the 4th and 3rd centuries B.C.) all that they absorbed into their system – whether by air, food or drink - was unpolluted and so there was little interference, from those sources, with bodily immunity. The animals they ate were unconfined and reared on natural produce without chemical boosters. No ecologically-unsound pesticides were sprayed onto crops, vegetables or fruits, and no artificial additives, colours, flavours or vitamins were added to their food. The food itself was neither stored for longer than the weather dictated, nor transported long distances, and there was no plastic packaging. Everything that was bought, bartered, or bargained for was fresh and, although sugar and 'comfort-food' addictions would have occurred then, as much as now, no artificial sugars, sedatives or other drugs were used to over-active or deaden the nervous system and medicines came directly from nature's herbal remedies, without the addition of manufactured ingredients. Moreover, there were no toxic emissions from large laboratories, factories or transport; the seas were clean; nuclear and carbon emissions were unknown; mechanisation had not taken over the world and the 'population bomb' had not exploded.

They were not, of course, without their psychological problems, for human nature has not changed and few would have paid heed to the injunctions to purify the energies of the Three Treasures. Their emotions would have been as adversely affected as ours by aggression, fear, envy, sexual rivalry, jealousy or the loss of a loved one. There would have been endless feuds over property and land and there were many wars; greed would have engendered corruption and fraud; the same strivings for political power, prestige, competition (with its attendant fear of loss) and enmity would have occurred as frequently as in our own society. The many servants of the wealthy would have worked wearily by day and late into the night, and the contrast between the landowners' wealth and that of their under-paid and under-valued servants would have been as vast as it is today. Thus, despite a widespread awareness of, and respect for, the Universal Laws, they would have had emotions as fear-filled and distraught as our own and suffered from the same depletion of *Ch'i, Ching* and *Shên* - and Taoist wisdom would have been as sorely-needed then, as it is today.

So, with many aspects of our lives mirroring those who lived over two and a half thousand years' ago - and with the aspects of both *Ching* and *Shên* manifesting on the physical plane only - these two Bear steps are far from 'pure' in their energy; indicate our inability to regulate how such energy is being used; the Bear is somewhat heavier in spirit (if not in body!), and the misuse of the spiritual elements of the Treasures of *Ching* and *Shên* leads us into further – and inevitable – Tiger activity.

156

35-37 Step Up and Deep Punch Down; Turn Body and Chop with Fist; Lunge with Fist and Swoop-Down; Twisted Step, Deflect Downwards, Strike and Punch

Attempting to repeat an earlier search; Tiger's rage; deep suffering, and a recollection of peace

We twist the fist and lift it high,
then turn and punch it low;
we draw it back and swoop it up
then chop it down below.
We lunge it out and twist it 'round,
unsheathed for its attack,
and then we strike another blow,
before we draw it back.
And then we punch with all the might
of Tiger's roaring rage,
tormented by a dreadful lack
that nothing can assuage.
And then, 'though blinded by our plight,
a light ahead appears;
whilst we're still struggling with the pain,
a light shines through the fears.

The next movement is not unlike that in the Search for the Golden Needle, for the back leans forward with a straight spinal slope and the right hand dives down deeply. Allegorically, the reason for this is clear, because, so stressed are we by our aggression and by our unbalanced energies, that we are recalling with yearning how much we had valued that golden time, that simpler, happier, more innocent time of the search for our creative gift and, having located it, of how fulfilling had been the joys of sending its results out into the world.

So we try to retrace our steps and attempt to dive down further, hoping to capture the past, while Tiger ("most-sensibly", or so it imagines), urges us on to a belief that, if successful, we could utilize our creative gifts in order to gain some prestige! But, because we are *seeking* rewards and deluding ourselves into believing that our only wish is to re-enact a previous, innocent experience, we go about it in the wrong way.

We know we went forward and down – and it feels similar-enough – but we are now so removed from the spiritual life and the pure creative process, that we cannot see that we are using a different arm movement and a *very differently-shaped hand.* For, whilst that earlier search stemmed from an open mind and a correspondingly open, divining hand, now the mind is closed and Tiger is guiding us with a clenched fist, revealing in the most potent of ways the marked difference between the two movements. Moreover, although that earlier, open hand rose-up high towards the heavens to make contact with the gods in a movement which was clear for all to see, this fist is furtive, brought upwards (almost hidden) beside the body, travels only as far as the head and thereby indicates calculation rather than inspiration, manipulation rather than innocence.

We then recall another significant factor: we had not meditated in advance of our search or quietly prepared ourselves. By rushing-in too swiftly, by heeding only the Tiger, we had failed to notice that there were no deep pools of wisdom into which we could spiritually dive, no depths of creativity to plumb, no recollection of 'action for its own sake'. Moreover, even if we had recalled some of those earlier wisdoms, our search would have been fruitless, because, although we can - and often do - repeat the same mistakes by continuing with the same psychological responses, we can never make the same things happen twice in exactly the same way - and we suffer accordingly.

Now, with a Tiger-filled fist, the battle continues. Not only has our search been a failure but, with wisdom ignored and our actions dictated by self-interest, we find ourselves mistiming procedures, misjudging intentions, confusing issues, distorting discussions, mindlessly and wildly lunging and plunging and causing great upheavals. In a terrible jungle of chaotic suffering, we find that Tigers abound, leap down from every tree, lurk furtively behind every bush, or - silently and stealthily - creep up on us from behind. Our inner turmoil is then so deep, so vast, so spiritually-annihilating, that we are blinded by the torment of Tiger's unyielding egoism and find no way of escaping the pressure induced by our self-centred activities, our self-loathing, and our self-pity - and we cannot come to terms with any of it. Older, but no wiser, our Tiger is not only as hurt, untrusting, and damaged as ever, but has grown so strong that we now repeat all the Tiger-filled movements we made after the Fan Through the Back movement, ensnared in a trap of our own making and responding with the same rage as do all caged creatures.

Roaring loudly with tongue-lashing, tail-swishing, eyes glaring and claws slashing, furious at the opposition we are arousing in others, shameful of the effect we are having upon them and ashamed of ourselves as well, the Tiger rages on, until the stark agony of the situation is so overwhelming that we feel the pain can go no further.

And then, somehow, from some place buried deep within us, we sense that there are other options, other ways of living, and one of these begins to surface and finally manifests as a slowly-deepening consciousness that: *it does not always have to be that way,* we do not always *have* to fight and attack and defend, justify and rationalise. And, from that deep, vast, 'somewhere' inside ourselves, we recall another period of similar behaviour and torment and pain - and of subsequent peace - and of how we were released from seemingly endless suffering. Out of our desperate, flailing agony, out of the blindingly-hot tears, that recollection has us hearing, as if from a deep reservoir, the inner voice of the higher realms of the spirit; has us seeing, as if through a vast expanse of arid land, a tiny dot of glimmering light that guides us to the remembrance that we *can* be free and the Tiger *can* dissolve – *if we let go.* And this momentous reminder, this arrival at the limit of our endurance of an intimation of peace, this light at the seeming point of no-return, releases us from our turmoil and leads us with a surge of relief and profound gratitude into the next, most expansive of movements.

38 Diagonal Body; (Double) Painting the Rainbow and Kick with Right Sole

Two-fold creativity from release for the spirit; a healthy kick at Tiger; 'will' and 'intention' in relation to aggression, and recognition of the next steps

With the recollection of peace, the fist is released. With the realisation that life *does not always have to be that way,* our next movement indicates such fullness of joy and expansion of spirit that we Paint *two* Rainbows, make *two* huge arcs of openness and creativity and feel doubly-blessed and doubly-radiant – for now we are using spiritual discernment, *as well as* creative intuition.

Now we see that we *can* live without aggression to others or violence to our own spirit. Now we know that we *can* be released from suffering if we release the fist, both physically and metaphorically *and keep it open.* And, with the re-awakening of the spiritual self, and having painted two deeply fulfilling, releasing and expansive arcs, to our surprise, we kick again! But, this time, the kick is filled with joy, for it is not borne out of frustration or pain or despair, it is not aimed with anger, but has arrived from a conviction that we must kick – and at what? - at Tiger itself (!) and all its distortions and masks, dissembling and rationalisations, at all its self-deceptions, double-standards, self-protections and self-justifications. And our kick must derive from a firmly-stable, centred base!

The full meaning of the Title of this movement then becomes apparent, for the action of the arms is double that of the previous Painting the Rainbow and the kick is made in the opposite direction. And why? - because a rainbow's 'double' reverses its colour...!

161

How portentous do these open, exquisite arcs and brilliant hues then become, for with clear skies appearing, yet again — albeit upon the heaviest of heavy storms - the double rainbow reveals the clarity of what is to come. We see that we can never go through such agony again and that now we must "come to grips with the Tiger": not once, not twice, but with more than double intent, and, most importantly, with a renewed and stronger perception of what is required. So, again, we turn to Taoist wisdom.

As already mentioned, the Chinese word *wu-wei* indicates action which is ego-free, whilst, when taking such action, another of the Ten Essential Points states: *"Apply your will and not your force"*. But, this has to be carefully considered, since the 'will' of the T'ai Chi Classics is not the 'will' of Victorian times, when the prevailing view was that a self-willed, strong-willed child, who - being stubborn, intractable and difficult - should have his or her 'will' broken, "for the child's sake and for that of society". Nor is it the 'will' of determination, duty, or self-discipline, of forcefully bending one's mind to accept ideas of how one should think or behave. How it is construed is that the purest energy of *Shên*, being ego-free, can direct the purest energies of *Ch'i* and *Ching*, in the same way as it does throughout Nature in the fulfilment of the Universal Laws. Thus, if one's inner perceptions are in harmony with such Laws, pure *Shên* can promote ego-less 'intention', rather than 'will', and such 'intention' — when applied to both the simplest or the most complex of issues — is then sufficient to fuel one's natural, highest, energies. Spirit is in charge of Matter, since, once an ego-less perception has arisen out of a state of spiritual awareness, it leads to an insight which is based on wisdom, and the action resulting from this will be both simple, as well as productive.

This simplicity is the opposite to our complicated self-defensiveness, for when thoughts are embedded in the realms of anxiety or self-interest ("Oh, I can't do that, I'd look silly, it's too risky, I'm not capable, it's not possible" or "I'd not get anything out of it for myself" or "what do others think of me and what should I be saying?"), the anxious self interferes with the perception of what is needed and the 'intention' becomes blurred, thereby confusing the action to be taken.

There is also a Taoist maxim offered by Lao Tzu: *"... let life ripen and then fall. Will is not the way at all"*,[1] which indicates that, if we can let go to 'will', as we know it in the West, we will follow the Way that is natural. Thus, the message of this maxim is in the same realm as that in the previous quotation, since it reveals that the best results are those which follow the Natural Laws of yielding and acquiescence and, by respecting these, we will know what to do.

We can also understand this more fully if we recall how we finally found ourselves kicking at our own Tiger, for – with barely a conscious thought - we had intuited that it was spiritually necessary, had formulated the intention, applied our energies, and carried out the action with the minimum of application and the maximum result – and there was joy in the outcome. We had known instability, unhappiness, and confusion. We had been deeply troubled and in spiritual pain. We had recognised its cause and realised that, if peace were to be found, appropriate action would be necessary. Most importantly, we had recognised that the solution was not "out there" in the midst of society's confusions, but within ourselves. And this is where the Taoist meaning for 'will', can be clarified further.

In his book "Beyond Violence", Krishnamurti said: *"There have been those who have said, 'Under no circumstance express violence'; that implies leading a peaceful life although surrounded by people who are very aggressive, violent; it implies a kind of nucleus in the midst of people who are savage, brutal, violent. But how does the mind free itself of its accumulated violence....?*

The source of violence is the 'me', the ego, the self, which expresses itself in so many ways – in division, in trying to become or be somebody – which divides itself as the 'me' and the 'not me', as the unconscious and the conscious; the 'me' that identifies with the family or not with the family, with the community or not with the community and so on. It is like a stone dropped in a lake : the waves spread and spread, at the centre is the 'me'. As long as the 'me' survives in any form, very subtly or grossly, there must be violence...[2]

Now, what have I to do? First I must not escape from it; let us be sure of that. I must not escape from the fact that I am violent – 'escaping' being condemning it or justifying it, or the naming of it as violence – the naming is a form of condemnation, a form of justification.

I have to realise that the mind must not be distracted from this fact of violence ... The mind must be absolutely clear that there is no escape from it; nor must there be the exercise of will which says, 'I will conquer it' – will is the very essence of violence".[3]

Thus, if we can understand that the 'will' which uses will-power, is *'not the way at all'*, and that *"will is the very essence of violence"*, we can take the next steps in the Journey. They are momentous ones, they will not be easy and they will take much time. But they are needed, for we have to closely examine and accept the causes of violence in ourselves and *know* them. One step has already been taken, for we have kicked out at many of Tiger's manifestations. Now, we need to look at other areas within ourselves that we do not 'like', whilst conscious that by acknowledging them without disfavour, we will be given the opportunity to face our ego as fully as our abilities will allow, with no Western-indoctrinated 'will to succeed' blocking our path – and, if this is possible, we will be able to come to grips with the Tiger in *all* its ramifications.

39-45 Hit Tiger at Left, Hit Tiger at Right; Kick with Right Sole; Strike Tiger's Ears with Both Fists; Kick with Left Sole; Turn Around and Kick with Right Sole; Twisted Step, Strike and Punch

Coming to Grips with the Tiger - and its reaction

> *"I am not a mechanism, an assembly of various sections.*
> *And it is not because the mechanism is working wrongly,*
> *that I am ill.*
> *I am ill because of wounds to the soul,*
> *to the deep emotional self*
> *and the wounds to the soul take a long, long time,*
> *only time can help*
> *and patience, and a certain difficult repentance*
> *long, difficult repentance, realisation of life's mistake,*
> *and the freeing oneself*
> *from the endless repetition of the mistake*
> *which mankind at large has chosen to sanctify."* [1]

The hard work of trying to free *"oneself from the endless repetition of the mistake"* now begins. We encompass seven powerful moves in an immensely long chapter which has to convey our ardent wish to come to grips with the "*wounds to the soul*" and, at the same time, be resolutely honest with ourselves. We have received and inflicted so many shocks, so many hurts, so many damaging effects of words and actions, that we are shaken, bruised and scarred. And the bruises and scars have become part of the ego. We have added them to the pile of self-images we have already created and, the greater the damage, the more the scars, and the more vulnerable have we become. But, we need to look at those scars, not out of self-pity, not to see how hurt or scarred we are, not in anger or with resentment or bitterness, but simply: to look.

We start with what we *can* do ("But I don't want to start this process AT ALL!", says the Tiger, in desperation. "It's ridiculous, we all have a Tiger, we all have a ME, it's just human nature!"), but we dismiss this interference and use the cathartic process of writing down what happens when Tiger appears, so that we can bring the areas of our damaged ego more clearly into consciousness, more directly into focus.

The movements themselves symbolise this shift in our spiritual Journey, for we now grip with both hands to represent the two aspects of intellect and insight, as well as both sides of the brain.

We begin with the critical, analytical, left side of the brain, so that we can "Grip the Ears of the Tiger to the Left", and we write down some moments when Tiger was mildly in action. Thus, when we, in the group, were asked individually to do this anonymously, these were the results:

"I looked up the word 'ego' in the dictionary... That didn't help, but the meaning of the word egoism seemed to clarify what I might write down. Egoism covers a few different things of which I am sure I am guilty every few minutes. I have a bad memory so I have tried to piece together some examples:

I thought I could make the breakfast better than he could. He was making breakfast and I came along and interfered. Understandably he got upset and left me to continue. Needless to say I over-cooked the eggs.

- - - - - -

I didn't want to stop working despite the fact that everybody was waiting for me to join them for lunch. My work was too important and I was too selfish to stop.

- - - - - -

She was telling me about some of her school problems but all I managed to do was draw parallels with my own school days and wallow in self-indulgence. I should have listened carefully to her problems and kept my mouth shut.

- - - - - -

I had thought of ending this with my name to prove that I was not worried about having my ego exposed... then I realised that would be pandering to my ego again."

"I notice the ego when I come to the T'ai Chi class:

> *wanting to be a favourite pupil;*
> *wanting to be the best practitioner ever;*
> *not liking to be corrected – taking it as criticism;*
> *not liking praise – do not deserve it;*
> *anxiety over new movement – can I do it;*
> *anxiety over known movement – am I doing it right;*
> *feeling bad if I cannot remember it – often!*
> *feeling good if I can remember it – rarely!*
> *feeling superior when others cannot do what I can;*
> *feeling inferior when I cannot do what others can."*

"Whenever the person I share a house with makes himself a drink, he leaves a dirty teaspoon on the kitchen work-surface which stays there unwashed. Sometimes I do not wash them up and all the teaspoons will accumulate. Seeing them there makes me angry and washing them up makes me angry.

The Head of Department is due to retire. I have worked hard in the Department for four and a half years and am the right age to become a Head of Department. It appears that I am going to be overlooked. My response is real personal antagonism towards the Head, combined with a feeling that I will have to leave if I have to work with a newly-appointed Head of Department. Coupled with this is a feeling of being under-valued and a sense of insecurity at the thought of changes.

— — — — — —

This is a recurring situation. I'll be walking along the corridor of the school where I teach when a boy who is not in my class blocks my way. He is a proud and conceited boy and he won't let me pass and he makes me angry."

"I start the dishwasher at night, turn it on and my kids empty it in the morning. One morning my son tells me that I didn't turn it on the previous evening and I deny it vehemently and swear I did and even kick the door shut after discovering that he was right – and break a cup.

— — — — — —

Practising the T'ai Chi and doing it very well, slowly, clearly, atten- tively, and then thinking how well I am doing it and then it deteriorating straight away.

— — — — — —

Massaging my brother's head as he has a severe headache. He says: 'It's working'. I think: 'I'm a healer, I'm really helping!' and after a few seconds, he says: 'It isn't working any more'."

"My Tiger seems to be quiet until I meet another Tiger. My shackles then instantly rise, and the bigger the other person's Tiger, the bigger mine become."

"I can never admit to getting anything wrong."

"My head is full of Tiger, seemingly all the time. I'm constantly imagining myself in different circumstances and my Tiger is always there, as if the whole world revolves around me, and me only."

"No matter what the circumstances, my Tiger says: 'what's in it for me?'"

"Tiger was present when I decided not to write about Tiger being present."

All the foregoing are examples of normal Tiger activity, and each contributor had a swift awareness of its presence. However, an example of Tiger totally in charge was:

"I had been circling the block and waiting a very long time for a place to park in a busy road when finally a space became vacant. I was about to reverse into it when a car from the other side of the road came across and went into 'my' space. I felt the anger rising, got out of my (doubly-parked) car, went up to the driver and said: "I've been waiting ages for a space to park and you just ....!" He looked at me as if I barely existed and then expressed with his face what is normally conveyed by the ruder-version of the 'V' sign, turned his back on me and walked into a supermarket. At that, I became literally mad with rage and, following him right into the shop, shouted: "YOU – ARE – A – RAT!". He simply walked away and I then realised what I had done and where I was; and my next thought was: "What if someone I know saw me!""

Thus, we start with ourselves, with what is near, and we find that, on the basis of 'that's human nature', Tiger is, of course, absolutely right: that is how we are nearly all the time and we could have described many such occasions in just one day. But, from having written about them (but not read them aloud), we find we feel different, lighter in spirit and, from knowing also that we are not content with our lives as they are and that it *does not always have to be that way,* we sense that we might be even-happier if we came to grips with the more-serious aspects of the unhappiness, depression, suffering, body-sickness and lack of peace which Tiger causes.

Tiger then retaliates by coming from another direction and, as we turn and face its response, states (somewhat aggressively!): "Asserting oneself and being aggressive are *necessary* to life – look at animals – they wouldn't *survive* if they didn't assert themselves. It's the same with people. They wouldn't *survive* if they weren't aggressive." and: "What would you do if someone came and took over your house, your land, your family? We can't just *let* everything happen. I have to be aggressive and assert myself and protect myself, and *you do, too*!".

We pay attention to the Tiger, but "Grip its Ears to the Right" and, with the inner wisdom and intuition of the right side of the brain, acknowledge Tiger's left-brain rationality and realism and obvious common sense, but know, too, that, if there is to be a balance in life, it cannot be arrived-at from viewing such concepts from one side only. So, although Tiger's assertions have a strong foundation and we recognise that, undoubtedly, there will be times when we have to assert ourselves, the question we are considering is how to peacefully lead our lives on a daily basis, and how to respond in a healthy, non-egoistic way to con-flict as a whole – for our Journey is concerned with wisdom, not with self-defence.

Tiger then reacts by saying that there is no point in doing all this probing, that ego will never go away, that it *makes* things happen and that we wouldn't *be* here if it weren't for the Tiger, so "why not just get on with living and stop worrying about it", sounding intelligent and full of common sense again, while hanging on for dear life and growling fiercely at our attempts to come to grips with the problems it causes.

While we are hanging on to *its* ears, however, we are discovering that, not only do we feel better for acknowledging our ego to ourselves in writing, but that, from later having read out each others' written ego descriptions and thereby had them all shared, we feel a spiritual release and an up-welling of actual joy and that, through this acknowledgement, through this crystallisation of what we so often camouflage, we not only contribute towards our own well-being, growth and maturity and assist our own damaged ego towards wholeness, but also help heal the psychological wounds of others. Moreover - and most-movingly - we find that we promote that vital element of trust which was mentioned so long ago. By openly exposing the Tiger, we promote the friendship and affection which brings us closer to the spiritual connection which underlies *all* relationship and, despite the underlying fear and natural resistance to being so exposed and, therefore, vulnerable, have been given the awe-inspiring proof that it was well-worth both recording and then sharing Tiger's activities, for we then were given the heart-warming and healing experience of pure joy.

There is, however, another unexpected element in this process: we find that (as with our earlier attempts to 'catch a Monkey thought'), when we no longer disguise our Tiger, but consciously describe and explain it to others it, it disappears! It is as if – by such a sharing - Tiger is held up to the light of the joy that results when we are released from its control and it then has no further reason for existing!

Sometimes, however, we cannot sense the dividing line between a Tigerish response and a healthy way of dealing with conflict, because the situation overwhelms us too swiftly. We then need to recognise these signs at an early stage. For example, the Tiger is certainly present when we become emotionally-heated over a problem; if irritation takes over in a discussion; when we expend an inordinate amount of repetitive Monkey Thoughts and energy on a difficult situation, or when we react to it with childish, erratic behaviour. Further evidence of Tiger's presence lies in the realm of how fixed we are in our point of view (since the healthiness of an ego is in proportion to the degree of its flexibility) and also by recognising how swiftly we become defensive of that viewpoint, regardless of what is true in what is being offered. For, more than anything, a healthy ego values truth higher than self-esteem and - when it senses that an ego problem is looming - deals with it swiftly.

There is also the physical factor. Psychological, emotional hurt is swiftly experienced in the body. Early-life traumas produce nervous reactions that continue into adulthood and the physical sensations can be so strong that we can feel Tiger's presence immediately we sense an 'attack'. The attack may, or may not, be intentional but - because of the multiple and genuine traumas of childhood - current feelings of stress and rejection can cause a physical malaise that is so acute that it can distance us from the actual problem and force us to mentally (and even, sometimes, physically) remove ourselves from the circumstances which have produced it. The mind 'goes into a spin', or we feel a sickness in the solar-plexus, a tightening of the muscles in the neck or back, or our legs 'turn to jelly' – and, if we are to succeed in coming to grips with the Tiger, we have to allow all this and wait until the physical disturbance is less acute. Recognising the familiar physical sensations at an early stage of Tiger's intervention, however, offers another way of handling the problem swiftly, for, by accepting that the malaise is Tiger-based, our intuition and the spiritual energies have a better chance of overcoming it.

When, then, we have trained ourselves to recognise the ego-nature of such emotional and physical responses, the next step is to try and locate the underlying causes behind our more dominant reactions and to ask why the influences of 'then' are contributing to such a degree to the responses of 'now'. This may not be easy if we have blocked the emotions concerning them, but, since the experiences happened to *us*, our memory of them will still be there, somewhere in the psyche, and might be traced back (perhaps through old photographs, diaries, letters, conversations with family or old friends, dreams, swift intimations and – not least – by writing), but, even if they cannot consciously be located, it is at least helpful if they can be recognised as physical and emotional reactions pertaining to ego-damage.

So, we meditate deeply on all of this and, when we next sense these 'attacks' on our system, we ask ourselves: are there emotional echoes from the past influencing the way we perceive someone's behaviour to us now? Are we perhaps responding with resentment generated from parental attitudes, which we have absorbed so deeply that they have become our own? Is our anxiety due to society's (spoken or unspoken) attitudes towards 'people like us', whatever we are? Are there basic anxieties, which may be giving rise to our current anxieties? The psychologist, Karen Horney, said that basic anxieties stem from: *"... the feeling a child has of being isolated and helpless in a potentially hostile world."* and that: *"A wide range of adverse factors in the environment can produce this insecurity in a child: direct or indirect domination, indifference, erratic behaviour, lack of respect for the child's individual needs, lack of real guidance, disparaging attitudes, too much admiration or the absence of it, lack of reliable warmth, having to take sides in parental disagreements, too much or too little responsibility, over-protection, isolation from other children, injustice, discrimination, unkept promises, hostile atmosphere, and so on and so on."* [2]

We ponder on this wide and daunting range of adverse factors and also bear in mind the vast number of unnecessary 'negatives' that so formed our view of ourselves in childhood and, thus, in later life - and we almost give up the quest. But, we continue Gripping the Ears of the Tiger to the Right, whilst trying to sense whether the unconscious memory of any such early traumas contributes to our troubled responses now, and discover that, by looking closely at some of the written descriptions of ego-activity, the teacher's anger (for example) at the child who was *"not in her class"* and was *"repeatedly"* blocking the way, may be seen in this way because there may be a hurt and rejected and, possibly, proud 'inner child' still active within that teacher, a damaged 'inner child' who is unwittingly blocking the adult teacher's academic advancement by 'not being in the right class', i.e. 'not good-enough' and doing so repeatedly – and that, perhaps, this has been recognised by those involved in deciding who should become the next Head of the Department. The three described incidents (of the dirty teaspoon, the child who blocks the way, and being overlooked in promotion) could then be seen as accumulated, symbolical reminders of earlier rejections, as well as lack of recognition of the child's (and therefore the adult's) intrinsic worth. Equally, as another example, a much earlier situation of 'total rejection' may-well-have motivated the disproportionate degree of rage experienced when a long-awaited parking space was taken so 'uncaringly' by another.

Thus, by sensing and writing, acknowledging, discussing and then probing as to whether such interpretations have meaning for us, we can bring buried memories to the surface and start the process of inner healing - and then (as we do now) aim another good and healthy Kick with Right Sole at the Tiger, in the process!

We then turn and "Grip *both* its Ears", linking both sides of the brain, using all our faculties and digging even more deeply into our repressed and unconscious areas. Inestimable help in this can be obtained from skilled psycho-therapy, dream interpretation and the reading of the lucid writings of those who have trodden the path before us and - by using as much as possible of our conscious understanding of the whole situation - we may be able to come to grips with the significance that the particular problem has for us, the recognition of which is sometimes even more important than the per-ception of causation, for - even if we cannot locate the cause - there is great psychological release from understand its meaning.

Another source of clarity can be obtained from the extensive range of symbolism and metaphors available in literature, for these can be used as bridges towards underlying realities, a situation which D.H. Lawrence clearly understood and expressed when he wrote:

> *"As a plant becomes pot-bound*
> *man becomes ego-bound*
> *enclosed in his own limited mental consciousness.*
>
> *Then he can't feel any more*
> *or love, or rejoice or even grieve any more,*
> *he is ego-bound,*
> *pot-bound*
> *in the pot of his own conceit,*
> *and he can only slowly die.*

Unless he is a sturdy plant.
Then he can burst the pot,
shell off his ego
and get his roots in earth again,
raw earth." [3]

Jung also used symbolism when viewing the problems of the ego, when he wrote: *"The conscious aspect of the psyche might be compared to an island rising from the sea – we only see the part above the water, but a much vaster unknown realm spreads below, and this could be likened to the unconscious.*

The island is the ego, the knowing, willing 'I', the centre of consciousness. But what belongs to consciousness, what I know about myself and the world, and can direct and control, is not fully conscious all the time. I forget, or I repress what I do not like, or what is not socially acceptable... I also have sense perceptions of insufficient strength to reach consciousness, and I experience much that is only partly comprehended or of which I do not become fully aware. These subliminal perceptions, together with the repressed or forgotten memories, make a kind of shadow land stretching between the ego and the unconscious which could – in fact should – belong to the ego; or, to use our other metaphor, it is a land which has not always been covered by the sea, and can be reclaimed."

Jung calls this shadow land the 'personal unconscious' (to distinguish it from the 'collective unconscious') and, because it belongs to the individual: *"... it is formed from his repressed infantile impulses and wishes, subliminal perceptions, and countless forgotten experiences; it belongs to him alone."*

Furthermore: *"The memories of the personal unconscious, though not entirely under the control of the will, can, when repression weakens (as for instance in sleep), be recalled; sometimes they return of their own accord; sometimes a chance association or shock will bring them to light; sometimes they appear somewhat disguised in dreams and fantasies; sometimes, especially if they are causing disturbances as in a neurosis, they need to be 'dug out'."* [4]

Thus, metaphorically, we can view ourselves as being 'pot-bound' by our ego, or as islands of personal consciousness, islands which not only separate us from each other, but from all other land-masses as well, whilst - with a 'pot-bound' Tiger in charge of each island - countless methods of territorial defence and repression are used in self-protection. All the daily effects of those darts and arrows of the early invaders, who shot at the young being with the negatives and admonitions of child-hood, are part of the island's history. All the long-term effects of the 'basic anxieties' just listed, form other parts. And, since Tiger believes that ceaseless vigilance is necessary to defend the island, much must be warded off. Many wounds remain buried in the land below sea-level, however, or lie in the shadowy waters around the island, and we try to pluck out the arrows. But, the tips remain, or they slip through our fingers, or the wounds re-open and never quite heal, or we cover them over with more defensive material, or we pretend that they don't exist. For the ways of Tiger's self-defence mechanisms are limitless and each person has to fully-locate her or his own sources of pain, in order to come to grips with – and dissolve - the Tiger's worst activities.

So, we continue our inner Journey and now move deeper into the shadowy-depths and, as we submerge ourselves, Tiger is convinced that we will not survive. But, the island remains, and what does surface is an awareness that, despite our habitual sense of separateness and our des-perate attempts to defend our territory, the more conscious we are of our wounds, fears and neuroses, the more the light of understanding shines through the waters, like piercing rays from the sun. The more we plumb the depths, the more we discover that, underneath the island, underneath Tiger's terror of annihilation, there is a unified land-mass of wholeness where *everything connects*. The deeper self then rises to the surface and consciously connects with the ego-self; the Tiger no longer feels isolated or fears extinction and the whole self can function effectively. And, said Jung, when this occurs: "... *a new centre of personality can emerge, dif-fering in its nature from the ego-centre*... [which]... *can include both the conscious and the unconscious. It appears to act as something like a magnet to the disparate elements of the personality and the processes of the unconscious, and is the centre of this totality as the ego is the centre of consciousness, for it is the function which unites all the opposing elements in man and woman, consciousness and unconsciousness, good and bad, male and female, etc., and in so doing transmutes them. To reach it necessitates acceptance of what is inferior in one's nature, as well as what is irrational and chaotic.*

This state cannot be reached by a mature person without considerable struggle; it implies suffering, for the Western mind, unlike the Eastern, does not easily tolerate paradoxes." [5]

Having written about some of our troubled, Tiger-based and 'inferior' responses, therefore, we see how the struggles disturb us less and we accept them - and what Jung called our "shadow" - more readily. By acknowledging Tiger's activities and submerging ourselves into the realms of what caused them and *recognising what they mean to us,* Tiger's grip on us weakens. Moreover, by bringing the Tiger into the light of day, so that we clearly can see our own shadow, we can more-readily acknowledge it, live with it, and allow others their own shadows, as islands in the sea have dark waters around them when the skies are heavy and storms abound, yet, irrevocably, are linked below.

Our Tiger then receives another kick, followed by a wide arc with a swinging leg which ensures that we have covered as much Tiger-territory as possible. And then we kick again, but with far greater balance and security, for every time we work well on ourselves, there is inner change. Each time we use our 'intention' to more-fully understand the source of our conflicts, the more balanced we become. The less blockage there is between 'within and without', the more the universal voice of the Tao can be heard, for - as Jung also said - *"I was not ever sure, except within the limits of a painfully prescribed comprehension, that man did all the thinking for himself. I had a feeling that even our own capacity for thinking shrank into painfully humble proportions compared with another kind of reality which was, as it were, thinking through us."* [6]

Thus, we cannot fulfil our spiritual potential unless we dig deeply and make contact with the roots of our being. Once we have *"burst the pot, shelled off the ego, and got our roots in the earth again, raw earth",* we can no more skip the various stages of growth than can a plant or tree. Change cannot be resisted and so we move with change, whilst the process, being a natural, organic one, is brought about by another Universal Law- "all things seek the light" - and so, by listening carefully to the voice within and by never donning any cloak of spirituality or truth that does not belong to us, we are led to ultimate self-awareness, or full contact with the Tao, with that other *"kind of reality which thinks through us"*.

But, *"Can you live in the world that way?"* asked Krishnamurti, knowing that it is relatively easy to live without Tiger when living alone, or on a Retreat, or surrounded by like-minded spiritual seekers, and that the hardest tests occur during the daily course of our existence. And another such test is looming now. There are two more instances of Tiger activity: a strike and a punch. It is as if, having arrived at an apparent plateau of spiritual awareness, we are fighting foes who see our spiritual flaws all too clearly and so Tiger fights hard to retain this foot-hold and ensure its permanence with a desperate attempt to eliminate the true self, rather than have itself overcome. Now its voice cries out with impatience at all this talk of 'self-knowledge', of 'the voice of the Tao', and of 'this other kind of reality', for, to the pragmatic Tiger, there is only one kind of knowledge: its own, there is only one voice: its own, there is only one reality: its own. And so, with the help of Monkey, it starts putting tremendous pressure upon us to cease what we are doing now, to find good cause to go somewhere else, to shift onto a different path, make a diversion, be tempted by a fascinating or sensual by-path or by a comforting conceit. Tiger's manifold self-protective devices are in operation again and we recognise them as such, even as we recognise the truth of other people's perceptions about us.

Our response to these tantalising pleas for its reinstatement has changed, however, for no matter how logical its reasoning, no matter how hard it tries, no matter how true may be some of its statements, Tiger's power over us is weakening, its fight, though still fierce, is of shorter duration and it only encompasses two manoeuvres. Tiger is tiring and this helps us to understand even-more clearly what this Journey is teaching us, for although we cannot eradicate Tiger – since, for as long as we are alive, it will be, also - we are learning how to reduce its potency until, much later, it will barely operate at all. And when *that* time comes, we will not only comprehend, but spontaneously live, the meaning of Lao Tzu's words:

"If terms to end a quarrel leave bad feeling,
What good are they?
So a sensible man takes the poor end of the bargain
Without quibbling.
It is sensible to make terms,
Foolish to be a stickler:
Though heaven prefer no man,
A sensible man prefers heaven." [7]

46 WITHDRAW (YIELDING) AND PUSH

The flow of opposites and the fifth Gateway to Wisdom

*"Sea-weed sways and sways and swirls
as if swaying were its form of stillness;
and if it flushes against fierce rock
it slips over it as shadows do, without hurting itself."* [1]

The natural and inevitable reverse of Tiger's last, but less-effective, strike and punch reveals itself now as the fist opens and the ego slips away, withdrawing from the struggle, sighing at what has become an unequal fight. Sinuously, almost without our volition, the mind and body soften too and, with the melting of the ego, we perform the beautiful yielding movement which must always follow any Tiger-induced trauma. We yield as water yields, we heed Nature's wisdom in her ability to adapt to circumstances, we let go and sway with the flow of life, just as seaweed sways and swirls with the tides.

We also yield to the pain we feel when our Tiger is hurt, we allow it, and we ponder upon it, and then we apply the T'ai Chi movement psychologically, by reviewing the written examples of Tiger's control. We let go to interfering; we let go to our problems when others are telling us theirs; we let go to comparison and competition. We withdraw our criticism when we believe others are 'doing things the wrong way'; we let go to ambition and conceit, to resistance and self-interest, and, most importantly, we let go to all the deep-seated feelings of rejection. We have had enough of all that.

We apply such yielding to other aspects of daily existence: to crowded trains and railway stations, large stores and supermarkets, over-populated streets. By softening our mind and body when surrounded by jostling, pushing people, we 'slip through the crowds like shadows' and remain unhurt. By retreating and yielding when someone meets us with force, we become so empty and 'still' that the other 'finds nothing there', and by emptying ourselves of the belief that we are more important than others, nothing within us remains to be hurt. Tiger's heat is diffused and softness fills the air around us.

Difficult to apply, but equally necessary, we yield when confronted with stupidity, ignorance, or prejudice, conscious that neither control nor criticism has any validity in the search for wisdom and that many authoritarian attitudes are born out of impatience, insecurity, and the malaise of irritability.

We flow with circumstances and yield to life, which, ultimately, means having trust that life is not malefic. Needing only to watch the pulse in our wrist as the blood courses through the veins of our body is enough for us to sense life's rhythmic order. Needing only to trust that flow as surely as one trusts a river to run when moved by the currents in the earth, is enough for us to trust life as a whole and have it lead us where it will. Nor need this be difficult if we value the words: *"...consider the flow of your mind to be the delegated adaptability of the Tao and be as alertly non-clinging inwardly as without"*[2], for it is the clinging to ideas, habits and responses which is, perhaps, the hardest lesson of all.

Some still may say that such yielding is not only unrealistic, but dangerous and who may cite, as in the previous Tiger's Ears section, the question of an attack upon our loved ones or our home as a good example of the unreality of such a premise. For those concerned about this dilemma, it may help to remember that those circumstances are rare; that such yielding is on the most spiritual of levels and that, for the majority of us who are far-from enlightened, it may be enough at this stage to know the difference between yielding totally - in the spiritual sense - and when it would be wise to cease making assumptions about others, for if we can manage the latter, we would already be quite far on the Way.

We also recall again our deep sense that *it does not always have to be that way,* and since examples of enlightenment can be inspiring, the following story may serve to show that 'yielding' to an oppressor is not only possible, but can bring further yielding in its wake.

During governmental changes in China in the 20th century, a Taoist monastery, its temples and lands were appropriated by the militia. The monks, in their gentle, *yin* way, showed no resistance, but welcomed the soldiers with kindness and compassion for their lot, and offered to share what little food they had and whatever sleeping space was available. When, however, even their own food, bedding and shelters were taken from them, their yielding went further and, quietly turning to fasting and meditation, they felt neither deprivation nor threat. It did not end there, however. Such egoless 'flowing with circumstances', such lack of resistance by the monks, brought changes in the consciousness of the *yang* military leader's mind and, softening, he arranged for all of the monks' requirements to be returned to them. The complementary qualities of opposites thus came into play through the military leader - having expected hostility and a defensive reaction – being met with the ultimate in yielding and kindness. *Yin* had yielded to *yang*, and *yang* then yielded to *yin*, and the latent spiritual elements in the oppressor - no matter how deeply hidden they may have been, or may be again – were given an opportunity to surface.

From all this, we learn anew: if egoless ourselves, no tiger's claw can tear us. If we see no ego in another, we are safe from harm. If we can yield and open our hand, withdraw from the fight, and 'change with change', we are nearer to ultimate trust and sanity. Recognising this yet again, we gently are led to the fifth Gateway to Wisdom and quietly sense the depth of its meaning with both wonder and gratitude.

47 CARRY TIGER TO THE MOUNTAIN

The union of Tiger with the Tao and the end of Part Two

> *"At the end of [each] third of the T'ai Chi Form... comes a wide*
> *sweep of the arms ending with crossed wrists and hands which*
> *always reminds me of the seraphim of Isaiah's vision, folding*
> *their wings before their faces.*
>
> *As I do this, I remember the impression that first came to me in*
> *observing and participating in T'ai Chi of the serene silence that*
> *accompanies it, a quiet that enfolds mind and body. In the heat*
> *and preoccupation of learning to practice correctly this*
> *impression tends to recede into the background, but the*
> *possibility of it is always there."* [1]

These words give us much to dwell upon. We have come to the end of
the second Third of the Form and, with Tiger resting, we now repeat the
movements of Embrace Tiger, Return to Mountain and can look back
and reflect upon the Journey in much the same way as we did at the end
of the first Third.

Recognizing that we are not, as yet, *spontaneously* living the wisdom
of 'letting go' on a daily basis, we nevertheless can perceive that much
that is positive has taken place. Our Monkey Thoughts have been recognized and dealt with to some degree; we have sought and found
the Golden Needle and we have painted glorious rainbows. We have
punched and kicked-out at life and then understood that Nature's circles can help us surround a difficulty, rather than punching, or wildly
kicking directly towards it. We have had the unparalleled experience of
Coming to Grips with the Tiger and the resultant, beautiful withdrawal
of ego in the flow of the Bamboos. We have gently pushed open no less
than five Gateways to Wisdom and have meditated upon their significance, together with that of clouds and galloping horses. But still we

seek that "*serene silence*" which we have, at times, known from our T'ai Chi, but have not yet fully-encompassed elsewhere. So, with much to meditate-upon and a deep spiritual yearning, we once more seek some space away from others, some peace and stillness, where we can integrate the many fragments of our many-sided selves and ponder upon the inner movements of the mind.

Again we cradle the Tiger, embrace it, acknowledge its elements of disharmony and, in this way, avoid the destructive duality of approval and disapproval. We accept what we are, as we are, and turn again to the abode of silence, to the stillness and peace of the inner Mountain, to the place of space. We meditate upon the means whereby truth is made more accessible than illusion and clear-seeing made attainable. We recall that Taoism teaches that it is the emptiness of 'the space between', which brings insight and clarity of thought and action, and that only in such space can we locate the source of life's movement and perceive what is essential.

"*There must be this space for beauty and compassion.*" said Krishnamurti. "*Everything must have space, the living and the dead, the rock on the hill and the bird on the wing. When there is no space there is death... Sound needs space. The sound of a word needs space; the word makes its own space, rightly pronounced. The river and the faraway tree can only survive when they have space; without space all things wither*".[2] And:

"*If rats are enclosed in a restricted space, they destroy each other; the small birds sitting on a telegraph wire, of an evening, have the needed space between each other. Human beings living in crowded cities are becoming violent. Where there is no space outwardly and inwardly, every form of mischief and degeneration is inevitable. The conditioning of the mind through so-called education, religion, tradition, culture, gives little space to the flowering of the mind and heart... The "me" has its being and its activity within the small space it has created for itself. All its problems and sorrows, its hopes and despairs are within its own frontiers, and there is no space. The known occupies all its consciousness. Consciousness is the known. Within this frontier there is no solution to all the problems human beings have put together. And yet they won't let go; they cling to the known or invent the unknown, hoping it will solve their problems. The space which the "me" has built for*

itself is its sorrow and the pain of pleasure … vast, measureless space lies
outside the measure of thought, and thought is the known. Meditation is the
emptying of consciousness of its content, the known, the "me".[3]

We ponder upon the spiritual freedom which such inner space con-
fers and its opposite, restriction, and we contrast *yin* with *yang*, light
with shade. The *yin* side of a mountain is that which is in shadow; its
opposite side is *yang*, full of light. It is our *yin*, shadow side that can offer
in-sight and it is through the light of the *yang* that we can assess the
results of that insight and take what action is necessary. The Mountain
then becomes a symbol of the universe, the light and the dark, the external and the internal, and it is the same with us, because - with the spine
and central nervous system housed, as it were, behind us, in the shadows - the light is always there in front of us, available to our scrutiny of
our every thought and feeling. We are then reminded of our previous
journey to the Mountain of Stillness and the importance of bringing the
spinal nerves to rest, since, only then, does the ego *"with its restlessness,*
disappear". And, therein, too, lies the importance of space, since the
nerves - those most delicate fibrous connections - are located in the
space between each vertebra and we are as much psychically damaged as
physically, when they are crushed or the vertebrae fuse together.

There is also the question of breath and its relevance to space, for, in
Eastern teachings that small space between each 'in' and 'out' breath not
only symbolizes Stillness, but also the Void, the Emptiness, the place of
wu-chi from whence, free from dualistic thought and differentiation, we
commenced this Journey. So, in order to reach such spiritual Stillness and
Emptiness, we see that we need powerful breaths to climb this Mountain
and that it is easy to succumb, inwardly, to the equivalent of altitude
sickness, avalanches, snow blindness and howling gales. And yet, we can
also perceive that, even though each crag and crevice, toe- and hand-hold
present real danger, they are moulding the soul, as much as, down in the
valleys, the souls of others are moulding our own, as we are moulding
theirs. Moreover, once at the peak of the mountain, in a space so serene
and yet so threatening, we need all our power and strength to withstand
the pitfalls occasioned by our fear of isolation, our fear of falling - and by
the Tiger's terror at the thought of its own demise.

So, we dwell upon formlessness and emptiness and, in order to understand both, ponder further upon the duality of their opposites in form and fullness. We realize that the T'ai Chi itself reveals these facets, for a pupil is given only one new movement at a time to learn and absorb very slowly, before moving on to the next. Its shape and form then become so familiar, and the practitioner so relaxed in its performance, that it becomes a natural movement made by a body which, ultimately, will appear almost weightless. And it is the slowness of the learning process which makes this possible, for, by learning something too quickly (or wishing to move-on, too swiftly and unheedingly), we cannot be sure of what we are doing, can be unaware of how heavy or light, full or empty, the body feels and can also – unwittingly - add to, or change, the movements. Equally, if the mind is moving too swiftly, we cannot be conscious of its many thoughts and of how filled it is with unnecessary material – and we then forget very easily, too. Thus, the slowly-increasing sensitivity to the *yin* and *yang* weight, or otherwise, of our physical movements, as well as to the weight of the clutter in the mind, allows a process to occur which transforms these states into their opposites and, from such sensitive perception, we then can make contact with the simplicity of Taoist non-duality. *Yin* and *yang* then merge, inner stillness takes their place, and the opposites in life lose their significance.

"...practise the art of <u>kuan</u> (inner vision) daily", advised a Taoist meditation master, for: *"This will still the restless waves of thought and sharpen your awareness. Awareness must be acute, but objectless. No looker, no looked-at, just looking... your mind must be indifferent to the objects it reflects, performing its function like a mirror. When there is no attachment, true seeing arises. With seeing comes serenity. Serenity puts an end to woe. In the absence of woe, joy will fill your body to overflowing. Certainty of the rightness of your doing and of the truth of your seeing will flush your cheeks and make your eyebrows dance".*[4]

With such a vision of joy-filled release, we embrace our Tiger and face North again, and enter into the silence and the source of our being. We discover the bliss of days passed in silence and are attentive to whatever arises: aversion, sadness, guilt, shame, hunger, despair – but with no longing for their opposites. We become aware of approval, joy, equanimity, elation, serenity, hope – with no attachment to any of these conditions. We learn about the actuality, the nature of things, not the idea of them. We meditate and receive replenishment and renew the eternal link between heaven and earth, restored by the spiritual elements of pure air and unblemished light. And, in the silence and stillness, when the self is absent, we find that truth can be glimpsed and held for a moment, but never attained or sustained through wish or will. We are restored to our original nature and the Tiger rests, no longer in opposition to spirit. We have become responsible for it, it belongs to us. And, because we have embraced it, given it respect and love and bestowed care upon it, it no longer resists.

Part Two is complete and symbolizes what can only be learnt through conflict, from the questing, duality-ridden adult psyche. Many of the more destructive passions are now behind us. Sustained tranquility is still ahead, but - without the turbulence of Tiger in Part Two - without the opportunities for spiritual growth and awakening which Tiger's existence gives to us, further serenity and wisdom would not be possible. And so, as Tiger sleeps:

> *"The pine shadows swaying green covers the level bank;*
> *I sit and play my lute to quiet the clamour of the world.*
> *Most at song's end, the world is still*
> *Clear of evening clouds, the green mountain stands tall."* [5]

PART THREE

MATURITY
AND
WISDOM

48a ELBOW STROKE, BRUSH (RIGHT) KNEE, AND FORWARD STEP

Coming down from the Mountain of Stillness;
the importance of accuracy; the paradox of
'spontaneity from repetition', and the shedding of
psychological and material burdens

"I realised that I had joined a pilgrimage to the East, seemingly
a definite and single pilgrimage – but, in reality, in its broadest
sense, this expedition to the East was not only mine and now; this
procession of believers and disciples had always and incessantly been
moving towards the East, towards the Home of Light. Throughout the

centuries it had been on the way, towards light and wonder, and each
member, each group, indeed our whole host and its great pilgrimage,
was only a wave in the eternal stream of human beings, of the eternal
strivings of the human spirit towards the East, towards Home." [1]

With Tiger still resting in our arms, our spiritual pilgrimage continues
and we turn Eastwards again, to that *"Home of Light"* and, although
we have now entered into Part Three, we repeat the movements of the
beginning of Part Two.

We have, by now, learnt much from the T'ai Chi and, from the
repetitions, have recognized how important it has been to perform the
movements accurately, since this has added a dimension to the Form
which we had not fully-appreciated. As one wisdom teacher put it:
"Beauty and efficiency flow out of accuracy. Efficient action implies mini-
mum energy and time-consumption...

After learning the art of accuracy, one should focus one's attention to
see that one does the necessary things at the necessary time. Postponement
of action is the seed of anxiety, fear and worry. Right action at the right
moment saves a lot of mental exertion.

The habit of postponing physical action gets crystallized, and distorts
perception. The same habit becomes a psychological attitude. Postponement
of decisions, laziness in responses to situations... grow in the soil of postpone-
ment. Postponement in responses leaves a residue in the subconscious. The
objective challenge degenerates into a subjective problem." [2]

We look at ourselves in relation to these words and realize, with a
sense of *'light and wonder'* - and *awe* - that the results of many months
of practice have spilt-over into daily life. Just by doing a specific thing in
a specific way: place a foot here, move an arm there, turn into a particular direction, co-ordinate the body in a clearly-defined way, and repeat
each action over and over again, we have become so familiar with 'doing
what we have to do', that, when something needs doing in our normal
routine, we do it in the same way: we just do it. Priorities are clearer
and subjective problems are less oppressive, and so the art of T'ai Chi's
accuracy, and consequent efficiency, has enabled us to resolve many of
our more-simple dilemmas. Moreover - and significantly - there is less

resistance or anxiety about dealing with a hitherto 'disliked' area of life and less concern over 'choice', which enables each issue, as it arises, to be dealt-with *spontaneously*.

There is thus a beautiful paradox in that the repetitiveness and precision required by T'ai Chi can lead to a spontaneous response in daily living, and that these two strangely disparate concepts – the value of repetition and the importance of spontaneity – can further our sense of well-being, for, although we are doing T'ai Chi according to a formula, we are no longer living one. We can also sense that if we were to use 'will' to impose discipline upon ourselves in the hitherto troublesome areas of life (because we were not 'getting things done'), we would be placing one layer of conditioned thought upon another, saying to ourselves: "I'm not doing what I should, therefore I must use more self-discipline", which would imply that a form of authoritarianism had been incorporated into the training through the forcing of the 'will', rather than the use of 'intention', and that a basic T'ai Chi premise was thereby being negated.

So, the art of T'ai Chi's requirement for accuracy – and our inner space on the Mountain - has given us further insight into the art of living, and we now move down onto the plains again and find ourselves viewing our world with different eyes. We see how much we have amassed in our homes and of how little we require. We recall our earlier climb to the Mountain and how heavily-laden we were with psychological burdens and of how we could be stripped of these by letting go to the many ideas, concepts, beliefs and vanities by which the Tiger had held us in thrall. We perceive that, in the intervening period, we have acquired other burdens, and not all of them psychological. We look at how we cling to the past and to our identity through our physical acquisitions and of how attached we have become to them - and then see what we have to do: we begin the liberating activity of 'shedding'. We start sorting out and sifting-through and disposing of what we no longer need and discover that the less we own materially, the more space we have, both psychologically and spiritually. We start off afresh and, aware of the dangers of *"stripping just to gain"* as Krishnamurti put it (for we often shed the physical and material vanities of one life-style for the spiritual conceits and vanities of another), we clear aside and brush away such obstacles and take another strong, bear-like step forward. And this more 'mature' aspect of Part Three is then confirmed, for we find that the hitherto-familiar daily split of the mind, the duality of those 'shoulds' and 'oughts', the aversions and the criticisms, the ground-swell of opinions and customs and prejudice, gradually diminish the more we allow accuracy and precision to move into the areas of daily living, where, together with the foundation for spontaneous right action, the real self can emerge.

Now, in contact with others who are on the same *"pilgrimage to the East"*, we are gladdened in spirit to discover how quiet and gentle they are, and of how great courtesy arises out of innate respect for others. From such contact, we then find that something else needs shedding, something else needs to be 'sliced-through', and this is because a very specific (and familiar) obstacle is presenting itself...

<hr />

48b Ward Off - Slantingly Downwards

The vanity in believing we can spiritually help others,
and the return of our inner 'Zen Abbot'

We have come down from the Mountain and are now in relationship with others again. Despite our previous contact with Zen admonishment, we experience anew that oh-so-familiar urge and subtle belief that we should influence others 'for their own good' and be of help to them, spiritually. For, although, for a while, the Tiger had hardly moved or barely blinked, it has begun to stir and that underlying conceit has emerged again. Still desiring that others should be similar to ourselves, it murmurs that we should impart to them what we have learnt and that this would help them, too. But, this time, Tiger's return is brief, cut-short by how swiftly we desist from that vanity and so it has only gazed around with sleepy eyes, conveyed its message with its familiar – but now weakened – self-interested air, re-positioned itself and settled back into slumber.

As if to reinforce this lack of Tiger's power, we recall the words of a Taoist adept who said: *"No man can help another beyond feeding him when hungry or tending him when sick, unless by setting him in the way of thinking things out for himself, which can be done better by example than by words, and very often not at all. This means that a man's first duty is to himself; for, unless he has cultivated the Way, what can he have to say that is worth the listener's trouble and what sort of example is to be expected of him? He must learn how best to live; then others, envying his content and well-being, will come of themselves to ask questions; some may even heed his answers, especially if he gives them sparingly."*

And: *"… find your own truth and live by it. In that way, you will save yourself trouble and perhaps draw a few others away from their senseless clawing at the slippery precipices of dualistic thought by convincing them that the sound of bamboos creaking in the wind is a wholesome substitute for concepts."* [1]

We absorb these words on a deep level and are grateful for their wisdom and find that, although Tiger continues to yawn out some egoistic intimation from time to time, he is blessedly soporific in the main and we are more conscious of our over-enthusiasms and more concerned to respond to others with interest and/or insight, rather than instruct them. So, blessed by what appears to be the equivalent of a Zen Abbot in our own psyche, who - acting in the role of clarifier - holds up that vital mirror to the soul, we look into that reflector before slicing across the strings which bind us to the illusion that we should influence, or spiritually be of help to anyone, except ourselves.

A further (and very large burden) is then disposed of and, even lighter in spirit, we flow again and softly sway and meditatively move with the interweaving rhythms of the fourth Bamboos and gladly acknowledge their: *"creaking in the wind as a wholesome substitute for concepts."*

48c Pull Back, Press
Forward and Push

The Bamboos: a developing sixth sense and the sixth Gateway to Wisdom

We move with the rise and fall of the breath and the dip-and-swing rhythm of birds' wings in flight. We move like waves in the ocean which respond to the ebb and flow of the tides which, in turn, are governed by the waxing and waning of the moon. We coil and loop, swirl and return as if in limpidly-slow eddies of water, and all the while sparrows sing and breezes murmur in the whispering Bamboos flow. And we relax, for in these timeless lulls, we harmonize with the Universe and, when so in-tune with the spiritual manifestations of life, our daily, separatist activities become unified with all the rhythmic movements of the Tao.

Another facet of life then unfolds, one of which we had been conscious before, but never so frequently, never so clearly. Now the world of psychic and extra-sensory phenomena reveals itself and manifests in telepathy, in coincidence (which Jung called 'synchronicity') and in precognition. We 'follow hunches' and find ourselves placed in circumstances which give much-needed information and which, or so it seems, would not have been possible to receive otherwise. We are prompted to go in a different direction from that planned and discover something of vital importance. We desist from a specific action and meet someone who plays a significant role in a decision we have to make. An old friend briefly moves into our aura of life and imparts some relevant information which helps us on our inner quest. At times, it is as if we are 'led' by unrelated and circuitous means to find what we were unknowingly looking for, as if a guiding hand were reaching into, and then pointing at, that which our unconscious knew we needed to know consciously. At other times, dreams – which can never lie, however complex they may appear to us - give us information about events to come, or information that we need to act-upon and, as this sixth sense manifests and unfolds in such an enchanting way, we marvel at the interweaving patterns which link us with other patterns and other people, even across vast distances. And, most significantly, we learn to recognize that some psychic experiences occur when we are labouring under deep stress or experiencing strong emotions, as if our connection to other people and to life itself had been heightened by the strength of our feelings. We then open ourselves up more fully to its influence and discover that, out of the emptiness of the inner space experienced on the Mountain, this exciting, intriguing and often mystifying extra sense is gaining in strength, with vibrations that, whilst emanating from our inner state, magnetically and, therefore, inevitably, draw similar vibrations from others.

We also read and hear about other psychic phenomena and find that the experiences relating to them indicate that a release from deep-ly-conditioned or repressive thought patterns has taken place in the people experiencing them. In some other people, we find that such deep conditioning has had little influence, as if it had somehow by-passed them and they had remained relatively-innocent of much of our usual 'programming' and were, therefore, more open. But, whatever the back-ground to this psychic phenomena, such flowing with life in such a timeless, 'mindless' way, enhances extra perception, and when events then occur which have deeper meaning, and things happen which are good things, we feel that we are being looked after and fewer obstacles appear in our passage through life.

Sometimes, however, when the Tiger wakes up and stays awake, we mistakenly view this sense of protective care, as if we were 'special' or 'different', whereas such things are happening all the time, without our influence. It is simply that our awareness has caught up with them through our having shifted onto a different plane of consciousness. We may try to analyze the situation logically, or intellectualize it by ration-alization, or embellish it by projecting various belief systems onto the circumstances, but such psychic events have only become so frequent because we have slipped into a different stream, a timeless space and so have become more aware of them. Neither the egoistic 'I' nor our spiritual growth has made these things happen, but being lighter in spirit, and having shed so many psychological burdens, we have arrived at the portal of a different plane of existence, and the more the clairvoyance manifests, the more we can harmonize with *its* flow and recognize that it is another aspect of our universe and, therefore, another of the Universal Laws.

On this then, the fifth of the Bamboos flow, we acknowledge the psychic stream in all its diversity and, smoothly and effortlessly, shift with its intimations of change with an extra awareness of their implications, whilst, at the entrance to the psychic world, glide into and open the sixth Gateway to the Wisdom of the sixth of the senses.

49 DIAGONAL SINGLE WHIP

The Bird's Beak or the Phoenix Stance: the dualisms of opposition, and a template for the next movements

"*We are two opposites which exist by virtue of our inter-opposition*" wrote D.H. Lawrence, meditating on light and dark, purity and passion and all the dualities which make up the processes of creation. "*Life is the foam*", he wrote, "*which is thrown off by the clash of opposing waves; it is the blossom which results from the struggle between sun and earth in the seed of the dandelion*" and when man '*falls into egoism*', then he fails to blossom and is given over to the '*flux of corruption*'."[1]

Now, as we sum-up the previous movements, we choreograph their meaning and again create the Phoenix Stance of duality, the *yin* and *yang*, which exist as just described. One hand closes to indicate Tiger's (albeit, lessening), power, the other remains open to symbolize the new, clairvoyant direction. Both arms spread as wide as wings and the head of the now more-psychic being turns to the open hand. The whole movement thus dramatically conveys the difference between where we were, when we performed this movement in Parts One and Two, and where we are now. For, the difficulties which were the result of our unbalanced, impure, physical *Ching* energy, gradually are being transmuted into the spiritual dimension of *Shên's* purer activities, and even though the duality of physical, as opposed to spiritual, will rarely be entirely absent (for it is truly the state of flux which is the very process of creation), once the impure energies have been mastered and the influences of Tiger diminished, a harmonious blending of both *yin* and *yang* can emerge from the struggle.

This is further conveyed by a subtle and important difference in the physical direction of this Phoenix movement, for – instead of facing West, as in all the previous Bird's Beak stances, thereby conveying our connection with the known - we have been steered to a different point on the compass, have veered towards the right like the shadow that forever follows the light - and now face the North-West diagonal. This clockwise turning away from the West, this movement away from what, according to the Chinese, is 'the home of the Tiger', this shift towards the more-psychic realm of the non-dualistic North, is thus indicative of the spiritual shift which Part Three exemplifies, and confirms that, slowly but without doubt, we are moving ever-nearer to the perfect balance symbolized by the home of the Immortals. Other repetitions of the Bird's Beak will follow that still have us facing West and we will continue to be influenced by our past, but the magical, mythical Phoenix, in this new, diagonal direction, heralds the more profound aspects of a psychically-orientated nature. It also acts as a template for, or harbinger of, the supremely serene – and diagonal – physical movements which immediately follow, and guides us towards two of the most important, inspiring and unique examples of the T'ai Chi's *"processes of creation"*.

"Among birds the phoenix,…
holds the chiefest place;
Cleaving the crimson clouds
the phoenix soars apace,
With only the blue sky above,
far into the realms of space;…" [2]

50 Parting the Wild Horse's Mane

An example of total openness, yielding and obedience to life's deepest orders, and contact with a reservoir of profound compassion

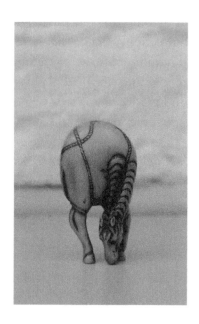

Each time we swayed with the Bamboos, we harmonized with the Tao and a Gateway to Wisdom appeared. Each time the Tiger yielded to the Tao, another Gateway came into view. And yet, on each of the two, latter, occasions, the yielding arose from an inability to cope with our inner turmoil, from having arrived at the end-most swing of the pendulum of emotional stress, and not from a spiritual realization.

Now we enact a different story. Now life is challenging us, as never before. Profoundly-disturbing, *external* forces are in evidence, forces which are far beyond any normal occurrences of conflict. Such a situation is not only new to us, but is fraught with violence. With extreme danger immanent, a confrontation takes place with the fiercest expression of the

Tiger in another, with a being whose fractured and tortured ego is so entirely in opposition to harmony and locked in its own '*flux of corruption*', that there can be no possibility of a normal exchange, nor even the barest recognition of a shared humanity. Moreover, if the Tigers within both participants were to react with equal ferocity, the two egos would become so locked in battle that they would become enmeshed in their own desperate blindness and, with very little to separate them, their very lives would be at stake. For, this is an aspect of war at its most ferocious and yet, when faced with the possibility of annihilation, a window to the soul is suddenly offered which reveals a profound spiritual reservoir upon which to draw, a reservoir of such unimaginable courage and power that, with neither intellectual debate nor conscious awareness, its existence confirms that the ego can dissolve in its entirety. And this is portrayed in the next, exquisitely-open "Parting the Wild Horse's Mane", the movements of which appear only once in the whole of the T'ai Chi Form.

To the Chinese, the image of the King of Horses is: "… *an ugly ogre with three eyes and four hands, bearing various weapons of warfare*"[1] and, when the Mongols raided China, their wild, saw-toothed, tiger-killing horses were the most fearsome of all, representing, amongst other images, the most primitive of forces and the kind of powerful and unbridled energy which, if manifesting in a person of great power, cannot be dealt with rationally.

Only a few exceptional souls can counteract such ferocity (and, metaphorically, come so close to such a horse that its mane can be parted), and such a situation, though much milder in comparison, has already been described when the militia took over a monastery in China and the Taoist monks yielded with peace in their hearts. Taoists are not alone in the practice of this wisdom, however, and many are the spiritual teachings that give guidance on how to yield in adversity, with the 'Let go and let God' maxim being one that is both frequently preached, as well as found to apply to all those spiritual teachings that indicate the wisdom of 'yielding', since whatever is seen as 'God', can also be seen as: 'T.S.I. - The Supreme Intelligence'.

Another such story comes from the life of Eric Liddell who, after his success as a world-renowned runner, became a Christian missionary.

Held behind enemy Japanese lines, he believed that his openness of heart and willingness to meet the Japanese soldiers as people, rather than enemies, would promote a peaceful exchange and, on an occasion when he was surrounded by hostility, the validity of his belief and the purity of his spiritual trust enabled a meeting to take place, which resulted in the soldiers showing him photos of their wives and children; weeping with him at the pain caused by separation from loved ones, and pouring-out their anguish at the brutality they were forced to employ. Conversely, as is well-documented, atrocities of such magnitude were committed by the Japanese (and other nationals) in World War II, that, for many, the scars have never healed, whether for tyrant or victim. Yet, out of such unimaginable and indefensible acts, there have come examples of such spiritual yielding and integrity of response that the lessons to be learnt from obeying the inner voice of truth and trust are profoundly awe-inspiring.

Such a story was given by Laurens van der Post when describing a situation during his imprisonment in a Japanese war camp in WW2. Each day, at a prescribed time, the captured British officers had to line up for a beating and the Japanese officer who took charge of the beatings was called Mori. On this occasion, there had been a rumour that many prisoners were to be killed that day and, since a machine gun had just been placed at the gate of the camp, the atmosphere was of acutely-strained attention. Laurens van der Post was in charge of the officers, and he wrote: *"...my turn came to face Mori. I walked towards him suddenly feeling strangely calm. It was as if I had become another person and somewhere far down within me, someone far wiser and with the benefit of having had to face this kind of thing ever since the beginning of man on earth, took command of me. I faced Mori, and this other self gauged Mori's blows and anticipated his kicks so accurately that it was able to make me move my head and body at the last moment before the blows and kicks fell in a manner not perceptible to the enraged man and his satellites, yet sufficient to rob them of their severity – to such an extent that I hardly felt them.* **

---

*In the martial arts, an ability to anticipate the blows and kicks of the opponent, yield to them, cause no harm, and not be damaged, indicates that the practitioner has reached the highest form of physical and mental activity.

Indeed, the physical aspect of what Mori was trying to do to me seemed so irrelevant that, during the whole time of his assault on me, this process within me of appraising the full meaning of the incident and searching my imagination for a way of putting an end to it all before it developed into something worse, even something which Mori himself might possibly not have intended, went on unimpeded, and if possible with greater clarity than before. The result was that, when Mori delivered his final kick and pushed me back to my place in the line and I once more caught a glimpse of the machine gun at the gates, it was as if I heard from deep within myself very clearly a voice of command from this other self, ordering me as if with the authority of life itself: 'Turn about! Go back and present yourself to Mori for another beating'.

Rationally, everything was against such a course of action. If there were normally anything which provoked the Japanese to extremes of punishment it was any action on our part that broke their rules and sense of order. Yet this voice that rang out almost like a bell within me was so clear and insistent that I turned about without hesitation, walked back and once more stood to attention in front of Mori before the next officer could take my place.

Mori was already in a position to beat up his next victim. He was on the point of attacking again when the realization came to him that he was being confronted with the very person whom he had beaten just a moment before. The shock of this slight variation in a process which he had taken for granted was great, and showed immediately in his eyes. He looked at me over his raised cudgel, arrested in its downward move, as a cliché would have it, like someone who was seeing a ghost in broad daylight. Indeed, so grave was the shock that it utterly broke up the accelerating rhythm of passion and anger in which he had been imprisoned. Slight as the irregularity was, it began drawing him out of the preconditioned processes of collective and instinctive reaction in which he had been involved and made him, I believe, suddenly aware of himself as an individual being. He stood there glaring at me, a strange inner bewilderment at this unexpected turn of events showing in the sombre glow of his dark eyes. Then, taking another sort of half-hearted swipe at my head, he grumbled with a kind of disgust that he thought the whole matter utterly incomprehensible and beneath contempt. He gave me a shove in the direction of our line, turned about, and still muttering tensely to himself walked away and out of sight...".[2]

From this most-moving of stories, it is clear to what extent unpremeditated, yet entirely *appropriate,* action can take place when a voice of such a spiritual dimension delivers its orders from within - and is obeyed. There was another component of Laurens van der Post's responses to Mori, however, and to the years of his imprisonment and harsh treatment, which he describes when writing about Jung's great insights into how necessary it is for us to bring the darkest areas of our 'shadow' selves to the light. For, to van der Post, the Japanese atrocities symbolized the unresolved, unselved actions, which form part of the chaos of that 'shadow'. Perceiving that the 'other' – in this case, Mori - was also 'himself', profound humanity and compassion were given to him to deal with the events he described, and his subsequent ponderings led him to write: *"I suspected that we would never know how to set about dealing with these dark forces until we knew more of their origin, nature and areas of growth. I was encouraged in this because of the extent to which I had achieved some understanding of these great non-rational imponderables in the Japanese during our years of imprisonment. And understanding helped me to invest our experience with some of the humanity that it so sorely lacked. What is more important, perhaps, it helped the two of us in the prison camp who were chiefly responsible for bringing some six thousand men through the experience, to do so not only without any feelings of bitterness for the Japanese, but with that extraordinary liberating conviction that our enemies had been forgiven because they truly "knew not what they did". One and all, we ended up, in the main, with nothing but compassion for the Japanese that they should have been so unselved as to commit such atrocities upon us...*

...Somehow, we have to understand the intimations which come at us out of our natures like lightning in the dark, and which are portents of great possibilities of new being, preparing to fall upon our arrested and arid lives like rain on desert earth. Accordingly it seemed more and more to me that we needed to serve and express them with all that we have of light, reason, endurance and fortitude." [3]

Thus, out of a situation that was violent, malevolent and fraught with the possibility of imminent death, a deep sense of shared suffering and humanity enabled van der Post to survive with the greatest sanity of all: compassion, that profound absorption into another's being which forms the basis of all spiritual teachings and without which such total yielding could not take place. His deep consciousness of *relationship* enabled him to connect with the inner voice of the Tao and gave him the foundation for right-action. He heard, and then acted-upon, the most insistent of orders and this resulted in an immense spiritual equilibrium arising within him and, in varying degrees, within those for whom he was responsible. And, by yielding totally to that inner voice, the lives of his men, as well as his own, were saved.

Now, the wide and expansive movements of Parting the Wild Horse's Mane (which surely must be one of the most-sublime examples of the meaning of "T'ai Chi Ch'üan", the Supreme Ultimate use of our energy and of the power to be spiritually open-handed when faced with an opponent), guide us as to how to make each 'parting and turning of the ways', with equally-sublime equilibrium. Moreover, by *fully* entering into the stream of life and, thus, by being at the very centre of the flood, we now can travel further than during any part of this Journey.

Carefully focusing our attention upon our rhythmic, shifting movements and, thereby, conveying the ultimate in gentleness, we perform the same movements as those in Diagonal Flying, but take them infinitely further, for we draw our hands and arms apart and up, apart and away, in arcs that travel further up and even further away - and only then, at the furthermost point of the body's vulnerability, do they turn towards each other and form the divine circle of wholeness and unity which so stabilizes and sustains the spirit. We then reverse the move-  ment and repeat the Parting by – again - shifting back and forth and turning into ever-widening diagonals, *opening* up ourselves as never before, and thereby symbolizing our total trust in the flow of the Tao.

Again and again, gently swaying and forming the circle, widely expanding and calmly turning, we separate the strands of the Wild Horse's Mane and yield up our essence to this perfection of movement and find that this is only possible when, symbolically, our very being is at stake, for only a crisis of the nature described above could takes us so profoundly to the heart of existence. Only then could we be shown how to live.

Thus, said Lao Tzu:

> *"'Do not invite the fight, accept it instead',*
> *'Better a foot behind than an inch too far ahead',*
> *Which means:*
> *Look a man straight in the face and make no move,*
> *Roll up your sleeve and clench no fist,*
> *Open your hand and show no weapon,*
> *Bare your breast and find no foe.*
> *But as long as there be a foe, value him,*
> *Respect him, measure him, be humble toward him;*
> *Let him not strip from you, however strong he be,*
> *Compassion, the one wealth which can afford him."* [4]

51 Grasping the Sparrow's Tail; Ward Off – Slantingly Upwards; Pull Back, Press Forward and Push

Heightened consciousness from total yielding; the Bamboos, and the seventh Gateway to Wisdom

We now Grasp the Sparrow's Tail of consciousness for the third time. Inspired by all that has just been described, we are aware as never before of the spiritual dimensions that can be received from heightened awareness and the most-supreme example of letting-go - and of how a total absence of ego-self can enable the human spirit to face the seemingly impossible.

We learn, too, from a very different source – the Third Law of Thermodynamics – that as activity decreases, order increases, and we see how this can be applied, not only to the situation related by Laurens van der Post, but also to one of the T'ai Chi's tenets: *use the minimum of activity for the maximum result*, for, when this maxim is applied in daily life, the T'ai Chi's *intended* slow and minimal physical activity leads, conversely, to a swifter and more-orderly mental response and physical agility. So we grasp this aspect of consciousness and enact the next movements with serenity, whilst understanding, even more deeply, the significance of their appearance, for - yet again - we are led into the curving flow and rhythmic harmony of the gently swaying Bamboos.

We abide awhile in a sweetly-whispering, softly-swaying grove of bamboo, shifting with an invisible breeze in one direction, changing course with another, and find again that such softly-fluid and peaceful movements harmonize the rhythms and energies of our own body with all of those flowing around us. Moreover, with each and every shift and change, we perceive that the enactment of our own flow must also allow for the possibility of a radically-different enactment in another's, and that this implies acceptance of another's dissimilar way of being, in the same way as Laurens van der Post 'accepted' Mori, albeit to a profoundly-greater degree. Thus, with each shift in space, the mind shifts, too, and confirms that, when a person remains true to his or her own inner knowing, even when faced with another's diametrically-opposite nature, a greater truth is revealed which - when held up to the light and as if suspended in time – fosters a profound recognition of the other's essence and of how best to meet it.

Flowing even further, we draw upon images of The Natural, of unhurried, physical self-regeneration, of a profoundly slow evolution which leads to an increase in capacity. We carry these images over as metaphors into every-day life, every movement we make appropriate to time and place, each action we take in accordance with our perception as to its immediate suitability - and find how fulfilling life becomes when lived that way.

Then, from all that was conveyed in the previous movements, we see that we have been given insights into a rare example of opposites and that, once this heightened consciousness has been fully absorbed, either from our own experience or from that of another, we can once again move forward into The Push and open yet another inner Gateway to Wisdom: the seventh in our Journey.

52 THE SINGLE WHIP

The Bird's Beak or the Phoenix Stance: the duality of a deep trust in the Tao, with its opposite: the most dangerous manifestation of shadow activity

The heightened consciousness just described is symbolized, once again, by that auspicious omen, the Phoenix, which, having a character of great gentleness, lives without crushing anything it alights upon, eats only seed and drinks heavenly dew and - most significantly to the Chinese - marks the birth of a Great Sage.[1] Its arrival at this stage of the journey is, thus, not without significance, since it represents and summarises the wisdom of refraining from injuring anything and epitomises both trust in the inner voice of mankind's deepest areas of compassion and how to deal with the magnitude of Tiger's violence in a situation of great crisis.

It also furthers an understanding as to why the Chinese ideogram for "crisis" comprises (amongst others) two important words: danger and opportunity, since, although a crisis does, indeed, indicate (sometimes extreme) danger, it also offers profound opportunities for growth, as well as the recognition that the deeper and more traumatic the experience, the greater the opportunity for heightened consciousness. Thus, the supreme compassion which can enable humanity to avoid causing harm, also enables an awareness to arise which makes allowance for the very worst shadow in another.

The violent actions of Mori went far beyond the accepted rules of warfare, however, and although it would seem - and with justice - that the part played by Laurens van der Post, as the victim of the violence, was blameless, he later described it from a different perspective through having become aware that, although mankind may view such events as deriving from external circumstances, they form part of our own, inner drama of spiritual development, stemming as they do from our collective ego, as well as our personal one, for – as Krishnamurti said – *"we are the world and the world is us"*. Thus, atrocities which form part of the human condition are not separate from, but are a part of us all and we are all responsible.

Laurens van der Post explained this in his book about Jung, when he wrote that we not only live our own lives, but, whether we know it or not, also the life of our time. He said that discounting this was: "…one of the most dangerous errors in our thinking." and that: "We assumed that "without" and "objective" were one and the same thing, as were "subjective" and "within". I believed that they were by no means synonymous and that there was something as objective "within" the human being as great as the subjective "without"."[2]

Thus, out of one of the most *subjectively*-dangerous, external situations which life can offer, the opposite of self-protection arose, and although, in the normal course of events, Laurens van der Post and Mori would have been vastly apart in terms of any true meeting of their inner beings, van der Post's response to his own deep truth, as well as his recognition that *his own shadow plays its part in the contribution towards mankind's suffering at large*, created the space which enabled Mori to make contact with an entirely-different aspect of himself. For, Mori – however unwittingly imprisoned within his own violent world – suddenly saw himself from without, perceived his own actions through the eyes of another and, despite himself, could not continue in his previous, desperately-locked role of destruction.

The Phoenix movement we now enact thus sums-up the symbolic dualities of life which, in this case, convey the opposites of external and internal, light and dark, good and evil, compassion and blind enmity. The head faces the open hand and the hand itself conveys the spiritual openness of an order rarely witnessed, whilst the closed hand, behind us, depicts the degradation to which mankind can descend, the shadow-side of human nature which, though often deeply buried beneath our consciousness, can easily be recognised in another, because we have it so firmly-established within ourselves.

Thus duality remains, and since compassion lies at the very heart of the events just described and forms the meeting point between these two widely-apart oppositions, the culmination of this important series of movements has the head of the Immortal Phoenix directing us towards a new and very different inner journey, one that will have no less than the "Goddess of Compassion" herself as our guide.

53 THE FAIR LADY WORKS
AT SHUTTLES

Kuan Yin, the Goddess of Mercy and Compassion, weaves through our lives in The Four Corners of the Earth

One of the loveliest of Eastern religious myths tells of Kuan Yin, the Goddess of Mercy and Compassion. Depicted in jade or ivory, fine gilded wood or rare porcelain, coarse china or plastic, on canvas, parchment or silk, the Goddess can be seen floating on a giant lotus leaf,

cradling a small child in her arms, holding a fish in a basket, raising a hand in blessing, standing in meditative serenity, or seated in the 'pose of lordly ease'. Sometimes she has a thousand arms, sometimes a few, sometimes only one which might hold a bowl stored with the sweet, honey-tasting 'Dew of Wisdom and Compassion', which only falls when a kingdom is at peace. Sometimes, to depict 'humility', she is portrayed in a long white robe which covers her arms and hands. At other times she holds one of the many emblems associated with her role as a deity who leads others towards illumination. At all times, those in distress can turn to her for comfort and peace, for Kuan Yin's name means: "The one who listens to the cries of the world and offers salvation from misery" – and she is a Bodhisattva.

A Bodhisattva is a highly-revered manifestation of the Buddha, a being who is filled with light and has attained a state of perfection wherein all vestiges of self-interest have dissolved. With deep compassion for human frailty and suffering – and in preference to joining other enlightened celestials in Nirvana, the State of Bliss – a Bodhisattva is one who elects to be of service to humanity by offering sentient, earthly beings opportunities for spiritual growth. In Kuan Yin's case, some of her messages would be to give up our assumptions, for then all things and forms would appear as they are; whilst moving, to be like flowing water; when walking to leave no trace; when at rest, to be like a mirror, so that our responses are as echoes, and, when thus appearing not to exist, we can pertain to the depth of reflection which arises from a crystal-clear mind.

In Buddhist mythology, Kuan Yin (whose Taoist name is Tara) was born on a thousand-petalled lotus and, as the "Mother of All Things", weaves in and out of our lives, guiding our intuition here, channeling our insights there, leading us towards higher, more spiritual realms. And she also spins. Weaving her shuttle in and out of our lives, she rescues us from error, or so places us that we may be given opportunities for more penetrating insights into more spiritual aspects - and she travels to the farthest corners of the earth to do so. We may resist her inner prompt-ings and feign blindness to the paths most clearly indicated. We may deny the wisdom presented to us and do all that is possible to avoid the attainment of spiritual liberation, but Kuan Yin continues her weaving with endless compassion for the suffering caused by our limitations and our unwillingness to learn from the circumstances that life presents to us; and she never fails to heed a cry from the heart.

Certainly all that Kuan Yin symbolises was there when Laurens van der Post responded to the Japanese with such profound compassion. Equally certain is that her messages of mercy entered into the hearts and minds of those other victims of the Japanese torture camp, when: "*one and all, we ended up in the main, with nothing but compassion for the Japanese that they should have been so unselved as to commit such atrocities upon us*". And when Laurens van der Post also said: "*somehow we have to understand the intimations which come at us out of our natures like lightning in the dark, and which are portents of great possibilities*", he was describing what the Buddhists call Bodhicitta, or the illumined mind, which heeds – and acts upon – Kuan Yin's messages of light.

Whether such spiritual intimations are seen as pertaining to mes-sages from a goddess on a lotus leaf or an angel on high or described in psychological terms as intuition or spiritually-based insight - or whether they come from our link with the holographic universe - the necessity for compassion undeniably weaves throughout our lives, for, without it, we would have destroyed each other long since. Equally undeniable is that a supremely powerful spiritual energy moves through the universe and forms an integral part of the tapestry of every human being's search for light, for such stirrings of heart and mind have occurred in every country and in every century since the beginning of human life on earth, revealing that, when free from the impure components of the Three Treasures, and when infinitely-more open and receptive than in our normal, mundane, egoistic state, wisdom and compassion can flow directly-into, and straight-from, the heart.

Thus, 'The Fair Jade Lady Weaves at Shuttles' through the four corners of the earth and, in so doing, encounters many cultures and different traditions, each of which has evolved in various ways in order to express – with the hope of fulfilling – our manifold human longings. And when the perceptive human mind provides 'answers' to our problems, through the many beliefs and creeds that have come down to us over the centuries, those who proffer such answers are sometimes set apart, put on platforms, revered, honoured, glorified, sanctified, and sometimes, even deified. If, however, they are wise-enough to repudiate the platforms upon which they have been placed, they can be of great assistance and, thus, if a skilled psycho-analyst releases us from a paralyzing emotional blockage, or a healer leads us to a different realm of perception, we – and they - are blessed by Kuan Yin's beneficence. If a gifted medium, a psychologically-astute astrologer, a spiritually-wise teacher, a sage or a mystic, is guided by Kuan Yin's hand to take us to a quieter and deeper place of insight, we have been led to the knowledge that is already available in the universe, but which we so often block by continuing to identify ourselves, on the mental and emotional planes, with the anxieties and fears which preclude clarity of vision and prevent inner wisdom from flowering. And, if these teachers, visionaries and conveyors of insight have succeeded in guiding us to our deeper levels, they, in effect, have become 'vehicles of Kuan Yin', conveying, through question and encouragement, that it is the seeker who can find the answer within.

214

Such guidance is sorely needed, however, for: *"...we have so little contact with, so little awareness of, the matrix of life from which the conscious ego springs – and so little understanding of the currents at work in the unconscious, shaping our lives and making our choices for us in accordance with the imperatives of the Self..."* [1] that: *"Many people become terrified at the first breath of impending change; in consequence they project it onto the environment, rather than acknowledging its true origin within themselves. As a result, external things begin to appear unstable and unreliable, and strenuous efforts are required to nail everything down, to ensure the immutability of one's personal habits, viewpoints, and property. And repression of natural psychic events of course provokes the unconscious, which, diverted from its natural channels of expression, must resort to indirect channels. These channels lead the individual to unconsciously invite the destruction of the very thing to which he clings. And the ensuring upheaval, which he has invoked himself, he proceeds to call adverse or hostile fate."* [2] or, in order to find it less threatening: "God's Will".

A situation such as this can be seen, however, as a preliminary to an awakening by Kuan Yin and can be utilized as such to bring about an awareness of the inner factors at work. And, when that occurs, we can sense: *"... the inner timing that regulates the endings and beginnings of phases, a knack of divining the moving forces of the unconscious."* [3]

Kuan Yin's intimations thus guide us toward a conscious recognition of the inner and the outer timing (which, as Laurens van der Post put it, is simultaneous), and, since, in reality, all the cells of our body are linked to everything else in the universe and are synchronistic with it, they also lead us to an awareness that we do not need to travel inwardly very far for such intimations to reach us, nor journey to the four corners of the outside world in order to gain such insights – for within and without are co-existent.

The term 'four corners of the earth' is used in the West, as well as in the East and is regarded as pertaining to geographical points on a compass, as well as, figuratively, places in our imagination. And yet, despite the circularity of our earth, one of the early discoveries of the space age was that the earth really did have 'four corners', or at least four recognisable large scale bulges[4] and that these were seen to be the four major mountain ranges of the Alps, the Himalayas, the Rockies, and the Andes, which, when viewed aerially (as by the first men on the moon), can be described as forming the 'square of the earth'. And, since the ancient Taoists also described our world as 'the square of the earth', it might not be too much of a flight-of-fancy to imagine that those ancients who spoke so knowingly of the four corners, had received this information from some of those highly-evolved, fully-enlightened beings who, as flying Taoist saints or Boddhisatvas, knew of the existence of these four mountain ranges (in whatever location they were then) from having viewed them with their own eyes, whilst flying in space between the dome of heaven and the circle of earth!

Painting of 'The Jade Lady Among Clouds'

We, however, being earth-bound, now continue our journey by travelling into the four corners of our own psyche, with the T'ai Chi's currently-intricate movements exemplifying this.

216

With hands that shape themselves into a square, and a circling body that has us visualizing Kuan Yin weaving in and out of our lives, we travel in rotation to the North East, North West, South West and South East diagonals.

The first corner, the North East diagonal, is described in the *I Ching*, as representing '*Chen*', the creative force, 'the Arousing', and such a corner could not be a more-appropriate place from which to start, for our journey in life began with the generative arousal which moved the seed which became the being, and so – through the application of that sometimes-searing intuition which we experienced when first our senses were aroused in childhood and adolescence – we now widen our insights concerning our sexuality, the warmth of our feelings, the passion of our emotions, our creative talents and our responses to Nature, since it is said in Taoism that, through the senses, the soul is free to mingle with the universe.

The next movement circles us around to the North West diagonal, to the corner of the *I Ching's 'Ken'*, a mountain, which, in this instance, guides us towards rock-like stability and the solid requirements of good health, food and clothing, shelter and financial sufficiency and, thus, all the material requirements of life which must be sought, sensed and savoured, provided we remember the Taoist maxim: *"He who has enough is rich"* – and that we actually need very little to have 'enough'.

With another circling movement we move to the South West corner, to the *I Ching's 'Sun'*: representing the wind, or air. Intellectual endeavour, the academic and rational mind, the brain's ability to function to its fullest capacity through analysis, logic, reason and mental agility are symbolized here, since it is as essential for our growth to develop these aspects of ourselves, as it is for us to seek warmth and stability, to fulfill our creative capacities, and to explore and refine our senses.

Finally, through another rotation of the body, we move out of that corner to the last and, in the spiritual quest, the most important of the four corners. We circle to the South East, to *'Tui'*, the joyous, the lake, symbolizing the fountains and springs of life which can lead us to the deeper, often mysterious and sometimes-unexplored pools of wisdom and serenity.

Our journey is usually seen as developing in such an order, for, once the early creativity and emotional self-involvement and physically-intense passions of youth become less absorbing, the energies are directed towards stabilizing ourselves through partnership, work, the acquisition of a home and the rearing of children. Later, if or when the requirements of financial security become less demanding and children more independent, opportunities for more intellectual development and travel can occur. Finally, if the intellect is seen as limited and unable to fulfill the search for inner peace, the path can lead towards wisdom. Thus, ideally, each of these symbolic four corners 'automatically' leads to the next but, as life does not offer the same journey to everyone, we can experience these aspects in quite a different order: passion and artistic fulfillment can come quite late in life; financial security can be given at birth; intellectual prowess can manifest at any age, and youth can have wisdom beyond measure. And yet, if any of the first three corners are over- or under-emphasized, the final corner of spiritual evolution cannot be realized, for a fully-enlightened being needs to experience and understand all levels of human existence in order to attain transcendence and ultimate enlightenment.

Kuan Yin's role is to weave and blend these four paths into one spiritual, centre-based whole and, in so doing, has us revolving, evolving, circling and turning four times over as we absorb the influences and movement of the ever-shifting stars that are guiding us through the four weeks in each month, the four seasons in each year and into as much of the inner and outer four corners of the world in which we live, as our circumstances and capacities allow. Nor is the number 'four' without further significance, for although, in the study of numbers, it is an 'earth' number, it also relates to the heavens. Thus: "… *if you want to describe the horizon as a whole, you name the four quarters of heaven...*"

said Jung, and with regard to our psychological and sensory responses: *"In order to orient ourselves, we must have a function which ascertains that something is there (sensation); a second function which establishes <u>what</u> it is (thinking); a third function which states whether it suits us or not, whether we wish to accept it or no (feeling), and a fourth function which indicates where it came from and where it is going (intuition)... The ideal completeness is the circle or sphere, but its natural minimal division is a quaternity."* [5]

These four ways of psychologically orientating ourselves also correspond to the four astrological 'types': the Earth signs of Taurus, Virgo and Capricorn which use the functions of the senses; the Air signs of Gemini, Libra and Aquarius which harness the powers of thought; the Water signs of Cancer, Scorpio and Pisces which have us 'feeling' our way through life, and the Fire signs of Aries, Leo and Sagittarius which further intuition. Thus:

"To our senses, the elements are four
and have ever been, and will ever be
for they are the elements of life, of poetry, and of perception
the four Great Ones, the Four Roots, the First Four
of Fire and the Wet, Earth and the wide Air of the world.

To find the other many elements, you must go to the laboratory
And hunt them down.
But the four we have always with us, they are our world.
Or rather, they have us with them." [6]

Nor, can it be denied that: *"they have us with them"*, for they manifest on the human physical plane as the hard and solid parts of the body that form the bones and cartilage and relate to the physical and materially-sensual element of Earth; as the breath moving in and out of the lungs and the mind's rational and intellectual capacities, as influenced by the element of Air; as the liquid and flowing parts which connect with the spiritual journey of the soul, through the flowing attributes of Water, and as the element of Fire, which expresses emotion and passion, sends warmth and heat coursing through the body and, thereby, awakens intuitive responses. Our equilibrium depends upon our ability to harmoniously discover and express all these elements by allowing them equal respect, and, if we can mange to be neither too earthy and physical, nor too airy and intellectual, too watery and spiritual, nor too fiery and emotional, we are doing well. As there are very few fully-rounded people on this earth, however, we can only attempt to uncover as many of those elements in ourselves as have been given to us by birth, by our experiences in life and by intuiting upon them.

Intuition – though usually swift - can sometimes flower in slow-motion, however, whatever astrological sign we come under and, blessedly, the slow-turning, explorative circling of these four T'ai Chi movements can help us part some of the curtains that may be blocking a particularly relevant corner so that we may see it more clearly. The 'circling around' can also heal us, since we are weaving a magnetic field around us (as in Dervish dancing), which is created by the circularity of the shapes we are making in space and by the union of opposites which occurs at the central *tan t'ien*, for, when opposites are united, they not only cause a rotation at their centre, but give balance to each other – and this can further physical healing. Moreover, whilst turning in such a circular fashion, we are aligning ourselves (again like slow-wheeling Dervish dancers) with psychic as well as cosmic, magnetic forces, which furthers our sixth sense. Thus we are integrating the circular symbol of heaven with the four 'corners' of the circular earth; we are generating a strongly-magnetic energy field in our own centre which links us to the universal rotation of the earth's axis with the heavens, and we are nearer to 'filling in' the circle of self-knowledge. And all this has us moving closer to *"the still point of the turning world"**, which we experienced at the beginning of this Journey, for, no matter how far our internal and external revolutions may take us, and whatever the circumstances, there will always remain the fifth point on the compass, the place of inner equilibrium, the realm of both spiritual and temporal reality - or what could be thought of as the midday point of noon, since that is the only place where the sun does not cast a shadow.

*From T.S. Eliot's "Burnt Norton"

Each corner thus contains a situation that has its reverse. Through suffering and self-knowledge, through living all the losses fully in order to experience the gains, some semblance of centredness can be attained. The key lies in moving into all these opposite directions without losing that centre, for only then can we be sure that we have paid heed to the intimations imparted by K'uan Yin and have travelled to the four corners of our inner world with her wisdom as our guide.

54 Grasping the Sparrow's Tail; Ward Off – Slantingly Upwards; Pull Back, Press Forward and Push

The potential for a highly-expanded consciousness; the Bamboos, and the eighth Gateway to Wisdom

Following upon our journey into the four-fold nature of much that we and our world comprise, we expand into ever-widening areas of consciousness as we Grasp the Sparrow's Tail for the fourth time. Still 'wanting to know' and understand all that is happening, that little bird of consciousness - in its fullest meaning - may still prove hard to catch, but Kuan Yin's weaving has revealed much and she offers us her mercy when we delude ourselves into thinking we understand, when we do not.

Prior to our recent exploration of the four corners of our inner world, however, we had already probed some of their aspects and had come to recognise that: heightened consciousness can arise out of non-judgemental meditation-upon and/or the writing down of, every thought and feeling; that contact with spiritual teachings, regular periods of silence, and specific breathing exercises can regenerate the sensibilities and promote self-awareness; that a retreat from the pollution of noise, smoke and destructive attitudes can calm the mind; that physical awareness and an even-greater joy in life can be implemented by regular exercise (not least when shared with others), and that a healthy and varied, organic diet cleanses, refines, and sensitises the system. Our sojourn with Kuan Yin, however, has shown that, if these already-absorbed components are combined with a rich variety of life-experience, there is, indeed, the potential for a highly-evolved being.

Such a being is seen as one who, with a psychological and spiritual awareness of cause and effect, has a far-reaching view of humanity and the Universal Laws governing it. These facets may not necessarily be in action during every moment of consciousness, nor under every circumstance, since the natural rhythms of the mind do not allow for continuous awareness (the mind briefly 'sleeping' every few moments) and because even the most-enlightened have their fallow times. A few such have existed on earth, however, and we have repeatedly been drawn to their wisdom teachings, either by the laws of vibration and synchronicity or because they have paid heed to our heart-felt call. Now, however, led by inner promptings in this evolutionary journey, we are conscious of something else beckoning, something that, appearing almost like a psychic 'order', can further our understanding of some other complex aspects of the mind.

The Journey has been preparing us for this and, although the wide and open Parting the Wild Horse's Mane had nuances and depths of spiritual meaning which may have been too profound for us to easily incorporate into daily living, we have at least sensed what it must mean to face the darkest side of humanity and yield *totally*. Moreover, the complex weaving of the Fair Jade Lady Weaves at Shuttles - which might have had us happily exploring only our more 'acceptable' aspects - furthered this message, by indicating the wisdom of exposing our darker, shadow side. Thus, if such a yielding or such a plunge into the depths of the unconscious were to occur, the liberation for the spirit would not only be a 'marvel' in itself, but would also reveal to what degree there is order in the unconscious levels. For, *"Where it was dark,"* said Laurens van der Post, describing Jung's exploration of his own unconscious, *"it had its own form of starlight and moonlight by which the probing spirit could steer. Its laws of order and determination were as precise as those that kept the stars in their courses in the universe without. The negations came only when man's conscious self ignored his dependence on this world of the collective unconscious and tried to establish some kind of independent tyranny over what ultimately only sought to nourish and increase what should be a partnership. The disturbance started in human personality when consciousness behaved as if it were the whole of man. There was nothing the unconscious world abhorred more than one-sidedness. When one extreme of spirit attempted a monopoly for itself, sooner or later another extreme in the unconscious rose titanic to overthrow it. That is why the history of man is so often a swing from one opposite of spirit into another..."* [1]

This description clarifies our resolve to heed the beckoning, and, as we come a little closer to what is sometimes called 'living and dying from moment to moment', we see that a journey into higher consciousness requires a plunge into deeper unconsciousness and, although we do not, as yet, know what form this will take – and there is some fear accompanying the quest – we recognise that we sorely-need a prior interlude beforehand, a fallow period for peace and harmony, before such a depth of probing can begin.

To fulfil this need, we slip once more into the flow of a rustling, delicately-whispering grove of Bamboos and all the swaying, pliant, yielding, bending, joyous freedom that they portray. As before, we glide smoothly into each *yang* movement before its reversal into *yin*; slip away from *yin*'s nadir into the zenith of the *yang;* sway with all the simplicity of Nature and the beauty of its form and, as always in these movements, harmonise the energies within our body with their outer, universal flow. By enacting the wisdom of the Tao that abides both within and without and is both immanent and transcendental, it is revealed yet-again that such a swing from one to the other can transform itself into a beautiful blend of opposites, as the day shifts into night and the sunbeams take-over from the stars. Moreover, as the disorders in the conscious mind merge with the order inherent in the unconscious - which, in itself, is part of the collective unconscious - we sense that all our corners can be rounded off as we harmonise the energies inherent in the two circles of the number 'eight' (which, according to the Chinese, symbolises 'riches', as well as the two circles of heaven above and earth below); unite our nature with Nature's own, and find rest in the Tao of small brown birds, pristine-white clouds in lavender-blue skies, in music, poetry, and peace. And then, as if opening a book of exquisite, gilded illustrations, or parting a silk curtain in order to gaze upon a breath-taking view, we find that the eighth Gateway to Wisdom has revealed itself.

"A jade kettle with a purchase of spring, *
A shower on the thatched hut
Wherein sits a gentle scholar,
With tall bamboos growing right and left,
And white clouds in the newly-clear sky,
And birds flitting in the depths of trees.
Then pillowed on his lute in the green shade,
A waterfall tumbling overhead,
Leaves dropping, not a word spoken,
The man placid, like a chrysanthemum,
Noting down the flower-glory of the season, -
A book well worthy to be read."* [2]

*"Wine, which makes man see spring at all seasons"

225

55 THE SINGLE WHIP

The Bird's Beak or the Phoenix Stance and the unfolding of androgyny

Again that auspicious bird, the Phoenix, symbol of duality and of peace in the land, alights and takes its stance. Again it is synonymous with the *yin-yang* symbol, for, as well as its other symbolic attributes, it combines the *yang* head of a cockerell, the *yin* back of a swallow, the eyes of the *yang* sun and a *yin* crescent-moon beak and is, therefore, a remarkably-androgynous bird. Furthermore, its wings represent the wind, its tail the trees and flowers, its feet the earth, and (after a maturation period of three years) it glows with the five colours of blue, yellow, red, white and black, which represent the cardinal virtues of uprightness, justice, honesty, benevolence and fidelity.[1] Thus, the richness, variety, and depth of symbolism of this magical, mythical bird becomes more apparent the further we journey into its meaning.

Its current arrival is the result of Kuan Yin's gentle intervention, and its presence - indicating the balance of opposites which our ever-deepening inter-weaving experience of life is unfolding - also embodies the form and character manifested in the wide-open Parting the Wild Horse's Mane movements. Thus, with an increasingly androgynous response resulting from the combination of both those highly-significant movements (and which explains why many mythological Gods are inter-changeable in gender), we find we are sensing with greater psychological accuracy exactly when a *yang*, male, more dominantly-active response is required, or when a *yin*, female, receptive and pliant way of being is necessary.

Sometimes, however, the situation is complex and produces a dilemma of levels, since we are not sure which is the more appropriate. Or, to cause further confusion, both responses may appear to carry equal weight, which can cause such misery in the mind that the Monkey goes racing around in circles. To give an example, a psychologist who practised in the last century and who, undeniably, could be deemed one of Kuan Yin's spiritual 'vehicles', described what she called the problems caused by the difference between 'focussed masculine consciousness' and 'diffused feminine awareness':

"How often one argues with oneself, getting nowhere, because the two inner voices conversing cannot meet." she wrote. *"What, for instance, should I do when a beggar comes to my door? "Give help," says one voice. "Don't be a fool," says the other. "No one need starve these days. It is a put-up job." "I can't possibly slam the door in his face," says the first voice. "You are only encouraging vagrancy," says the second. And, as I reluctantly shake my head and close the door, another voice says, "Inasmuch as ye have done it unto one of the least of these, ye have done it unto me."*

I return to my interrupted work feeling baffled and ashamed. That voice which said I should be encouraging vagrancy was certainly right, and yet how could I possibly have been so callous? It might happen to any of us to be in need. How dreadful to be refused, house after house, and go home hungry.

But it is no use answering the voice of one level with that of the other. They are both right. Only the two truths do not coincide. They do not even impinge on one another. It is as though the voices were speaking two different languages and neither could understand the other. As though there were two people trying to shake hands across a gulf.

We are literally impaled on this dilemma. For those who are able to stand firmly on the basis of rational common sense and the moral code of the day, there is little difficulty. They will shut the door in the beggar's face, more or less politely, convinced that the slight, just discernible twinges of guilt at their own lack of charity are mere signs of childish sentiment which they should have outgrown long ago. This is the attitude of our masculine culture, the fruit of our focussed consciousness. A fruit we have won at the cost of hardening our hearts.

But for those who stand firmly on the level of awareness that all life is one, and that what is done to any is done to all, it is inconceivable to refuse the beggar. This is where little children live, until we educate them out of it, educate them to be more sensible." [2]

Such wisdom then shows us that, for our own sanity and spiritual peace of mind, we need to heed the voice of that small child and incorporate it into our daily lives, whilst, at the same time, also recognising that: *"Over awareness of feminine values may make action impossible in the outer world. While a too focussed consciousness renders the wisdom from the feminine layer of our psyche invisible."* [3]

Out of the inherent harmony at the centre of the Four Corners movement, however, we can, at times, sense our errors more subtly, recognise more swiftly when we have acted in too *yang* a manner and caused ripples of distress, or when we have been too compliant and *yin*, thereby inviting disharmony or even, sometimes, danger – and, from this awareness, we can return to the centre more rapidly and can even change the course of our confused responses. For example, if we had refused that beggar (with a Tiger-influenced 'sensible' masculine *yang* response), we could – on second thoughts - have run after him, whether he were fraudulent or not, and given him some money or food (which would have been a feminine *yin* response) and thus returned to our centre of balance with peace of mind and without those significant *"just discernible twinges of guilt"*.

But, there is also the problem of how we view a problem. For instance, someone asked the Indian wisdom teacher, Anandamayi Ma (who always adjusted her responses to the needs of the individual and in accordance with the questioner's religious background): *... whether it was proper for him to engage in a suit, in view of the fact that he had been cheated in a business deal. In reply, She stated that one could argue that one must go to court to teach the culprit a lesson and to keep him from further* *crime. On the other hand, who is really cheating? "Are not all forms, all beings manifestations of Him? What I have been deprived of was evidently not my due. It is God who has taken it from me". Another way of looking at the problem is that through generosity and forgiveness one might bring about a transformation in the criminal. Or one might refrain from going to court, considering it sufficient punishment that the villain had caused bad karma for himself. Finally, one could reason that one would not go to court if the wrongdoer were one's own brother. "Whichever of these points of view appeals to you, according to it you should act".*

When someone complained to Ananadamayi Ma about Her unwillingness to give clear-cut answers to problems, She retorted: "At least you have understood that there is a state where problems are no longer settled in any particular way …no solution is ever conclusive…. The resolution of a problem arrived at by the mind must of necessity be from a particular point of view; consequently there will be room for contradiction, since your solution represents but one aspect." Only by transcending the region of multifacedness can one arrive at the one solution." [4]

From this discourse, we could (if we wish) extract which attitudes were *yin* and which were *yang* and, perhaps, then find that *the* "one solution" might lie in Laurens van der Post's: "compassion for the unselving of the other", since that would indicate a response from one's centre that would combine all aspects of one's spiritual being.

We can also more-fully appreciate how deceptively simple, and yet subtle, is the *yin-yang* circular symbol itself, since it depicts the complementary opposites in the human condition, but does not indicate their spiritual resolution. Thus, whilst an exploration of each side of our nature would have us more-fully able to appreciate the small circular ray of its opposite, and all aspects of light and shade would be acceptable as part of the dualism inherent in our nature, it is clear that spiritual discernment – and enlightenment as evinced by Immortals such as Kuan Yin - can only be found in the purest of hearts – which, perhaps, is why those ancient Chinese philosophers who designed the *yin/yang* symbol omitted a area which would indicate spiritual fulfilment, since such a state is not part of human nature and is only attained by those who have transcended duality within themselves.

For us now, however, we portray the summing up of the previous movements with the crescent-moon-shaped Bird's Beak hand which – in outline - so resembles each half of the *yin-yang* symbol and which indicates, in this case, the half that encloses the underlying, sometimes hostile responses which are activated from the *yin* shadow that resides behind us. On the other, sun-shaping, open hand, we convey the *yang* light-filled circle of that same symbol and the responses that arise from compassion. The movement, as a whole, is thus a summation of the androgynous symbol of opposites and - although the central place of balance where all contradictions converge still is conveyed, in the physical body, as the *tan tien* - it is only from the unconscious that *the* answers may arise from its depths.

56 Wave Hands like Clouds

Three sideways steps: thinking, meditation,
and contemplation

"Just as a white summer cloud, in harmony with heaven and
earth, freely floats in the blue sky from horizon to horizon,
following the breath of the atmosphere – in the same way the
pilgrim abandons himself to the breath of the greater life that
wells up from the depth of his being and leads him beyond the
farthest horizons to an aim which is already present within him,
though yet hidden from his sight." [1]

It is time for another Cloud Arms, time
for another fallow period of spiritual
reflection. Quiescence does not only fol-
low-upon intense activity, it also precedes
it, and, given that our more-strongly
awakened psychic senses have divined
that there is a *greater life that wells up*
from the depth of our being which is
leading us *beyond the farthest horizons*,
we again wave our hands and arms like
clouds which slip across the azure heavens, whilst 'letting' them softly rise and
gently-sink and subtly-form and then disperse in the same way as clouds do – and,

again, we are given a message from the Tao. For, whilst balancing our
body, forming the magical circles which give lightness and ease, enjoying
the quiet rhythms which the harmonising patterns of this movement
bestow upon us, we are drawn out of our habitual patterns of thought
into areas of meditation which, in turn, take us into free-flying realms of

231

contemplation – and we then find that these three sideways steps could be seen as symbols of these three aspects of the mind, which are (as far as we know) unique to mankind and which, though appearing so similar, yet are so different.

Thus, *Thinking*, which is essential for the organisation of our daily lives, can convey so much in just one moment, yet can also roam, mindlessly, without focus or guidance. It can be as blanket-heavy and slow as many a leaden cloud and yet can penetrate into abstractions with perceptions as sharp as rays of light. It can meander into avenues that are crystal-clear and yet also can block and twist itself so out of shape that the results of its tangles can cause irrevocable harm. It can take us to profound depths of wisdom and then plunge us wildly, incomprehensively, into an abyss of emotional pain. At other times, it can appear to function with no purpose at all except, perhaps, to fill the gaps created by our fear of silence, or make more interesting what might appear to be a life of stagnation and boredom. Or it can move us away from an intuitive, wordless perception by then filling the mind with knowledge and facts, out of an apparent need to do just that. And yet, like clouds, however variable, *Thinking* has good reason for its passage through the mind, can be well-utilised and is deserving of respect.

Meditation requires thought as help-mate, using it initially as a means-whereby the mind can focus, and then rest. If the practise of such one-pointedness continues over time, thought can dissolve and a state closer to emptiness can take its place. Peace can then arrive swiftly, with lightness and certitude, although (as has been mentioned), there will always be a residue of thought remaining in consciousness. At other times, thought can interfere with the meditational path by moving like a restless monkey in a wind-lashed forest, or travel slowly like sluggish or stagnant water in heavy, water-logged clay. Alternatively, a specific thought can become the focus-point in meditation with the sole purpose of solving a personal problem, but if the problem remains, such thinking has not fulfilled the purpose nor led to meditational depth. When one-pointed focus has been achieved, however, and thoughts are allowed to slip into consciousness with clarity and wisdom, answers can rise up out of the wisdom of the Tao. *Thinking*, then, can be used in meditation to keep an end in view, but can only bear fruit when sufficient practise has succeeded in eliminating all outer and inner disturbances.

Mystical *Contemplation,* however, which has consciousness combining with insight in order to fly in freedom, is without the hindrances of conditioned thought or goal-orientation. Having no motive, it neither toils, nor does it spin and can hover upon the heights like a majestic bird that views its landscape with unlimited perception and is at-one with all it perceives. Abiding in stillness and arriving unsought, it is wordless. Being nebulous, it has no objective, needs no result, requires no reward, observes without an observer and looks without an 'I'. *Contemplation* is the 'quiescent watchfulness' that can sojourn in the spaces that arise when a mind contains no fruitless thought, and can relate to a spirit that has no body, and thus it is that - like clouds – it both fulfils the Tao and is fulfilled by it.

Thinking could be regarded as being synonymous with Part One of this Journey, when life was new; when the processes of thought were essential to enable the child to function safely within its environment, and when it was the tool which was needed to handle the countless daily necessities which life has to offer. *Meditation* - of the free-wheeling Vipassana and 'writing-down' varieties, as well as of the 'one-pointed' kind - was revealed in Part Two, and its aim, which is implicit in the training of would-be meditators, offers direct insight and self-knowledge (although a practised meditator comes to understand that peace from the mind's journeying – as with the passage of the clouds – requires no more than an arrival at a state of serene 'non-striving', and of 'not-minding' whether meditational 'success' has been achieved, or not).

Now in Part Three, without losing-sight of the essential qualities of thought, and of the meditational techniques that have been of such assistance, we are guided towards *Contemplation* and the state of peaceful wonder which transcends them both. Floating like clouds, free from judgement, exempt from duality or ambiguity, the contemplative mind senses the wonders of the universe, ponders upon its manifestations and forms no conclusions. It simply observes, sometimes in stillness, sometimes circling in space, sometimes flying. But, when it flies, it does so as swiftly as do the clouds when ushered along by the equally free-wheeling wind and then views with equanimity the endless shifts and changes in life - and shifts and changes with them. Detached, it makes no attempt to remain in any one place or plane, but disperses, gathers, floats, sinks, draws near, drifts away or becomes as empty as the skies when clouds have passed and left them cleansed with the air which, though filled with *Ch'i*, appears so empty. *Contemplation* thus fulfils the Tao by requiring nothing more than to follow its own serene flow as it moves through space.

Now we can view the path ahead. The 'lens of differentiation' which, mentioned so long ago and which normally blurs our sight, has – for the time being – been lifted from our eyes and, with the enactment of the cloud-dance which links the earth with heaven, the microcosm with the macrocosm, human life with the world of the spirit, there is direct perception of that which is to come. Roaming free, *Contemplation* now takes us towards the source of what will become the essence of existence as it floats us through space to a place unknown, to areas within which have always been there, but which, hitherto, have remained unattainable. It guides us to an awareness that, soon, we must release ourselves from the realms of 'thinking and knowing' and even to the limitations of memory itself.

57 The Single Whip

The Bird's Beak or the Phoenix Stance: the duality of 'thinking and knowing' with 'contemplation and no-knowing'

Once more the Cloud Arms movement ends with a beautiful, upward-floating hand and leads us into the Phoenix Stance. For the seventh time we form a closed Bird's Beak with one hand and, having acknowledged it with a turn of the head, look to the direction of the other, open, hand. Again, the movement creates a dwelling place for the deeply-perceived, but not yet fully-manifested aspects of ourselves to which we have been guided by all the previous movements, the last of which floated us through the emptiness of *Contemplation* towards an important – but, as yet, unknown – process of illumination.

The balance required by the movement is also clear. We recall that, only in a condition of total equilibrium and filled with light, as if standing in the brightness of the midday sun, would we would have no shadow to cast, and yet our brief glance back towards the closed Bird's Beak has re-confirmed the existence of the darkness still remaining. We are also again facing West and, recognising our human fallibility, we sense that enlightenment is only rarely glimpsed, let alone ful-ly-attained and so we are grateful to this Phoenix Stance, because it confirms the reality of where we are now and that there is still much to come.

It also offers us a vision of the next stage of our Journey, for, whilst still seekers, still pilgrims, still moved by the call to the East, our increasingly-androgynous understanding and our burgeoning psychic awareness, are indications that the path ahead is becoming clearer and, moreover, that we have to answer a burning question:

"Are you willing to be sponged out, erased, cancelled,
made nothing?
Are you willing to be made nothing?

dipped into oblivion?
If not, you will never really change.

The phoenix renews her youth
only when she is burnt, burnt alive,
burnt down to hot and flocculent ash.
Then the small stirring of a new small bub in the nest
with strands of down like floating ash
Shows that she is renewing her youth like the eagle
Immortal bird." [1]

Universally representing resurrection and immortality, death and rebirth, the Phoenix now guides us – with the longest step yet taken – into an acceptance of the fact that we have to 'let-go' even further. Phoenix-like, we have to 'die' to be re-born and have to dissolve a human attribute which we have been taught to respect from childhood, but which profoundly hinders the spiritual life: we have to let go to *thinking that what we know, is what is*, and to the belief that knowledge itself is of supreme importance. For, "*the word is not the thing*", says Taoism and, from the bright glow shed by the Phoenix fire, this message is clarified. Its brilliance also reveals that it is a two-fold insight, for it is not only the confusions and vanities inherent in knowledge that can cause malaise to the soul, but it is our attachment to 'knowing' that hinders something that is vital: a freshness of perception and the capacity to look at life, as if we had never seen it before.

58 THE SNAKE CREEPS DOWN INTO WATER (SQUATTING SINGLE WHIP)

*Letting-go of 'attachment to knowing', by
entering the Waters of Wisdom*

*"Do you think it is easy to change?
Ah, it is very hard to change and be different.
It means passing through the waters of oblivion."* [1]

Our Cloud Arms' reflections have given us an insight into the functions of *thinking, meditation* and *contemplation*, and have indicated that *contemplation* is a condition that would not have a scratch of memory, nor a word, nor a conclusion that could distort perception. Our difficulty in accepting this – even as a concept - is in direct proportion to the satisfaction we receive from the use of the mind's intellectual capacities, and so we might now be fearful that, for us, spiritual enlightenment could mean the loss of all that the *third* of the Four Corners of the Earth represents.

It is to that corner that now we look, however, and in so doing, we find that there is much to discover that is both admirable and yet hazardous, for, despite the phenomenal capacities of the brain and the wondrous feats of the intellect - and to what degree we thrive upon all that they offer – there is the factor of pride to bear in mind. Having been taught that the intellect, as such a remarkable aspect of mankind's evolution, *should* be something of which we are justly proud; that the furthering of knowledge *should* be sought and highly-prized, and that the ego-enhancing ability to recognise ourselves through our intellectual insights *should* be given the greatest respect, we have come to accept that the capacity of the brain to perform all these feats is valued above all other capabilities. Yet, still we overlook the fact that these magnificent attributes are freely-given gifts of the Tao and, whilst recognising that they are necessary and valuable factors in our existence, we consider them as 'ours' - and are deeply attached to them.

From this it can be seen that such an attachment can blur our awareness of the deeper levels of existence and that we must let-go to the strings which bind us to our ego and to our insistence on our superiority - for Tiger's use of ego-boosting, intellectual 'cleverness' is too destructive to humanity's spiritual endeavours, as well as to how we use and abuse the air, the seas, the earth and the creatures (both human and otherwise) on this magnificent planet.

The wisdom in our current T'ai Chi movement thus has us releasing ourselves from such bondage and, although the Tiger (having been in exile for some time), now swiftly slips into our consciousness to hold forth and ask most searching questions as to *WHY* we need to delve into this third corner and disengage ourselves from something so precious - and, of course, sounds as convincingly sane, balanced, perspicacious and *mature* as it always attempts to do - we pay no heed to its outpourings, but continue to be concerned with the kind of spiritual response which, by using the Stillness at the heart of wisdom instead of the intellect, furthers 'becoming one' with what is being viewed.

So, we turn again to Taoism and recall the 'loss is gain' messages that have come so frequently through these pages, for the wisdom teachers and the sages of all ages have said that, if ego-free action is to take place, there must also be *contemplation* and that, for this to occur: *"Knowledge, discrimination, logic, analysis, reason and every variety of conceptual thought must be banished. None of them will serve. Therefore the need for perfect stillness, outside and in. Without, there must be no boundaries, the mind being free to penetrate all objects and perceive their interfusion; within, self-consciousness must be annihilated. The fruit of such intuition is a liberating transformation; the mind, freed from the tyranny of dualism and self-assertion, roves at will, transcending self and other, recognising the ego as a ghost of what never was nor ever will be. Pure harmony results, a limpid perception of the seamless unity of the formless Tao and its myriad forms, be they people, animals or objects. Profound compassion stirs. Fear and anxiety vanish. Henceforth, ups and downs, good and bad, life and death, are one."*[2]

Nearer to our own level of experience, the inner-questing psychologist, Joanna Field said: *"... I discovered that there is all the difference in the world between knowing something intellectually and knowing it as a 'lived' experience... The more I read scientific books on psychology the more I felt that the essential facts of experience were being missed out.. [and]..it was the uneasy suspicion of this gap between knowing and living that determined the first steps in the development of my method. Remembering Descartes, I set out to doubt everything I had been taught, but I did not try to rebuild my knowledge in a structure of logic and argument. I tried to learn, not from reason but from my senses. But as soon as I began to study my perception, to look at my own experience, I found that there were different ways of perceiving and that the different ways provided me with different facts. There was a narrow focus which meant seeing life as if from blinkers and with the centre of awareness in my head; and there was a wide focus which meant knowing with the whole of my body, a way of looking which quite altered my perception of what I saw. And I found that the narrow focus was the way of reason. If one was in the habit of arguing about life, it was very difficult not to approach sensation with the same concentrated attention and so shut out its width and depth and height. But it was the wide focus way that made me happy."*[3]

And that word, *"happy"*, is a key word here for, even if we were not using such words as 'spiritual' or 'deeper meaning to life' in relation to our inner impoverishment, we all say that we want to be happy. And we *have* experienced happiness: in childhood, when totally absorbed in something creative or new; as adolescents when, without any conceptualisation, we have sensed the tremendous potential for life and the vibrant energy within us; as adults when our consciousness has been heightened by a liberating experience such as looking at an exquisite view, a flower, the face of a loved one after a separation – none of which has anything to do with the intellect. And, also, at those times when - metaphorically or otherwise - we have been flowing with the Bamboos and have slipped into an unassertive, fluid, pliant, unconditioned state, in harmony with the energy of others and the rhythms of life and, intuitively, with the truth inherent in the Tao.

Most intellectuals would say that they valued truth more highly than themselves and, if they have utter integrity, this would be the case when it comes to what they are actually working upon. But, when it comes to protecting their own 'corner', Tiger's shackles rise, it rears-up upon its hind legs and it most-vehemently asserts itself and fights to retain its supremacy. Worse, it has been known to accept praise, and even awards, for work of which it had no part. The third 'corner' is then expressed in the most negative of ways, and sometimes results in a wide range of repressed information, rationalisations and justifications, with, occasionally, dangerous results to the psyche, as well as to the field of research. For, as has been said before, the unconscious mind requires conscious recognition of its content and when the intellect successfully blocks the promptings of such 'messages' - as offered through nightmares, dreams or symbolism, the words of a friend or foe, a passage in a book, the words of a song, or from any of Kuan Yin's many intimations – the intellect closes its ears and builds-up barriers to protect its self-esteem.

Once asked which people he had found most difficult to heal, Jung answered instantly: *"Habitual liars and intellectuals…"*, since: *"…the intellectualist was also, by constant deeds of omission, a kind of habitual liar. He was untrue to other equally important and valid aspects of himself. He tended to lead a highly compartmentalised existence, creating concepts to shield him from reality. As fast as they were challenged he invented new ones to take their place."* And, because Jung felt that: *"Spirit was so much greater because it included all the feeling values as well as other non-rational sources of awareness in man"*, he described with some dismay how he observed the *"…intellectualist's success in identifying intellect with spirit"*.[4]

Thus the intellectual's unwillingness to listen to the 'sensing' responses of the non-intellectual approach, has her or him using Tiger's defence-mechanisms of: "let's analyse this", "define your terms", "what exactly do you mean by that?", "let's look at this rationally" etc., and this acts as an impediment to the natural resonance of the wider focus of awareness described earlier, as well as to the swift comprehension and acceptance of the meaning inherent in what is being said. The wise maxim of 'loss is gain' thus continues to be an essential component to spiritual liberation and, whilst respect is given to all facets of the intellect, wisdom teachings recommend that no special importance be attached to any of them.

Now, having understood that we cannot find peace or happiness through abstractions or concepts, we *let-go* to the mind's distorting interference in the mystical realm and move into one of the most dramatic movements in the whole of the Form: the very significant and highly-symbolic: "The Snake Creeps Down into Water".

Not easy to perform (though it is less difficult if we retain consciousness of the 'pull' of the silken thread at the crown of the head that connects us to the heavens, and thus remain light in our being as we sink down in the movement), it is also clear that both its meaning and its symbolism are equally difficult to absorb. And yet, it is essential to our Journey that we do so, for, whilst the Snake lures us with the mistaken belief that knowledge is paramount, it is also associated with healing, with physical and spiritual rebirth, and - through periodically renewing its skin - with new life and resurrection - and all these elements have already formed, and still are, part of our Journey.

Creeping low, the Snake glides us away from the world of theories and abstractions and slips us into water, that symbol of wisdom so beloved of the Taoists and, again - as in the Search for the Golden Needle at the bottom of the Sea - we see why. For water flows wherever the contours of the land dictate and fills all hollows before continuing upon its course. Non-discriminatory, it makes no distinctions between high or low, pink cloud above or mud-filled pool below, mountain or valley, ocean, stream or rivulet. Sinking, it seeks its own level; rising, it floats as mist through the land; settling, it is the sweet dew which renews and revives. Never climbing, it yet changes its nature and fills the clouds and flows down from above to unite heaven and earth as rain, hail, sleet or snow. Reflecting, it mirrors the heavens and yet, once plumbed, can be immeasurably deep. Yielding, it moves around obstacles, forms no attachments, never clings, yet wears-away obstinate stone. Stagnant only when held in check by human bondage, when pure, it is essential to life and composes seven parts of our body. Totally adaptable, yet persistent, it is a source of energy and a medium for power; immensely strong and also heavy, when solidified it is almost impenetrable. Forming rainbows when the vapours of sun and earth meet, it also ebbs and flows with the tides in response to the power of the moon, follows the patterns of the seasons, and moves, always moves, with and towards the larger flow of life. And it is the Snake, which has the ambivalence of character which is open to so many interpretations, that now uses its many-faceted powers to guide us into the depths of such water - and we are almost annihilated.

We 'let-go' and we sink down and we almost drown. We cut the ties that bind us to our endlessly analysing self, to our egoistic opinions, to our self-importance and self-praising 'insights', to our ego-inflating ideas and certainties, to our intellectual conceits and our belief in 'our rights', and to the very processes of thought which we had always relied upon to lead us to the answers to life. And this letting-go, this plunge into oblivion, is carried-out with supreme consciousness, as well as *intent,* in its most-profound Taoist meaning. Through one of the T'ai Chi's most demanding movements and its hardest lesson, we enact this 'loss', this shedding of layer upon layer of thought and conditioning, by dissolving the intellect, by discarding the known, so that all those hitherto-binding strings of attachment soften, weaken, bend, are broken and float away, and we are lost in the Waters of Wisdom, submerged in their cleansing, purifying, healing depths. And we find that:

> *"Oh seekers, when you leave off seeking*
> *you will realise there was never anything to seek for.*
>
> *You were only seeking to lose something,*
> *not to find something,*
> *when you went forth so vigorously in search."*[5]

242

We then realise that some of the deepest spiritual truths are learnt through the loss of self in that desperate 'dark night of the soul'. Symbolising a process towards enlightenment and a fully-experienced state of highly-developed insight and penetration, the movement represents a major spiritual breakthrough such as Laurens van der Post experienced when he yielded up his inborn sense of self-preservation, entered into the stream of universal consciousness and obeyed its orders. We have not 'arrived' at enlightenment, nor are we, as yet, nearer to relative freedom from the ego, but the movement indicates that we have been transported onto a different plane of being. Other transformations may take place, some dramatic, some less so, but a mutation has occurred in the mind, the psyche has altered, and although life will continue in much the same way as it has always done, such a mutation cannot be erased. Furthermore, by delving so deeply into the unconscious and 'letting-go to knowing', no further transformations will be desired and - if they do occur - they will come of themselves.

59 THE GOLDEN ROOSTER
STANDS ON ONE LEG

Emerging, new-born, with the Herald of the Dawn

We are now at the dawn of a new and very different phase of our spiritual development. The Snake, having entered the Waters of Wisdom and taken us through a transformation of radical psychological and spiritual dimensions, now changes course and we slide up out of the Waters and then swoop up in a wave of spiritual consciousness, shedding our skin and fulfilling the renewal which the seasons and patterns of Nature consistently reveal. Re-born, baptised, transformed, the process symbolised by the previous movement has been a crisis of near-annihilation and has been dangerous, but true spiritual growth could not have taken place without it and, whilst both the Phoenix and the Snake have symbolised re-birth, now the "Herald of the Dawn", the Golden Rooster itself, makes its appearance for the first and only time in our Journey and confirms that such a different way of seeing may not necessarily manifest in an altered life-style, but could certainly reveal a markedly-different outlook.

As with the Golden Needle movement, this Rooster is linked with the creative element of gold, the gold which is strong and *yang* and which is transmuted out of baser metals by fire, much as the Phoenix is born out of the ashes. And, in the same way as the sun rises and furthers the life of the universe, the Golden Rooster, a bird of the sun, represents warmth and vitality and, with the birth of a new day, lifts us onto a different level of being.

We rise upwards and the Golden Rooster stands on one leg – on the left, *yin,* earthly, female side of the body – and then, just for perfection in balance – shifts its weight and stands on the right, *yang,* heavenly, masculine side. Furthermore, when the left leg is so earthed and the left hand faces the ground, the right leg and arm are raised towards the heavens and, when standing in the same way on the other leg, the opposite takes place, so that further balance ensues and the necessary contrasts are firmly established.

Physically-complementary, since the Snake glides down and the Rooster rises up, both movements affirm renewal and regeneration, resurrection and reconciliation. They also herald a vision that is clearer, a heart more compassionate, a mind more finely-tuned to the wisdom of the Tao, or Love, or God, or The Supreme Intelligence – call it what we will, for the words are immaterial. For the Snake of Knowledge has crept into the Waters of Wisdom, so that we may

'*know that we know nothing*' - and this is our salvation - whilst the Golden Rooster has offered us our new direction by confirming that:

> "*The only salvation is to realise that we know nothing about it*
> *and there is nothing to save*
> *and nothing to do*
> *and effort is the ruin of all things.*
> *Then, if we realise that we never were lost,*
> *we realise we couldn't be saved.*
> *For you can't save that which was never lost...*"[1]

60 STEP BACK AND REPULSE THE MONKEY

Meditating-upon the Monkey Thoughts and 'letting-go'

Some time later, when the elation following upon such entirely new and extraordinary experiences has somewhat subsided, we almost unconsciously find ourselves beginning to wonder about this rare transformation and ask questions of ourselves and of others concerning it and then start probing and reading about the enlightenment experiences of others and begin to see how it all happened and how it could happen again and then decide that the thousand and one events in our life which preceded the experience had gradually but surely been leading up to just such a transformation and we conclude that not only had it been inevitable but it was also of course quite unique and very splendid and that we must be very special indeed and that we must tell everyone else all about it!

Then – suddenly – illumination is born in the mind. Oh! Monkey! Monkey! Monkey! This is fast-talking Monkey-talk! When we would least have expected it (which is a Monkey Thought in itself), that mischievous Monkey had started to play all its old tricks, re-playing the events, tracking them forwards, hopping them back and - jumping and leaping about with lively swings and exhilarating bounds - had taken us by paw and tail into exactly the same pathways of the mind as it did when we later attempted to analyse, and then share, the sensations of peace which we had experienced on the Mountain of Serenity! The subject-matter and its accompanying thoughts are different, but the analysing, the wanting to dissect, the wanting to know, the self-praise and the attachment to the process are all the same and we see how swiftly we had moved away from the earlier experience, how briefly we had 'let-go' to our attachment to the mind's capabilities, and how soon, even after such a potent transformation, had the Monkey taken hold of the branches of analysis and reason, of logic, comparison, and conclusion and had even purloined some of Tiger's vanity, so that, with its habitual speed and energy, had us swinging happily from one branch of the Tree of Knowledge to another. And we had thought (*Monkey* had thought) that the new clarity would have lasted *much* longer than that…

Can we catch that little Monkey? Again? That special Chinese term for ego-free activity, that *wu-wei* of right action, is also referred to as "Monkey-free activity", because it is composed of the character *wei* - which stems from the symbol of a monkey and a claw-shaped hand - and *wu,* which conveys emptiness or nothing. "*Wu-wei*", therefore, translates as no clawing after knowledge, no wish to fill the empty space, no monkey-ish interference with the wisdom teachings. And we recall that – long ago – when we *did* catch that little Monkey, it was because we directed our meditations to the Monkey Thoughts themselves *as they occurred* and, as it were, focussed a beam of light upon them from the mind's eye, so that they gradually subsided and then disappeared. By focussing upon them, we had annihilated them, and so had discovered that the pure and natural state of the mind was total attention and that, when this occurred, Monkey no longer clung to illusion, had no branch of reality upon which to land, and had ceased to 'reach for the moon'.

Hakuin appended to this painting:

The monkey is reaching for the moon in the water,
Until death overtakes him he will never give up.
If he would only let go to the branch and disappear into the deep pool,
The whole world would shine with dazzling clearness.

(Zen Master Hakuin, Japan, 18th c.)

247

Now we see how swiftly Monkey can side-track us, enticing us with the memories of the unusual nature of the recent events and then wanting the delight of experiencing them all over again. The brain remains the magical store-house it has always been and the intellect still comprises one of mankind's most astonishing features, but we see that we took one long and important step forward with the Snake, only to take three steps back with the Monkey, and that we need such reminders of how easily this can happen in order to pay full attention again and recognise anew that, although we will inevitably house the Monkey occasionally, it need not be a permanent resident.

We reflect again upon the *Thinking, Meditating, Contemplating* processes which are so much a part of the wonders of the mind, and heed the warning we have just received. We see that, in spite of Monkey's manoeuvres and of how rarely we can sustain clarity, meditate serenely, or contemplate in freedom for any length of time, it is essential to sanity for the human psyche to understand what is happening to it, to experience the psychological ease when this occurs on a deep level, and to recognise that, despite its antics, the Monkey can be overcome. We see, too, how *words* can interfere with truth and how dangerous they can be, for, once they have been spoken and given life and their arrow has reached its target, they can never be unsaid. And so, at peace once more, both alert and yet quiet, we see how we can hold on to focus by the use of thought *and* can let-go to Monkey to retain our soul.

> "Shall we let go,
> And allow the soul to find its level
> downwards, ebbing downwards,
> ebbing downwards to the flood?
> till the head floats tilted like a bottle forward tilted
> on the sea, with no message in it;...
> Must we hold on?
> Or can we now let go?
> Or is it even possible we must do both?"[1]

61-66 REPETITIONS: "CHANGE WITHIN NO-CHANGE"

61 Slanting (Diagonal) Flying: *heightened senses*

62 Step Up and Raise Hands: *combining both sides of the brain*

63 The White Crane Spreads its Wings: *sacred, ritual dance, linking heaven and earth*

64 Brush Knee and Twist Step: *cutting through spiritual materialism*

65 The Search for the Golden Needle: *creativity in the Chinese arts*

66 Fan through the Back: *sending the results out into the world and up to a spiritual mountain*

Our individual, human patterns include much repetition, providing opportunities for psychological growth each time we attract someone or something that is familiar, in whatever different shape and form, by the psychological vibrations of our own psyche as well as by our unresolved, neuroses. The face of a new lover may be very different from the one who came before, but, if the previous lover had been discarded because of our own lack of psychological stability, the core of the new one is likely to be similar to that of the predecessor and we are likely to make the same mistakes in the new relationship. We may change a job, but the new employer or colleague may have similar characteristics to those previously disliked in an earlier situation, and 'cause' us similar disruptions. New neighbours may be like the old ones in the difficulties 'they' inflict upon us, and we will re-act to them in the same way as we have always done, or we may continue to criticise others when, in fact, what we are criticising lies within ourselves. Until, that is, we step into another psychological dimension; observe and accept our conditioned responses with greater depth, and learn how to integrate the underlying causes.

The next six movements in this Journey are repetitions of those which followed the Monkey Steps in Part Two and, although their form is the same, we learn from them what the Taoists call: "Change within

No-change", which clearly can be seen within all of Nature's patterns and seasonal changes, but which we now apply to ourselves.

Firstly, we find that our awareness of Monkey is more-than usually acute throughout them all – and that is not only understandable, considering the recent Monkey Steps' experience – but is change indeed! Secondly, our attitude towards the repetitions is different, for, although they offer us the opportunity to correct any errors, as does any true learning process, this time the Tiger does not attempt to prove that we are better than we were when we first performed them, or better than others, or – because they are repetitions – that we need pay no heed to them. So, we appreciate what has changed; enjoy the aspects that are changeless; discover more about the variety of their symbolism, and learn more about ourselves in the process.

The perfectly-balanced and beautifully-harmonious *Slanting (Diagonal) Flying* comes first. Once more our hands form the circular symbol of wholeness and unity and, with the Monkey Thoughts subsiding and the inner self flying free, we part the arms wide and move into the realms of *'hearing with the spirit'* - which (as well as the physical movement itself) is the 'non-change' in the movement. The 'change', however, is that, although we may never be able to put our ear to the ground and hear far-off sounds as do aboriginals, or pick-up 'messages' in the same way as do birds and animals, we are, nevertheless, *hearing* more acutely on both the psychological and the physical levels. Subtle, delicate messages are being relayed by the inner spirit that are more-intensified and have wider import and we more-accurately tune-into the meaning in another's spoken or unspoken words. The extra mental space we have gained from meditational interludes in peaceful places, now allows what is known as the 'silence beyond sound' to become more-accessible and we sense the singing of the stars and the music of the spheres, and not only in places that are far from human habitation. We are conscious of the whisper that follows a slight breeze like an echo, and the 'rustle of silk' that seems to continue even after a bamboo has ceased its sway. Conversely, we are aware that much of the 'civilised' world is much noisier than that of our ancestors and that this increase in sound, as measured in decibels, is harmful. We discover that a whisper is about

20 decibels; ordinary conversation about 60; painful noise in a factory is 100, and that many public indoor places far exceed this level. We discover that a gun fired near the head is 160 decibels and that even brief exposure to such a noise can cause giddiness and nausea; that anyone attending a particularly loud party, discoteque or rock concert will have slightly impaired hearing and lowered concentration throughout the following day, and that, if exposure to such a loud noise is prolonged over time, it can lead to permanent, albeit partial, deafness. We also find that, because the ear and brain are so delicately linked, loud noises can so disturb the brain that the hearer feels as though the brain were 'turning to jelly'. This sensation is because Nature reacts to an over-loud increase in decibels with a physical method of defence, attempting to protect such a finely-tuned and essential part of our sensory equipment from too-much damage by - temporarily – 'closing' a small component in the ear when any such 'attack' occurs. This small physiological reaction is not enough, however, for sufficient evolution to have taken place to withstand the vast increase in the level of sound in our modern world and, thus, this represents another 'change within no-change', which has distinct disadvantages.

With this exquisite movement of balance and beauty, however, we now repeat those established ways of avoiding outside clamour by turning towards the North and 'diagonally flying' to our own 'inner mountain', or to the peaceful realms of a quiet park, lakeside, seashore or hilltop, or by joining fellow travellers in meditation.

The remaining four senses of taste, smell, sight, and touch have also been heightened and, as well as discovering that this improves our vitality, we discover that they relate to the four elements mentioned in the Four Corners of the Earth: water, earth, fire, and air. Thus, because taste-buds are activated by the juices of saliva - which, to the Chinese is known as 'Honey Dew' and which, apart from its function as a tenderiser, has healing components and is why we lick our wounds - we see how *taste* is dependent upon liquid and that this faculty has been refined by the 'baptism' in the Waters of Wisdom. Moreover, by having been released from some of the intellect's strings, we can savour life's spiritual manifestations more-fully, whilst on the physical level (if we have been able to cleanse the body with organic foods and liquids) we can now enjoy food that has become more flavour-full and can more-sensitively savour its many varieties and of how much longer their pleasant taste remains on the palate.

We next find that the sense of *smell* does not arrive "just out of the air" and into our nostrils, but has its foundation in the elements of the earth and what it produces - and that it also furthers our ability to live in the moment in the most remarkable way. This is because odours are not processed by eye or ear, and so - by the miracle of creation - when we sense the perfume of a flower, a piece of sweet-smelling fruit, sniff wet earth or new-mown grass, or any of the myriad smells of the earth and its products which please us (or even otherwise), we are transfixed without thought, engrossed in the aroma and profoundly in touch with our earthly roots and the 'ground of our being' and - at such moments - lose awareness of the other senses. The scent is expressing its spiritual nature, its inner essence, whether it be divine or deadly and, moreover, even fifteen-seconds of a pleasing smell can reduce high blood pressure and, thereby, ease stress. Equally, we ourselves put-out a strong scent when constrained by fear or panic, which can be picked-up by other people as well as by animals, and this 'product' from our essence not only conveys our anxieties, but also whether or not we are 'well-earthed'. Thus, the strength or otherwise of our bodily odours, is in direct proportion to what we are thinking, feeling, doing or sensing, as well as to what we have eaten from the products of the earth.

The next element is that of *fire,* which creates light out of darkness and warmth out of coldness. Our ability to see clearly – and with in-sight – requires such light and, when we are 'filled with light', our inner sight is infinitely finer and far-ranging, our behaviour more illuminated and we can live with a greater degree of joy and lightness of being. Like a flame, lighting and lightening life with its glow and warmth, an en-lightened spirit views the outside and the inner world with the fire of a clear mind and heart – just as invisible ink is made visible by heat – and, thus, the whole of life is enhanced by this increased capacity to 'see' more clearly.

Touch relates to the effect of air upon skin, and the more we touch and stroke and hold (whether it be a person, an animal or even matter), the more we are soothed into calm and are less 'touchy' from nervous tension. Notice how we need to finger what we see or might buy, when shopping, and how even a light 'hand-hold' onto a leaf, or a slender branch of a tree, improves focus and can rectify an imbalance in walking. Notice, too, how we like to hold a letter in our hand and take in its message and can then recall it easily – and, if it is a long letter, enjoy sitting down to absorb it more fully – whereas, if the message is on a machine and is long, we note its length and then quickly skim through it and often forget much of what we have read. This is because the energy in air links with mind and matter, through the sensitivity of fingers and hands directly from the central-nervous system and this latter, in turn, is stabilised by physical, tactile contact, bringing healing to the psyche as well as to the body. Moreover, a heightened sensitivity to touch, through awareness of other physical sensations, such as the breath travelling through the nostrils; the expansion and contraction of the lungs; the food on our tongue and the liquid in our throat; the coursing of blood as it pulses through our veins; the shape, size, discomfort or otherwise of our feet in shoes; the feel of a ring on a finger, spectacles on a nose, a too-tight belt, our clothes as we move in space – or, more painfully, the sharp 'attack' of a thorn or a bee on flesh – all can lead to a deeper awareness of the life-force, of the breathing, moving, sensing, living Tao which touches us all.

Thus we 'fly in space' in this repetition, as if – through the increase in sensory awareness - a curtain has been lifted on a stage, a portal opened upon a magical room, a special space created for the heightening of the senses – and this brings us a little closer to the more-acute sensitivity of the ancient Taoists and to the spiritual awareness which accompanied it.

Still facing North, we next *Step Up and Raise Hands,* and again unite the opposites of left and right, the spirit of the East and the rationality of the West – and the functions of both sides of the brain. Released (to some degree) from our attachment to the reductionist activities of the *yang* left-brain, which highlights the 'change', we can combine left-brain words, such as self-control, structure, tradition, discipline, duty, authority and obedience, with others of the *yin* right-brain, such as ebbing and flowing, sensing and wondering, feeling, intuiting and trusting, for – as mentioned in a previous chapter – an over-emphasis of the *yang* elements, impoverishes the spirit inherent in those of the *yin*, whilst too much of the latter creates an imbalance in practical daily living. Thus, the Taoists considered that a rigid structure of self-control and duty was unsafe, psychologically, since the spirit which needs to meditate and function in peace and which utilises the right *yin* side of the brain to give the subtle signals for passive non-action, is over-borne by the rational mind's wish to control and impose rules for every circumstance, thereby setting up a fixed schedule for daily existence which pays no heed to the changing currents of life. Moreover, if the left *yang* side of the brain is telling us what we should or should not be doing (when there are other more-important *yin*-based things to attend to), we may end up doing far less, since the conflict between what we think we should be doing, and what we intuitively recognise is necessary, causes a loss of psychic, as well as physical energy, whilst such procrastination can lead to depression. With a combination of both sides, however, and if listened to attentively, the subtle intuitive right side of the brain can be utilised by the efficient activities of the left side, and, by that wonderful illogicality referred to when 'the art of accuracy' was mentioned, can create an efficient – and even disciplined – daily way of life, which can be seen as either another instance of 'change within no-change', or as a repetition of that which we had earlier understood.

Thus, in this, the second of the current repetitions, we draw our hands in towards each other in a process which blends both these complementary opposites, and then form another circle of unity and harmony, before facing West again.

We then step into the repetition of *The White Crane Spreads its Wings.* Of these birds, Karen Blixen wrote that the crested cranes are: "... *birds*

of good omen, announcing the rain; and also by dancing to us. When the tall birds are together in large numbers, it is a fine sight to see them spread their wings and dance. There is much style in the dance for… they jump up and down as if they were held on to the earth by magnetism. The whole ballet has a sacred look, like some ritual dance; perhaps the cranes are making an attempt to join heaven and earth like the winged angels walking up and down Jacob's Ladder… When, after the dance, they lift and go away, to keep up the sacred tone of the show they give out, by the wings or the voice, a clear ringing note, as if a group of church bells had taken wing and were sailing off. You can hear them a long way away, even after the birds themselves have become invisible in the sky: a chime from the clouds."[1]

We, too, now are earthed, as if 'by magnetism' and we, too, are linked to the heavens in this, our second encounter with the fascinating Crane-bird, for this repetition of the arrival of the Messenger of the Gods offers again the connection between the physical and the spiritual, the earth and the sky and the opportunity to soar upwards and let our spirit fly once more into the weightless, free dimension of a spirit unburdened by conditioned thought – and that is the 'no-change'. We also recall that which we assimilated when we first spread our wings, for, when the White Crane Spreads its own Wings, love and trust shine through to us, promoting a new release of energy which brings joy and gladness. Having learnt much from the many movements that have led up to this one, we thus are not held back by the doubts and uncertainties we experienced in Part One and cease to project onto others those aspects which we lack or deplore in ourselves – and that signifies the 'change within non-change'. Moreover, thanks to the entry of Kuan Yin in our lives, we feel an even greater depth of love and compassion than when we first encountered this magical creature.

Our upward-curving, winged-hand then moves down from sky to earth, to cut through 'spiritual materialism', for we have become acutely conscious of Tiger's interventions and of how we can become

255

as attached to our spirituality as to any of our belongings. So, we slice through any new attachment, which is the 'change' and move ahead into the repetition of the *Brush Knee and Twist Step* which is the 'non- change'. Another spiritual practice is then reinforced and we take the now-familiar wide, strong, bear-like steps to brush aside the obstacles, whilst each of the three steps forward take us a little nearer to the time when we can say 'no', instantly, to our habitual responses and transform our thoughts and actions at the very moment when such transformation is needed.

The spiritual seeker now is led towards the areas of his or her creativity as, once again, we *Search for the Golden Needle* and, in so doing, find that the creative process is sometimes akin to the process of the seasons:

the preparation of Spring, the activity of Summer, the productivity of Autumn, and the apparently-fallow period of Winter, each part of Nature's patterns necessarily and inevitably reinforcing our awareness of the self-perpetuating forces in creation. But, the great sages of Chinese Taoism apprehended the meaning beyond the seemingly obvious, beyond the world's immediate appearances, sensing the spiritual energy of a bole on a tree, a worm under a stone, a snail resting upon that stone, the scurry of a bird, or even the soul of a simple man. The

Chinese artist attempting to convey this, then would ponder upon what was being perceived and, if she or he were successful at 'becoming one' with the object to be painted, would hope to express the underlying spirit in the less-obvious aspects of Nature's artistry, rather than realistically-portray only that which was visible. There would then be no dividing line between the spirit within the tree, worm, snail, bird, or simple man and the spiritual energy of the artist; the resulting work of art would be inspired, and it would convey that, at those moments of creativity, thought was not present. For:

> *"The mystery of creation is the divine urge of creation,*
> *but it is a great strange urge, it is not a Mind.*
> *Even an artist knows that his work was never in his mind,*
> *he could never have thought it before it happened.*
> *A strange ache possessed him, and he entered the struggle,*
> *and out of the struggle with his material, in the spell of the urge*
> *his work took place, it came to pass, it stood up and saluted*
> *his mind..."*[2]

The essence of Spirit and its manifestations in Nature were also depicted in Chinese art as whorls and coils and feather-like ripples and these offered the viewer a sense of the rising vapours and threads of mist that conveyed images of the perpetual motion of clouds in the heavens, the gentle or dynamic sway of *Ch'i*-filled branches, the bounce or flow of a stream over pebbles, or the deep currents and high tidal waves of the ocean.

Thus, the Chinese artist would attempt to convey the *yang* and the *yin* of Nature, with the *yang* elements frequently conveyed by the sun and its streams of light and by turbulence in the skies, swelling seas and soaring mountains. These latter then, in turn, might pierce the delicate *yin* clouds, whilst *yin*

vapours and mists might be seen as arising out of the valleys and streams of the feminine, *yin* dark earth, or in exquisitely *yin* swirling mud-flat tidal formations.

To the Eastern mind, there is nothing in Nature that is neither *yin* nor *yang,* and even fruits, vegetables, flowers, bushes, trees, birds and insects are classified as one or the other, by taste, smell, colour and shape, texture and sound, as well as by the essence of their intrinsic feminine or masculine nature. Everything is of significance, but the profundity of Nature's dualistic world can only be expressed in art through the skill of one who can combine great spiritual insight with the delicacy and refinement of heightened awareness.

Another aspect of Chinese art lies in the system of geomancy, or the land-orientation known as *feng-shui.* This system was based on the discovery and utilisation of the *yang* ley lines, or 'Dragon Veins', which flow through the *yin* earth, and also from the realisation that, by using a magnetic compass, a dowser could detect the invisible currents of earth's vital *Ch'i* energies, the information about which was so highly-regarded that a Chinese diviner could be asked to locate them and then give advice as to which location would be suitable to protect them from whatever man-made purposes were being considered. Thus, through the information obtained, the spirit of the architect could be in accord with the spirit of Nature, and the Chinese temples, tombs, palaces, important Civic buildings and houses could be placed in harmonious relationship to their natural surroundings, without blocking the energies of the earth. In the same way, Chinese artists could, themselves, or through a dowser, locate earth's ley lines and then portray the harmonious blending of man-made establishments with the *Ch'i* energy inherent in Nature, by painting rippling patterns to convey the 'invisible' energies flowing in the landscape which surrounded any edifice.

An understanding of such earth energies also relates to the Chinese view of what influences us internally in relation to external conditions, for it has long-been established that seasonal changes affect the subtle energies of the human body and that our emotional and mental balance can be as influenced for good or ill, by the shifting energies and temperatures in earth, sea, air and sky, as much as the earth can be damaged by a cement building or road when placed without regard to the Dragon Veins. Thus it was taught that the veins and arteries in the human body were akin to the earth's natural irrigation systems of channels and streams, for, if the latter were free from blockage, water could run freely and, by the same token, if the veins and arteries of the body were not blocked by strong emotions or other impairments, the energy would run smoothly. Acupuncture then became part of Chinese medicine, for it had been found that, by placing needles of certain lengths and thicknesses in the spaces between certain parts of the body in an atmosphere of moderate temperature, the body could – in time – be restored to balance, and that, in the same way as a magnetic dowsing needle could locate the natural currents of the earth in *feng-shui,* the skilled acupuncturist could 'feel the pulse' of the 'white tiger' or the 'blue dragon' in the human system, and – having already been trained in, and have a clear knowledge of, its meridians or pathways – would endeavour to harmonise the *yin* of earth with the *yang* of heaven through the vehicle of his or her Golden Needle.

Of all artistic skills, however, the Chinese regard calligraphy the most highly, for, although the calligrapher's brush-pen produces written characters in the same physical way as an artist puts brush to canvas, the calligrapher (who may be a sage or an eccentric, an intellectual or a skilled, but unwise person) is said to influence the calligraphic gift by the calibre of her or his own mind and spirit. Thus, if a person were reading the works of one of China's greatest poets or philosophers and it had been calligraphically-written with deep spiritual comprehension as well as great artistry, far more would be absorbed by the reader than wise words, profound thoughts and beauty of form, for the *essence* of the calligrapher would take the reader further than the meaning in the text alone. Moreover, the combination of the calligrapher's mystical intuition; the Golden Needle of the calligraphic pen; the profound sub-ject-matter, and the spirit of the Tao, would convey that both sides of the calligrapher's brain were in use and that every aspect of body, mind and spirit had been united in the creative process and, thus, great, indeed, would be the effect upon the reader of the noble work produced.

So, we repeat the Golden Needle movement and find that the 'change within no-change' lies in how we perform it. From all that we have absorbed so far, we now can portray the union of the 'economy of movement with the minimum of energy needed for the maximum result' with the portrayal of the Chinese artist's calligraphic *yin* and *yang* brush-strokes. With an ever-deepening absorption in, and response to, the meaning in the movements we are making - and with simplicity and conscious intent - we can unite the earthly mind with the mind of heaven. As we raise one arm up to the *yang* dome of the skies; lean forward and down, and then guide that arm and hand into the depths of the *yin* waters of the sea, we can divine both the splendour of the heavens and the depths of the spiritual ocean, as we search for the dualistic symbol of their union in true creativity.

We then convey a repetition of *Fan through the Back*, which directs the results of our search – in print or canvas, music, word, deed or spirit – out into the world; and we send them in spirit upwards also, in gratitude to the spiritual mountain. But, which mountain? There is a choice of many (which is what is new to us) and find that there are nine sacred mountains, or *shans,* in China, five of which are Taoist. So, of the five, which shall we choose to receive our gratitude: *T'ai-shan*, which lies in the Province of Shantung and which, coming under the geomantic rule of the Green Dragon - known as the Lord of all the Springs and Streams that are fed by the clouds that are gathered on its summit – stands supreme in the veneration of the Chinese agricultural society? *Pei-yüeh,* of the remote *Heng-shan* range in the North *Shansi* - known as the 'Northern Guardian' of China - where the sun is lowest in winter, which also comes under the element of water and to which annual sacrifices are made for well-being and eternal life? *Sung-shan*, 'the Lofty', lying in the heart of China's long civilisation and soaring up above the fertile plain of Honan, which contains many archaeological and historical vestiges of China's long past and of its legendary rulers? *Chu-jung Feng*, the highest peak in that remove *Heng-shan* range, named the 'Blessed Fire Peak' for lying in the southern quarter of the universe where the sun is highest in summer, and coming under the geomantic influence of fire and 'red'? Or

Hua-shan, which, soaring upwards in the *Shensi* Plain, where the Yellow and Wei Rivers meet, is known as the 'Flower Mountain', the Taoist gods of which were witness to much of China's history and who, in due season, received the sacrifices offered by the dynastic founders, when they assumed 'the mantle of Heaven' with which to rule their empires?[3]

Clearly, the choice is wide, and since each mountain or range has its own shape, colour, form and spiritual significance – and like everything on earth – is unique, it is up to the Chinese artist to choose the one which is most capable of captivating his or her capacity to convey onto canvas the human spirit and the spirit of nature - and up to us to decide which one might inspire our gratitude and awe.

The repetition of the movement, which is also known as *"Holding up the Mountain"*, also offers an opportunity to ponder further as to whether there has been 'change within non-change' within ourselves. For example, one pupil initially disliked the movement because its alternative name made her feel as though she were: "carrying all the burdens of the world upon her back". She later discovered from the repetition that she no longer felt that way and could positively enjoy the sense that she could choose her own mountain and let its strength and power send her own gifts out into the world. So, that, indeed, was 'change within no-change', for the burdens of life rarely change, whilst our attitude towards them can.

As participants in a T'ai Chi or yoga class who silently move in space; as monks in meditation who are enclosed in a world of peace; as ramblers who pause to admire a flower; climbers on a mountain peak who gaze at a distant view; swimmers in a warm, turquoise sea; members of an orchestra combining their talents, or their audience absorbing what is being offered - all are conveying pictures of great beauty. Together in a group, all share in the various repetitions of life and, in many-coloured garments and of differing contours, their bodies form pieces in a kaleidoscope which make wonderfully clear pictures composed of sharply bright or softly hued shades and shapes, each appearing separate, yet all, in truth, deeply connected and glowingly so. A soft saffron here, a bright green over there, a deep blue with honey-dew far across the room, a lavender, a purple, a cyclamen and red, a clear white, a deep pink, a turquoise band on head: colours, so many different colours, each one moving or remaining still, each one offering rich, glowing harmony and multi-faceted hue. Then, suddenly, there is change, a shift in awareness. Some of the T'ai Chi practitioners have lost their place, forgotten the movement, become fragmented. Others follow suit and laughter bubbles over. One of the meditators stirs, gets up, and others do the same; the ramblers continue their walk; those on the mountain top collect their packs and slowly move down into the valleys. The swimmers return to the shore and dry themselves with coloured towels. The members of the orchestra conclude the performance and, as do those in their audience, turn to speak with each other, smile, stand up, move around, move away. And all the colourful disarray of all these people is as much a marvellous sight as were their slow, deep, magical, movements as they swam in air or in the warm, turquoise sea; as was their stillness as they sat in meditation; as they gazed upon beauty in the plains or contemplated the world from the top of a mountain - and as was their focus in the concert hall. Colours abounding, synchronization shifting, stillness changing, movement altering, patterns adjusting – all beauty is there, in both the inner, silent worlds and in the colourful array and sounds of their outward appearance. Themes and motifs, refrains and repetitions, the familiar with the new: these interlace and become 'change within non-change', the constant within the fluctuations, the repetitions of patterns within the ever-changing varieties of form – and the Tao continues to reveal them all.

67-68b Further Repetitions, With an Important Difference

67   Turn Body and Chop ('Plunge') with Right Hand: *Lack of pride*

68a   The White Snake puts out its Tongue: *Piercing the eyes of illusion, saying "YES!" to the sight inside, and another movement towards non-differentiation*

68b   Twisted Step, Strike and Punch: *the brief, but stormy return of the Tiger*

Change within No-change has been experienced and will be so again. Shifts have occurred in the psyche and further mutations have taken place in the mind. We now move away from contemplation of our chosen mountain and, having sought and sent out the results of the search for our creativity, we repeat the impressive: *Turn Body and Chop ('Plunge') with Right Hand*. And, whilst this is performed as before, there is a small, but infinitely important difference at the end of the body-turn and the fan-like, high-circling arc : no fist is made and the absence of Tiger is confirmed. Instead of, as hitherto, forming the Tiger's Mouth, the downward-plunging palm stays open, no pride in achievement takes place and the creative gift remains pure. Slowly, over time, the true artist – or the artist of life – has achieved the heightened perception to see what has to be done, and when, without ego, vanity or ambition clouding the gifts of creation. The results of such activity are praised as 'masterly', because the free-flowing brush-strokes (or their equivalent) have offered the sensitive onlooker a cameo of life, a moment in time which is complete in itself and is a true reflection of the master-craftsman whose mind is equally free-flowing, yet whose hand is firm and whose intention is pure. Such an artist then receives praise, but – being also a master of life – such praise has no effect: it is heard, but left behind. The familiar pleasures of commendation no longer carry weight and because of this subtle, important 'change within no-change', we then make another movement, which – briefly contained as it is, between two repetitions – is not only dramatic, but is entirely new.

It is known as: *"The White Snake puts out Tongue"* and, initially, it can serve as a reminder that, sometimes, we lapse into mindlessness (which is *not* new!), because the current repetitions are – again - so familiar. Nor, if such a lapse occurs, is it immediately obvious, for, although we might 'fist' out of habit instead of keeping the hand open, we then continue as before, on the assumption that no conscious awareness is required in the repetition. And then, if still unaware of the error, we continue with the moving fist until we sense that something is wrong, look around in confusion, find that we are not at the same place as some others and try to catch up as quickly as possible. Eventually, however, we learn to keep the hand open at the end of its downward plunge and this marks the imminent – and vital – arrival of this next powerful and swift movement. But, a *white* snake? Surely that is so rare that the physical movement must be rare also? And it is, appearing only once in the Yang Style, Long Form (and not always in that) and scarcely in any other Form, martial or otherwise, which, given that the index and middle fingers part like a snake's forked tongue and then forcefully shoot forwards and up, "to pierce and then gouge-out the eyes of an opponent", it is obvious to what degree it is a fierce and physically destructive movement and that omitting it might be with good reason.

Its brief appearance offers a symbolic meaning of some spiritual consequence, however, since – rather than portraying such destructive elements – it conveys that, finally, we are: *"piercing 'the eyes of illusion' and saying a deeply-felt and sorely-arrived-at 'YES!' to the sight inside"*. For now we no longer wish to be caught up in the manifold tricks of 'heedlessness', nor be trapped by the illusions that mindless thought can create. What we do want is to focus the mind, even when – and maybe especially when – there are repetitions in life and, as a corollary to this, we do want to pay heed to our intuitive, inner vision.

These positive affirmations have arisen naturally, not by precept, and take us on to a new development, for this strong, clear movement, this 'YES!' to the sight inside, offers another conundrum concerning the mind's desire to differentiate between one thing and another and

– since everything has its opposite - to a pondering on what else that powerful '*YES!*' might imply. Such an extension of thought then has us turning to the Taoist wisdom of having neither a 'no' nor a 'yes' and this is the direct result of the 'no-knowledge' meaning in the previous, and profound, Snake Creeps down into Water movement – for the purity of water offers reflection on the ties that bind us to our dualistic assumptions and reveals things as they are, without comparison of one thing with another. So, no matter how far we may be from applying this complex, spiritual concept – or even fully-understanding it – another transformation is indicated by the current movement. By virtue of an intuitive shift in consciousness towards non-differentiation, by an awareness that the same thing could have a '*NO!*' that has as much merit as a '*YES!*' and that, paradoxically, by having both, the one cancels-out the other, we perceive that the incisive movement of the White Snake's Tongue also reveals that discrimination between opposites can lead to illusion. The day, for example, is no more 'right' than the night and, thus, to a Taoist (as has been mentioned before), by having preferences, we are not accepting that there is neither good nor bad, but just 'what is'.

The very whiteness of this rarely-seen snake confirms this perception, for 'white' symbolises clarity as well as purity and so, instead of absorbing what could have been a dark force behind the White Snake's penetrating movement, we are given the trust to hold-fast to the purity of our inner vision. For, to the Taoist mind, everything has its place and season and reason for existence, and, as Kuan Yin (who has led us through so many corners of our inner and outer worlds and who, in this movement, now manifests as "White Tara") continues to guide us towards a time when such perceptions permanently abide within us, we become more of our own person and try to speak our truth without bias. And, since it is the *tongue* that the White Snake thrusts forward – that important part of ourselves which, as well as having vital taste-buds and curling around dry lips, teeth and mouth to salivate them, conveys our thoughts and emotions in speech, can be sharp when cruel, thick with alcohol, slip into a cheek when lying, slide back and forth across the lips when nervous, rest on an outer lip when concentrating, and thrust itself forward when discourteous – it no longer wishes to convey mechanical, conditioned thought or the restless antics of the Monkey-mind. It no longer wishes to produce mis-remembered facts, nor misapprehended knowledge from a mind that is dominated by ego's wish for its own omniscience and continuity. It no longer wishes to convey choice between one thing and another. What it does want is for its speech to pierce *illusion* – or ill-vision. Moreover, the swift dynamism of this short-lived movement also acts a template for the dynamism in many of the new and major spiritual movements still to come.

Another repetition then follows, which appears as if White Tara were already testing our newly-born sense of the value of choiceless-awareness. For we find that, inasmuch as the Monkey so swiftly followed upon the transformation of the Snake Creeps Down into Water, so too does the Tiger immediately follow upon the action of the White Snake's Tongue. Certainly, there was not even a swish of a tail, a lift of an ear or a twitch of a whisker to indicate its presence when praise was recently bestowed upon us, but now, well-rested and after a long absence – and sensing critical danger to its finely-tuned, discriminatory powers – it cannot resist returning to the fight with a *Twisted Step, Strike and Punch* that is aimed in fierce retaliation at such an 'appalling' concept as a movement towards non-duality! And so we have the brief, but stormy, return of the Tiger.

Again we use our powers of acute penetration to injure the self-esteem of others. With a twist of vanity, with a strike of ice-cold superiority, with a punch of judgemental arrogance and a tongue as forked and lacerating as is its counterpart in the martial-art application, we demean and diminish and deny other (different) viewpoints, with a cool certainty that not only lacks White Tara's compassion, but conveys how desperately and deeply Tiger wishes to control this area of possible transformation. But, none of this lasts long. Perhaps by White Tara's intervention, perhaps by our recent ability to say *"YES" to the sight inside*, we soon become aware of this unjust, discriminatory attitude and bow to the wisdom of 'not-knowing'. Tiger's return has been harsh and undeniably lacerating to all concerned, but has been so swiftly overborne that we immediately make amends to those we have wronged.

Thus the situation was weighted with danger to the spirit, but was also fortuitous, and it is not long before the calm after the storm arrives and we can move into the next repetition of Painting the Rainbow, which, with the beautiful opening of the fist, releases us (and others) from our Tiger, and reveals anew the beauties of this many-hued arc of existence.

69a (Single) Painting the Rainbow
69b Grasping the Sparrow's Tail;
Ward Off – Slantingly Upwards;
Pull Back, Press Forward and Push

*The Rainbow as a portent; an exploration into
clairvoyance and mysticism, the Bamboos and
the ninth Gateway to Wisdom*

*"Even the rainbow has a body
made of the drizzling rain
and is an architecture of glistening atoms
built up, built up
yet you can't lay your hand on it,
nay, nor even your mind."*[1]

The White Snake's forked tongue has pierced the illusions created by Monkey's heedlessness and the mind's desire to differentiate. Tiger's brief presence and its *yang*, dramatic brain-storm have been dealt with swiftly and been dispersed. Now, we can accept our Tiger's return with neither approval nor disapproval, whilst the archway of *"glistening atoms"*, that beautiful radiant arc which spans its prismatic colours across the horizon after a rain-storm, beckons once more and draws us towards another dimension. Then, with this exquisite rainbow before our eyes, we trace its shape in space and paint it again with both awareness and sensitivity.

Unlike the countless trees, birds, flowers and insects, the desert sands, the many lands that contain those sands, the raindrops in space, the fish in the seas, the animals on land and the numbers of people on earth, a rainbow is different. Usually there is just one, and that one seen so rarely in comparison with the majority of Nature's wonders, that we marvel at it, gaze with awe at its almost-mystical nature of shape, colour and size, point it out to others and – apart from understanding that the sun's rays have created it out of moistened air – we ponder on its meaning, for it is sometimes regarded as a portent of possibly more than better weather to come.

It has already been mentioned that, by the omission of violet and indigo, the Chinese name only five of the rainbow's seven hues, i.e. those of: blue, green, yellow, orange and red, and that - of our own senses - we have but five that are considered 'normal'. Moreover, due to the various physical and spiritual activities that we have put into practise, these five senses have become crystal-bright and sharply defined. Long ago, however, or so it seems, we began to experience something of the sixth sense of clairvoyance, or what is known as the 'paranormal', a sense which grew out of a deepening, intuitive, non-analytical 'seeing' and from an emptier inner space. And this awareness of a different dimension, though sporadic, has not diminished, whilst the recent experience of our Tiger's sharp-tongued battle has not only reaffirmed our perception that non-discrimination is an essential component of the spiritual quest, but, from our experiences of synchronicity or so-called coincidence, of telepathy and related paranormal phenomena, we have begun to understand that there is a link between non-differentiation and clairvoyance - and that both relate to mysticism. And so, having also been led to perceiving the vital connections between the inner and outer realms of meaning, as manifest in Parting the Wild Horse's Mane, we now find that some of these less-acknowledged manifestations of the Tao have not only become more frequent, but have gained in significance.

Laurens van der Post mentions his, and Jung's, awareness of this, when he wrote: "*Coincidences, instinctively, have never been idle for me but as meaningful, I was to find, as they were to Jung. I had always had a hunch that coincidences were a manifestation of a law of life of which we are inadequately aware and which, in terms of our short life, are unfortunately incapable of total definition. Yet, however partial the meaning we can extract from them, we ignore them, I believe, at our peril. For as well as promoting some cosmic law, coincidences, I suspect, may be some sort of indication as to what extent the evolution of our lives is obedient or not to the symmetry of the universe. Coincidence was nothing if not an expression of a symmetry of meaning."*[2]

This description resonates with us and, awake to such 'a *symmetry of meaning*', we find ourselves apprehending more of the cosmic laws and becoming clearer about events which, whilst appearing to reach us through what is known as our sixth sense, also appears to have come from 'outside' ourselves. We then allocate meaning to such events and try to sense whether our interpretation of their significance is 'right' – which it sometimes is – whilst, at other times, we incorrectly attribute to so-called external, universal forces, those influences or manifestations, which, in fact, are aspects of our own psyche that are endeavouring to arise from within. These latter, then, might relate to truths that we have suppressed or rationalised and which might lie embedded in the unconscious, and it would be 'wrong' to describe them as proof of *only* external psychic events or messages from the holographic hemisphere. Regardless of the psychological difference, however (and despite the importance of recognising this), the emergence of psychic gifts, at whatever age, together with our ability to accurately recognise the link between the events which are happening in our personal life and the *"symmetry of the universe"*, are indications that such phenomena not only occur, but seem to do so more reliably when we are obedient to cosmic law and its orders, and disobedient to the Tiger and the Monkey. Another facet then emerges in that, whilst clairvoyance has been ascribed to a sixth sense, and the state of mystical union could be described as a seventh, these two senses are similar in essence and share the same sense of unity.

This similarity is borne out by the many descriptions given by both clairvoyants and mystics, and the following summation of some of these reveals that the central aspects of clairvoyance relate equally-well to the mysticism experienced by those who have achieved union with the 'godhead'. Thus:

"There are four central aspects of the Clairvoyant Reality:

1. *There is a central unity to all things. The most important aspect of a "thing" is its relationships, its part in the whole. Its individuality and separateness are secondary and/or illusory.*

2. *Pastness, presentness, and futurity are illusions we project onto the "seamless garment" of time. There is another valid view of time in which these separations do not exist.*

3. *From this other view of the world, evil is mere appearance: when we are in this other understanding (a term which originally meant to "stand under", "to be part of"), we do not judge with the criteria of good and evil.*

4. *There is a better way of gaining information than through the five senses."[3]*

and, most significantly:

> *"It is the unity of all things that is seen as most important, their relationships rather than their individual and unique characteristics, that are seen as crucial."[4]*

Another example of the similarities is given from the same source: *"In the Clairvoyant Reality, say the sensitives, time takes on quite a different structure. All events are, they do not happen. The past, the present, and the future are all equally in existence, even though we can ordinarily only observe those events located in the present. It is as if one were describing what happens when a movie is being shown. All the events of the movie are in existence: they are on the celluloid film already, but we can only see a very narrow slice of the film at any one time. As the frames of the film pass behind the lens of the projector and flash on the screen, it looks to us as if the events were happening, but in reality the entire film and all the events on it (those that have already "happened" on the screen and those yet to "happen") already exist. All these events can (theoretically at least) be observed. None can be acted on any more than we can act on the events in the film, even if we were an actor in it. This is similar if we are an actor in a play. The events exist in the script. We can participate, feel, observe. Any attempt to change the events as they occur (if for example we were playing Romeo and "wished" he would not take the poison) would disrupt and end the play. Any attempt in the Clairvoyant Reality to "change" events disrupts this reality and returns us to Sensory Reality…*

… all events of the past, present, and future exist; it is only the narrow window we usually look through that makes them seem to "happen", that makes only the present visible".[5]

The indisputable correspondences between the clairvoyant and the mystic thus relate to their experiences of unity and timelessness and go even-further in their shared recognition that any differentiation between 'good' and 'evil' is irrelevant to deeper perception, whilst Taoist and Buddhist sages regard such judgemental words as a movement away from the pure spirit inherent in a non-dualistic approach to life.

Despite such basic agreement, however, one major difference between clairvoyance and mysticism lies in the warning that the mystic and the sage give with regard to the pitfalls that can endanger the clairvoyant. For, it is said that, if self-knowledge and psychological-awareness be lacking in the clairvoyant, her or his psychic perception could lead to a spiritual *cul-de-sac*. Thus: *"In one area, there tends to be real disagreement between the mystic and the medium. This disagreement centres on their attitude toward the paranormal. For the mystic, concentration on, or interest in such things as telepathy, precognition, clairvoyance, and psychokinesis tends to move the individual away from the path of psychological change… The mystics, particularly the Eastern mystics, report that paranormal abilities naturally arise as the person moves into the perception and being of the world of the One. However, the mystic tends to believe that interest in them prevents further growth."*[6]

Mystics, therefore, do not advise an impassioned furtherance of what the Hindus call the '*siddhis*', or psychic powers, suggesting, instead, that one must respect them, but only insofar as one would the phenomenon of any of the other five 'normal' senses. Thus, no *siddhi* is wrong, but is viewed as being neither more nor less significant than any other gift and neither more, nor less, miraculous. Undue interest in clairvoyant phenomena – however fascinating and valid it may be in its own right – is, therefore, considered spiritually unwise, and any sustained involvement with, or *attachment to*, the paranormal is described as a 'half-way house up the mountain of divinity'. Nor is it hard to understand such an attachment, since the delights of that 'half-way house', the richness of the psychic experience, the seemingly-certain awareness of a deeper meaning to life, the visions of unity, and the deliciously-omnipotent feelings such experiences can evoke, can be so exciting and rewarding that the Tiger can quickly find a fresh foothold and the remainder of the journey up the mountain can sometimes be postponed, or even permanently laid aside. Consciousness of the Oneness of the universe then diminishes in proportion to Tiger's influence and the person experiencing the clairvoyant phenomenon may even see him- or herself as being 'further along the spiritual path' than others who are less psychically gifted (or who are not psychic at all), whilst the ego, enchanted by the psychic phenomenon, desires ever-more experiences of that nature. True mystical union with the Tao then is abandoned (albeit often unconsciously) and the psychic stays bound in her or his psychological patterns of thought, preventing further growth. Thus, it could be said that the mystic is primarily intent upon the dissolution of ego, whilst the clairvoyant might be enriched by the gift of extra-sensory perception, but be unaware of the degree of Tiger's participation in the experience.

For the same reason, it is said that there are dangers to pure spirit if expanded consciousness, spiritual euphoria, or any deepening of the clairvoyant gift, have been induced by the taking of drugs or allied substances, by hypnotism, sustained dervish dancing, the frenzy of revivalist meetings, the beating of drums, violent dancing, loud singing, shouting, or even fasting, for even when these inductions heighten the senses, increase energy, expand consciousness and/or increase psychic abilities, they have been induced and are limited to sensation only and are, thereby, considered unwise.

All this implies, yet again, that the wisdom of the mystic lies in the important messages of ego-awareness and non-attachment. Thus, whilst mysticism can arise from the same source as clairvoyance and is often as indistinguishable from it as indigo and blue are from violet, the mystical state differs from clairvoyance in some respects and can, justifiably, be classified as a seventh sense. Such a premise then connects with the work of colour therapists and others involved with what are known, in India, as the spectrum of the seven "chakras" (or, in China, the seven energy "*choils*") which have been allocated to seven different areas of the body and which have been observed – by those who have a sixth sense – as sharing the seven colours of the rainbow.

For example, the first chakra, which is situated at the base of the torso, relates to sexuality and love on the physical plane, and to all the passions. Its colour is vermilion, or the 'red' of the rainbow's longest wave-length and, as it is furthest away from the most spiritual chakra – which is at the crown of the head and coloured violet - it is also furthest away from the violet in the rainbow. The sixth chakra, which is known as the 'third eye', is located in the middle of the forehead, just above eye level, and is coloured indigo (a mixture of red and blue), which is the colour of the rainbow's second-shortest wave-length. Its function is: questioning, inner vision, intuition and dreaming and, therefore, relates to the sixth sense of clairvoyance and insight. The colour violet, however, which has the shortest wave-length and, thus, is the first colour of the rainbow, has been allocated to the thousand-petalled chakra at the crown of the head; relates to the mystical bliss of the non-discriminatory 'acceptance of all that is', and to the understanding of divine purpose. It thereby connects the area of the body which is closest to the heavens with that of the seventh sense of the mystic's highest and holiest state and it is through indigo's link to violet and their relationship to clairvoyance and mysticism, that we now use all the colours of the rainbow in our T'ai Chi movement.

Released from Tiger's lacerating red tongue, with its (mercifully brief) verbal onslaught, and through our body's *chakra* connection with the rainbow's seven colours of the spectrum, we relinquish the fist and once more paint the rainbow's glorious arc, using all five fingers to delineate the five shades of red, orange, yellow, green and blue in an imaginative portrait of the five senses, whilst visualising the 'third eye' and the crown of the head as streaming out the remaining two colours in a virtual display of the sixth sense of spiritually-linked wisdom and clairvoyance (indigo) and the seventh sense of pure, ultimate mysticism (violet). Symbolic of the splendid union of *yin* earth and *yang* heaven, we outline each hue of the rainbow's arched span across the skies and then, on this, the seventh occasion of Grasping the Sparrow's Tail, see that our search has not only been for a deeper understanding of the unconscious and for the relationship between psychic manifestation and mysticism, but for the end of the rainbow, which, rather than residing in a pot of gold, rests in a grove of sun-filled bamboos…

Again we flow with this exquisite movement and re-discover that: *"To be among growing bamboo in a grove is to be surrounded by a sense of peace. This experience does not come from a dead stillness: the branches and the leaves far above are unresting, and the vitality of the young sprouts in spring is almost tangible. It is compounded of the silence, of the colour – sunlight, delicately reticulated through foliage, shifting on the new green of the leaves – and the architectural regularity of the surrounding bamboo pillars, evoking recollection of quiet cathedrals. One can absorb in this mood the tapering strength of the great shafts which culminate overhead in a trembling plumage, and be gladdened also by their bright freshness and simplicity."*[7]

Thus, in the mystical '*quiet cathedrals*' of the great shafts of the bamboo pillars, we ponder upon the *siddhis* in all their extraordinary manifestations, as well as muse upon the doubly-earthed rainbow, that portent, as well as vehicle, of our spiritual exploration. Soaring high, its bright, seven-hued rising curve gathers up our seven senses and has us move our limbs and body as quietly in air as does a sable brush when placed on silk by a skilled Chinese calligrapher, and we focus particularly on the spiritual colours of indigo and violet as they emanate from our 'third eye' and the crown of the head. Then, with the rainbow's arc gently lowering us down to earth again, we reside amongst the shimmer of the young green leaves and the golden sunlight on the bamboo stems and therein become aware of yet-another Gateway to Wisdom, the ninth in our Journey.

70 THE SINGLE WHIP

The Bird's Beak, a White Peacock in place of the Phoenix, messages in sound and silence, and the 'ordinary' in relation to clairvoyance and mysticism

> *"Birds are the life of the skies, and when they fly, they reveal the thoughts of the skies...*
>
> *You shall know a bird by his cry, and great birds cry loud, but sing not. The eagle screams when the sun is high, the peacock screams at the dawn, rooks call at evening when the nightingale sings. And all birds have their voices, each means a different thing."[1]*

We now form another Bird's Beak with the hand behind us, retain openness with the hand ahead, and, having explored the realms of the sixth sense of second sight and the seventh sense of mystical experience (and, not least, those qualities that those two extra-senses have in common), the present movement sums this up.

We also use the White Peacock in place of the Phoenix, having discovered that these two birds share many attributes through the renewal of their plumage and the incorruptibility of their flesh, their symbolism of rebirth, resurrection and immortality and their link with compassion.

They share excellence in beauty also, attracting constant admiration and wonder from all who behold them - whether in reality or in artistic depiction - and each has been blessed with an exquisite tail, the phoenix displaying waves of coloured, feathery plumes in elegant trails behind it, whilst the peacock's long and many-eyed feathers spread-out widely in one of the most glorious arcs of creation.

There are three important differences between these two birds, however, which is why the White Peacock is more applicable than the Phoenix in this particular summing-up. Firstly, whilst we can appreciate the beauty and many variations in colour and design that artists have ascribed to the phoenix, it lacks the symbolism of the all-seeing 'myriad eyes' in the peacock's wondrous tail. Secondly, the phoenix is mythical and the peacock's reality is powerful, not least for the third reason, which is that, since: *"all birds have voices, each means a different thing"*, we have become aware that the White Peacock has a message for us, and - realising that we cannot know how the voice of the phoenix would sound in contrast to that of the peacock - we find this might be fortuitous, because the latter bird's voice is so 'telling' that we register how potent sound can be and are made all the more aware of the special beneficence of the silence which follows upon its *"scream at the dawn"*. We are, therefore, acutely conscious that we must pay attention to its forthcoming message!

To the mystic, however, no emanations of nature are haphazard or unpleasing to the senses, and even though (despite modern recording and sound-comparison systems) we are not sufficiently in-tune with Nature to fully-intuit what is being conveyed in their various and distinctive calls, we can be filled with wonder at how birds recognize the meaning in each others' sounds. Moreover, for as long as they fly in the skies and *"reveal the thoughts of the skies"* and convey meaning in the sounds they send to other birds, we can at least imagine that - as they sing their melodies from tree-top and branch - they are also carrying messages to us, and can only hope that they are as receptive to our delight in them, as we are to their perfection of shape and sound.

So, the White Peacock has arrived and, as it slowly turns around in its perfect 360 degree circle, its eyes not only view our ordinary world with compassion for our earthly errors, but also foresee the future, thus symbolising the rare combination of a calm perception that is down to earth, *as well as* one that is psychically-aware. Its presence thereby confirms, for the eighth time, why the Bird's Beak movement offers such a summation of duality as we now convey the narrow focus of ordinary reality, which uses the five normal senses, with the wider sixth and seventh senses of clairvoyance and mysticism. The closed hand then represents those very-human times in our lives when we are blind and deaf and dull to the meaning so often conveyed through the psychic or mystical states, whilst the open hand – to which the head is turned - symbolises our consciousness of that which is transcendental. As always, however, we unite both, for each is to be found in the other in that central point of the *tan t'ien* where – holistically – they meet.

Now we understand how the messages of the gods are to be found in the song of a bird by day or night, whilst, at twilight – that mystical, magical time when day and night blend into one – a bird as small as a nightingale can inspire us with some of the 300 love songs it has in its repertoire. We can also be reminded at those moments of exquisite sound that, if we would only close our eyes and truly listen, open our ears and truly hear, we could be transported to the realms of the divine each time a bird opened its mouth and sang its song.

71 Wave Hands like Clouds, or the Heavenly Horse-Riding Steps

*Further symbolism of the Horse and contemplation
on the rhythms of the universe*

*"The sunlight must be moving the waves by itself;
the sky is calm, and there is no wind.*

*With each passing moment, the clouds change colour –
now yellow, now purple, now deep blue-green.
I sit and watch the clouds floating in the blue sky..."*[1]

The gently swaying, sideways floating, exquisite movements of Wave Hands like Clouds now offer us a further opportunity for contemplation. We emphasise the shape and energy in the hands with *yin* and *yang* contrast as they move in front of the upper chest and the lower *tan t'ien*. We rhythmically rise and sink and slowly turn the head from right to left in harmony with that rotating centre, and we let it guide the body three times-over in side-stepping, circling formations as we move like serene, slow-motion clouds across a wide and peaceful sky.

For the third time, we take part in a three-part dance and discover that there are three primary cloud formations: *cirrus, cumulus* and *stratus** and that we could, if we wish, call these three lovely movements by those three beautiful names. We discover yet again how the rhythms and patterns of the movements induce a strong tingling of *Ch'i* in hands and body and that the emergence of this energy relates to the rise and fall

---

*There are now ten internationally recognised cloud forms which were classified at a later date from these three basic forms and which might explain why, apart from the increase in Ch'i induced by repetition, some T'ai Chi Forms have the Cloud Arms movement performed ten times over…!

of the movements, the rounding of the arms and legs and by the rotation of the *tan t'ien*. We also recall that, from observing others perform these steps and seeing how similar their circular rhythmic movements are to those of a superb, slowly-cantering horse, why they are also called "The Heavenly Horse-riding Steps" and why the power, strength and beauty of the horse is so meaningful to so many cultures and in so many countries.

History relates that when the first legendary Chinese Emperor, *Fu Hsi* (2953 B.C.): "*...was seeking to combine the characters proper to express the various forms of matter, and the relation between things physical and intellectual, a wonderful horse came out of the river, bearing on his back certain signs, of which the philosophic legislator formed the eight diagrams* which have preserved his name.*"[2]

In India, the Buddhist Winged or Cosmic Horse is known as "Cloud" and it is said that the Buddha left his home on a white horse. In China, the winged horse bears the Book of the Law on its back, and Kuan Yin herself can portray a part of, or the whole form of a horse in some of her many emanations.[3]

In Taoism, 'The Superlative Horse' is one that "*...raises no dust and leaves no tracks — is something evanescent and fleeting, elusive as thin air...*"[4] - an image which carries even further import when we consider that, to Taoists, 'dust' can imply mental clutter and the trivial and bothersome distractions that disturb the mind, whilst the clear-minded sage is said to 'leave no trace' in any of his or her activities.

To the Hindu, the horse is the body's vehicle and the rider the spirit, whilst the black horse is an attribute of the rain god. White horses draw the chariots of the Greek gods, Mithra and Apollo, across the skies, whilst one winged horse can represent the sun itself. Clouds are the steeds of the Valkyrie; Poseidon, the God of the Sea, emerges as a horse out of the ocean, and the Four Horses of the Apocalypse symbolise our doom if we destroy, or interfere with the balance in this perfectly-created earth.[5] A pure white horse also represents the natural, the unblemished and the innocent and it is considered unwise to let the artificial obliterate the natural by, for example, putting a halter on a horse's head or a ring through a bullock's nose.

* The eight Primary Trigrams of the *I Ching*

With these rhythmic, swaying movements we dwell upon 'the natural' and ponder upon the innocence inherent in those words. We meditate upon the rhythms of life, and of those in the physical movements we are making. We sense how each beat of the heart follows a pattern and that the harmony of those heart-beats is in accord with the rhythmic movements of the Cloud Arms' movements. We see how each rise and fall of the body relates to life's endless ebb and flow and how each circular step we take recalls the balanced circularity of movement conveyed by galloping horses - and of how their rolling eyes reveal their innocence and high sensitivity and of how superbly 'the natural' is conveyed in their free, rhythmic lope.

We re-discover how wave-like is the combination of the gentle turning of the *tan t'ien* with the sideways-stepping leg movements, and recognise that the arm movements and the rising and sinking of the body are both wave-like *and* circular. We experience again to what degree the currents and energy-waves that are made by the intersection of the arms across the *tan t'ien,* energises that psychic field and – for the third time in the Form – of how such a dynamic, yet stabilising, interplay of all the body's variously combining rhythmic and circular movements reflects the basic rhythms and stable order of our living world. Thus, as one Quantum Physicist put it: *"Process and stability… are compatible only if the processes form rhythmic patterns – fluctuations, oscillations, vibrations, waves. … [and that] fluctuations are crucial in the dynamics of self-organisation. They are the basis of order in the living world: ordered structures arise from rhythmic patterns.*

… Rhythmic patterns seem to be manifest at all levels… Plants, animals, and human beings undergo cycles of activity and rest, and all their physiological functions oscillate in rhythms of various periodicities. The components of ecosystems are interlinked through cyclical exchanges of matter and energy; civilizations rise and fall in evolutionary cycles, and the planet as a whole has its rhythms and recurrences as it spins around its axis and moves around the sun."[6]

Thus, thrice-blessed when performing these three rhythmic and stabilising movements as well as by conveying to others the natural rhythms, flow, oscillations and fluctuations in the waves they create, we see how they offer us a sense of the perfection of harmony in the universe and of how: *"These moments of perfect rhythm, when everything feels exactly right and things are done with great ease, are high spiritual experiences in which every form of separateness or fragmentation is transcended."*[7]

We enact the endless cycles of self-renewal which are fundamental to the dance of life, whilst the *tan t'ien* becomes the vortex, or moving part within the moving whole that centres us in this interweaving poem of rise and fall, light and shade, rhythm and form. Then, with such a flow of energy streaming through us, we complete the series of three steps with a circling, upward-flowing arm movement which, gently, and with great simplicity, symbolises all the circles just portrayed, before we glide into the next, and penultimate, Bird's Beak of our Journey.

72 THE SINGLE WHIP

The White Peacock foresees the future, and
the necessary tension of opposites

"Homer was wrong in saying, 'Would that strife might pass away
from among gods and men'! He did not see that he was praying
for the destruction of the universe; for, if his prayer were heard,
all things would pass away – for in the tension of opposites all
things have their being -"[1]

The White Peacock of renewal and clairvoyance arrives on our path again. Having slowly spread its exquisite, all-seeing tail before us and, equally slowly, turned around in its magisterial way, this splendid bird then suggests – somewhat alarmingly, for its voice is like a warning – that there are 'winds of change' ahead and it would be wise if we were to provide a *résumé* of our past and of all that we have learned so far! Furthermore, (and this was said with unadorned, portentous severity, somewhat in the manner of a High Priest), some further repetitions might be necessary and, if so, the culmination of our spiritual quest would entirely depend-upon the degree of wisdom we revealed when responding to this intimation!

With due deference, we bow our head and heed the advice of this wise old bird, and, with neither humility nor vanity (since we sense that the former might be seen as a cloak for the latter, and we wish only to speak the truth as we see it), we look back upon our Journey. We recall a baby's eyes as it absorbs, and has imprinted on the cells of its being, the contours and colours of the home it resides in and the atmosphere created therein – and we identify with (and mourn the loss of) the innocent wonder inherent in that simplicity of observation. We sense the arising of the 'consciousness of opposites', which the young child received from the many physical changes and the arrival of the Tiger's cub. We recall the sense of joyful freedom so often experienced, as well as all the unnecessary admonitions which a child receives and which promote such a lack of self-worth - and of how this subtly-resides within us as adults, to the destruction of trust. We sense some of the inhibitions and self-justifications that follow such a loss and how significant they are in relation to the numerous challenges which reveal them. In contrast - *"for in the tension of opposites, all things have their being"* - we sense that, if such unnecessary negative admonitions have not been too destructive, they might have contributed positively to the many sub-cultures which have proliferated in teenage and young-adult lives throughout the centuries and, perhaps, shaped some of the rebellious, anti-authoritarian, anti-religious, non-conformist, and/or artistic endeavours of many of our great poets and writers, artists, thinkers, philosophers and liberators, without whom life would be far-less inspiring and interesting.

We recall with pleasure the many satisfactions and joys which a child can experience when there is recognition of success well-earned; of physical or psychological validation; of intense friendships; shared understanding; harmony with Nature; a sense of self; a sense of fun and, perhaps, some interludes of quiet introspection. Inevitably, however, memory cannot overlook how, from early childhood, there also were the many opposite emotions of anger, resentment, jealousy, fear, trauma, shock, grief, and the strains of repressed fury (all of which can engender physical and/or mental illness), together with the belief that others can betray, can cause dismay, and trick us into being the opposite of our true nature – and of how helpless a child can feel against such injustices to the spirit. We recall the times when we lost sight of our connection with others and only 'went through the motions' of living, whilst walking, talking and moving around with a semblance of normality, yet feeling emotionally-numb. And we realise that even if there were a spiritual or psychological framework upon which to hang our suffering, it hardly seemed to matter whether our inadequacies or misfortunes were viewed as coming from our behaviour during that day or week or year; from the failings of our parents; from childhood trauma, illness, or adolescent angst; from other people's behaviour; from the result of current social dictates; misunderstandings; religious concepts; astrological influences;

universal synchronicity, or from any of the many other 'reasons' which our more adult-self had hoped might rationalise, justify, or explain our pain. For the pain was all-consuming and it was only when the suffering and the trauma had eased, that we tried to understand the problems and soothe ourselves by placing them in some appropriate section of our particular attitude or philosophy, hoping that our earlier ignorance (or, our ability to ignore much of what we had learnt) might lead us to find answers to our problems by seeking possible causes.

All this then has us focussing-upon the ego and of how the Tiger over-shadows the human condition. We look at our own, actual shadow as it rests on the ground and ponder upon its purpose, why shadows exist at all, and realise that, because it is our body that intercepts the light, this is symbolic of our quest, for our shadow will *always* be attached to us for as long as we are dense. We recall how often all those stresses, traumas and shocks which the Tiger had promoted, were overcome whenever we let-go to whatever was causing the emotional suffering, and of the great joy and relief which accompanied such yielding and of how we then were enabled to fully-absorb the meaning in those many Gateways to Wisdom.

We begin to see that there can be no blame, nor any complete answer as to 'why' problems occur; that we (whilst still in human form) *never* will fully-understand the results of the total interweaving of all the days of our lives; *never* have full, conscious knowledge of all the millions of moments of cause and effect upon the emotions, of all the trillions of words that have been imprinted upon the cells of the brain, of all the facets of our genetic and ancestral inheritance which have culminated in whatever we are now. For, apart from the fact that memory is selective and mostly subjective, it has never been given to the majority of humans to find out the answers to everything, but only occasionally to delve into the personal psyche and/or discover a few significant connections from the holographic universe.

We recall our Bamboos' connection with the rhythms of the universe and our long-delayed acceptance of life's contrasting cycles and opposites, since these have confirmed that - without them (and the other repetitions) - we could not have explored the dualism in the few rich gifts that the human mind and body can access, nor perceived that neither fear nor expectation need arise in relation to any portent that may be predicted.

This then has us pondering further and we perceive that this latter part of the *résumé* indicates that all the wisdom teachings and all the repetitions have been guiding us to just one thing: an invincible acceptance of all that is, as it is – and that fully-understanding this will enable us to let-go to whatever is behind us and accept whatever the future brings.

It also is clear that the recent, but long period of peace, learning, and creative activity, which was interspersed with only one brief Tiger-induced storm, is over. Some disruptive 'test' is looming which, as ever, will indicate that such tests are part of the rhythms and tides of life. We have yielded often-enough to understand these patterns and so, if and when *"coming events cast their shadow before"*, * we should be able to sense for ourselves in some small degree – and then accept – whatever lies ahead, in a similar way to all the other creatures on this wonderful planet, sharing with them some of the extra-sensory perception that can tap into the holographic information which fills the universe. Nature produces violent storms, plagues of locusts, fires, floods and droughts that are so death-producing that we regard them with dismay, but, long term, they produce new life on this earth. And so, for us, in the areas of our own psychological and spiritual development, having been stripped bare, we too can don fresh clothes.

Now we are prepared for any further 'change within no-change', which the White Peacock may have foreseen. No longer disturbed by the shrill cry of this remarkable bird, we understand that the significance of *'all things have their being in the tension of opposites'* does not only apply to the Universal Law of the survival of life itself, but also to spiritual maturity, in the same way as a seed in the dark earth, which might be under a stone and seemingly blocked from growth, seeks the light in order to produce a flower...

To confirm all this, the White Peacock now lowers its head and then lifts it again, as if nodding assent to and, therefore, being satisfied

*Thomas Campbell (1777-1844) in "Lochiel's Warning"

with our response, but, before it departs with its serene and measured tread, we physically sum-up this ninth and penultimate Bird's Beak of balance and unity. Thus, the necessary, but disquieting tensions that were indicated in our *résumé* of the past, rest in the closed hand behind us, whilst the sixth sense of second sight – and the possibility of the seventh sense of mystical fulfilment – continue to reside in the open hand ahead. Moreover, whilst we accept that we may have a long way to go in evolutionary terms, we do see that:

> *"The surest test if a man be sane*
> *Is if he accepts life whole, as it is,*
> *Without needing by measure or touch to understand*
> *The measureless untouchable source*
> *Of its images,*
> *The measureless untouchable source*
> *Of its substances,*
> *The source which, while it appears dark emptiness,*
> *Brims with a quick force...* "[2]

73-76 High Pat on a Horse; Cross Palms and Lunge; Turn Around and Kick; Twisted Step, Fist, Brush (Knee), Low Punch and Circling Fist

Three dynamic repetitions in four movements of power which, with our altered response to 'attack', indicates another major landmark in the Journey

The White Peacock's 'examination' is over and its prognostications were accurate. The aforementioned repetitions have arrived and we now move into the High Pat on a Horse which appeared in Part Two of our Journey. Then, we had less self-knowledge, and any perception of our destructive attitudes of self-defence was limited. Ego was strong, but we had not yet felt the need to come to grips with it, and the pent-up energy, power and dynamism inherent in that earlier, swift, High Pat movement served only to reinforce the strength of our ambition and competitive self-assertion.

That power is portrayed again, but is of a different order. The body's rise, the swift thrust-forward of the hand, the pawing of the ground: all these are present, but we still recall the pain of that earlier battle and can restrain ourselves from any egoistic action. We are also profoundly-thankful for the spiritual opportunities and energy-given components which the recent interlude and gentle repetition of the Cloud Arms, Heavenly Horse Riding Steps has given us, and so, as before, we proffer our gratitude with a high 'pat of thanks' onto the head of the heavenly horse which transported us so serenely across the skies and gave us such an opportunity for further reflection.

This takes us smoothly into a new movement: "Cross Palms and Lunge". Firmly pressing-down the 'patting hand', the action is followed by a sharp, forward, upward thrust of the other, indicating quite a degree of inner power and an understanding of *wu-wei*. Similar to the White Snake puts out its Tongue and almost as dramatic, the movement conveys the results of that earlier learning process, but its power lies in our continuing ability to say "*YES!*" to the sight inside and in the almost-clairvoyant awareness we have of what is going on around us – for this now reveals itself by an uneasy sensation in the solar plexus and by a tingling in the back of the neck. Does this relate to any 'impending trouble' which the White Peacock might have divined? Has our 'cut and thrust' action been precognitive of something similar to come? Did the action (in itself) promote antagonism from some source, through its strength and dynamism, or is someone irritated by what could be construed as an unpleasant egoistic element in our bearing?

Recalling the stately Peacock, we turn around slowly, as if carefully sensing the air, for the attack, though not as yet recognised, is coming from behind. Aware of possible confrontation, our Tiger awakens, stirs with the familiar response of wariness and self-defence and, feeling vulnerable, we cross our arms in front of our chest and consider what form of retaliation we should take. But then… we pause… and lower our arms, for something has changed. We are assimilating our Tiger's responses as they arise and then evaluating the consequences of any Tiger-action on our part. Using insight and our awakened senses, we find that, although the war of nerves in the solar plexus has dispersed, there are still some signs of tension in the neck and upper back. So (as suggested in the previous Kicking section), we gather together as much information as possible to assess the situation and find that, yes, an 'attack' is indicated. Still watchful of our Tiger, however, and with each moment occurring as if it were in slow-motion, we appear to have an infinity of time to focus-fully on the situation, only to find that, although Tiger had stirred sufficiently to cause the psyche to feel uneasy and the body to tense, it now opens its mouth in a wide yawn, circles around, and relaxes its vigilance, dissolving – as we have already discovered it does when so fully-focussed upon – until it barely exists. We then find that, although the 'attacker' has arrived and there is much verbal exchange, the situation has ceased to be dangerous, each participant has entered into the cause of the problem and there is a genuine desire for resolution.

This dramatically changes the course of the final confrontation and, although it now is recognised on both sides that a firm and stable, albeit symbolic, 'kick, strike, and clenched fist' is necessary to resolve the serious issues at stake, we simply don the cloak of whatever is appropriate and deliver what is needed. Quieter within and with no desire to hurt, the retreat of our own Tiger has changed the responses of the Tiger in the other and we give and receive of our information with the firmness which emerges from a fair and just foundation. Both parties have presented the salient facts straight from the *tan t'ien* , the problems have been resolved with the integrity inherent in *wu-wei,* and the Eighth Essential Point then comes into its own, for now we can fully co-ordinate and unify the power of the inner psychological state with its outward physical expression.

And so, yet again, the value of repetition is confirmed, for we now are nearer to mastering the Tiger each time it arises and putting into action what we were taught so long ago: that, although attack and defence are as fundamental to daily life as they are in any martial art, the basic teaching of both, paradoxical as it may seem, is to take appropriate action without causing harm, for:

> *"… Quick action bruises,*
> *quick grasping loses.*
> *Therefore a sane man's care is not to exert*
> *One move that can miss, one move that can hurt."*[1]

All these, apparently fighting, movements, whether verbal or physical, again become indicative of the difference between a healthy ego's response and that of an unhealthy ego – and so another paradox occurs. Having finally learnt how to kick and apply *wu-wei* with stability and spiritual consciousness, we never kick again! Having at last absorbed and been able to apply all the lessons offered in the first Kicking section, there is now no need to do so. There is, however, another indication of 'change within no-change': instead of following the kicking and fisting with a punch to the solar plexus, its aim changes course. Brushing aside illusion with one hand, we plumb the depths of Tiger-based activity with a penetrating, downward punch and then make two more moves which, again, are new to us. Using all our resources of wisdom and spiritual power, we turn the fist to face down – thus denying Tiger any residual interference – and powerfully pull it back towards the *tan t'ien*, like a lever to its fulcrum. Drawing it closer to our centre to convey that we are in charge, the other hand – simultaneously – extends outwards with a gentle strength, as if recognising and moving towards something of supreme importance. And these two movements reveal that we are nearer to our goal. Truth has been valued beyond ego and no-one has been hurt.

To signify this, we now make a slow and lovely circle with the fist as it moves towards the other upward-turning, returning hand, as if to meet another person more-than half way. Then, having drawn the fist over that receptive, open palm, we let it go and raise it high and find that the Tiger's Mouth is akin to the head of the Cheshire Cat, which lingers awhile in the air and then quietly fades away. No ego-body is left, not even an elusive smile remains.

77 Grasping the Sparrow's Tail; Ward Off – Slantingly Upwards; Pull Back, Press Forward; Two Half-Steps Up, and Push

The final, eighth Bamboos; the Zero Point Field; the direct, unhampered rhythm of initiating action, whilst in 'step with the Tao', and the tenth Gateway to Wisdom

> *"Sages, poets and artists all dwelt, when possible, in the bamboo forests where the rustle of the leaves in the breeze is the murmur of the voice of remote places, of mountain gorges and deep groves; the voice of the silence, wisdom herself. The bamboo is all the qualities of the soul of man and of nature epitomized. Seldom painted in other than black and white, throwing into relief darkness and light, expressing power and delicacy, it is the yin-yang symbol of the universe."[1]*

Our opened hand has risen upwards to the heavens in an expansive movement of joy and release and we now Grasp the Sparrow's Tail of heightened consciousness for the last time. We sway into a softly-murmuring forest of bamboos and sense the delicacy of those most-fine and noble plants. One arm curves up through the air with purity and grace and the other awaits the power of its lightly turning, downward flow. Circling smoothly from our centre, we swirl, loop and return, flow, eddy and sway, move forwards and back and right and left, and thus – for the eighth time – shift in harmony with the bamboos and their whispering, rippling music.

Moving in unison with those green and supple plants as they send out such sweet melody, always has signified that we have relinquished our individuality and been absorbed into the larger order of the universe and, thus - with simplicity and in accord with Nature's beauty and rhythms - have moved with the energy that moves the breeze that obeys the wider laws that rule the universe, in the same way as water surges with energy in the middle of an ocean and, at the other end of its flow, has waves bursting their bubbles on a distant shore in a never-ending symphony of sound.

Moreover, to harmonise with such a source and to be so linked with each other, also has always been a supremely significant experience, and this time is no different and yet is profoundly so – and for two main reasons. Firstly, there is the significance of the number 'eight'. As this is the eighth Bamboos, we recall that some spiritual teachings view that number as the 'soul of the world' and that, because it symbolises the two circles of heaven and earth, it has become a sacred number. In other religions, 'eternity' is seen as circular, since, as with the figure eight, it has no beginning and no end. In mathematics, 'eternity' and 'infinity' are symbolised by an eight, placed sideways, whilst the number 512 – which adds up to eight – is known as an ideal number, being eight times eight times eight, or eight-cubed. Nature also – and enchantingly - portrays the importance of the 'eight', when just one worker bee, with the odour of recently-found food on its body, uses sublime awareness of the sun's rays on the earth, the buzzing sound of its swiftly beating wings, the various directions it can face in relation to the honey comb and its body repeatedly outlining a figure of eight, to indicate to other bees the exact distance and precise location of the food it has found. Thus, the bee conveys the distance between itself and the food with its mathematical knowledge of where the rays from the circular sun link with the circle of the earth, whilst its magical 'pattern of eight' dance furthers its survival - as well as our own.

Another example of the use of a circle is made by the most innocuous and pallid of fish – the male Japanese Puffer fish – which (it could be said) has nearly all the characteristics of an enlightened being! It is so translucent as to be almost invisible; lives in the element of the Waters of Wisdom; applies awesome patience, perseverance, dexterity and zeal to create the most perfect, exquisite sand circle (albeit to entice a female into it); uses its 'wings' to 'adjust' that sand on the sea-bed in order to create astonishing and mathematically-accurate, mandala-like patterns within that circle and, god-like, takes six days to do so; rests on the seventh and, having successfully impressed the previously-absent female with the delicate beauty of its craftsmanship, invites her into the circle and (if she acquiesces) there impregnates her. She then insouciantly swims away and it proceeds to fulfil its androgynous nature by nurturing the results of the successful encounter, whilst, in true Buddhist fashion, quietly accepting that the perfect, circular 'world' it has created is dissolving into a shapeless mass again.

Circles of eight, and circles in general, thus have great significance in the spiritual, the mathematical and the natural world and on this, our most significant Bamboos – which has us forming similar circles - the second reason why it is different becomes apparent. For, we now take two half-steps, for the first and only time, in the *middle* of the circling, swirling movements, before continuing with the universal stream, thereby (like the bees) conveying *yang* action *at the same time* as moving in a *yin*-based, circular flow. And this means that we are not only *yielding to,* but are *initiating* action. By the taking of these two small, half-steps, we have made one whole step that could be seen as akin to taking a 'quantum leap'. Nor is this analogy made by chance, for, in quantum physics, there is what is known as the Zero Point Field, which - together with the holographic wave (which contains the memory and language of that Field) - is regarded as the Source of everything in the universe, including the Primary Reality mentioned earlier on this Journey and Jung's 'collective unconscious'.

In that Field: *"There is no 'me' and 'not me' duality to our bodies in relation to the universe, but one underlying energy field. This field is responsible for our mind's highest functions, the information source guiding the growth of our bodies. It is our brain, our heart, our memory - indeed, a blueprint of the world for all time. The field is the force, rather than germs or genes, that finally determines whether we are healthy or ill, the force which must be tapped in order to heal. We are attached and engaged, indivisible from our world, and our only fundamental truth is our relationship with it."* [2] Thus: *"...we and all the matter of the universe are literally connected to the first reaches of the cosmos through the Zero Point Field waves of the grandest dimensions".*[3]

The Quantum pioneers who reported on this Field also discovered that their own physical process, their own: *"... involvement with matter was crucial. Subatomic particles existed in all possible states until disturbed by us – by observing and measuring – at which point, they'd settle down, at long last, into something real. Our observation – our human consciousness – was utterly central to this process of subatomic flux actually becoming some set thing..."*[4] and that: *"Much like the undulations of the sea or ripples on a pond, the waves on the subatomic level are represented by periodic oscillations moving through a medium – in this instance the Zero Point Field. They are represented by a classic sideways S, or sine curve, like a skipping rope being held at both ends and wiggled up and down".*[5] The Field thereby contains *all* that has ever-been, is now, and ever-shall be, and each curve or wave, once they have collided: *"... contains information, in the form of energy coding, about the other, including all the other information it contains. Interference patterns amount to a constant accumulation of information, and waves have a virtually infinite capacity for storage."*[6]

Thus, instead of stepping aside from the *yang* of life into the *yin* Bamboos' flow, we, too, now oscillate like waves in our S-shaped curve in a field of energy which is composed of universal information. We not only affect subatomic matter by adding that whole, new step (as an '*interference pattern*'), that other new piece of information to the universal whole, but, by being so '*in step with*' the Tao, we actively *become* a part of its fundamental nature. We have not interrupted its flow. We have not unsettled its inherent patterns. We have not disrupted the Universal Laws, but have added ourselves to their universality.

So this final, eighth Bamboos conveys a vastly different response to life as hitherto we have known it and, from now on, the remainder of the Journey becomes swifter and simpler as we finally leave behind those places to which we do not wish to return. Having explored so much of what we had thought separated us from everything in creation and from having, at last, travelled beyond Tiger's domination, we now have fully-absorbed to what degree we are an inseparable part of all that exists. Moreover, through our own, fallible *human consciousness*, we have fluidly *stepped into* the holographic wave of our own volition – and, most importantly – with no differentiation taking place between one state or another.

Now, as our bodies send out ripples of energy, as well as psychic forms of invisible communication, we become both active and passive, creative and receptive. We have moved together so often in these beautiful movements that, in the depth of the silence, we have influenced the rhythms of others, as well as been influenced by theirs. We have learnt that any separatist or egoistic movement can send ripples of what could be seen as 'disarray' through the whole group; that, although Tiger can fight as hard as it likes for its independence and domination by doing things its own way; could wish another person were further away in the room (or, even, not there at all), or could block the rhythmic connections by Monkey forgetfulness, we can absorb those ripples. By so doing, we then find that – like a scatter of rain on a pool of water – they soften and merge with the whole and thereby contribute to it, and that (as mentioned in an earlier chapter) we then can move in harmony with whoever is near us, silently modify our movements to theirs, and accept that - if the spirit is to be liberated and harmony achieved - such modification is not only necessary but *inevitable*. Real movement towards ultimate enlightenment then arises, for we now can use our energies in directions not governed by the past, are free from man-made indoctrination, and can enter into the 'time free' zone of the mystics and the underlying Laws of the Universe. Now, much nearer to the fulfilment of all that the wisdom in the T'ai Chi Journey represents: the emergence of the selfless state where love and compassion result through rhythmic relationships with each other and pure contact with the Tao, we see that the burdens along 'The Way' have become lighter, or have dropped by the wayside, and, following upon our two half-steps-up, we now understand the full meaning in the Tenth and penultimate Gateway to Wisdom.

78 The Single Whip

The final, tenth, Bird's Beak or the Phoenix Stance,
and the yin and yang of the breath

Flowing Eastwards once more in waves of rhythmic, silent harmony, our deep connection with each other continues, as does our link with the pulse of the universe. We have repeated such themes over and over, since – as with any art form, all specialised techniques, therapeutic method or the hard work of serious research – a transformation cannot take place, a breakthrough cannot occur, nor a step be taken into an expanded state of consciousness, without repetition. Such a transformation – as well as being a 'quantum leap' – is akin to the flowering that happens each time ego is absent (and, perhaps, we have at long-last produced sufficient flowers for a small bouquet), but the wisdom of Nature dictates that the bamboo flowers only once in its, sometimes, very long life and that its flowering is its 'swan-song', for it dies thereafter (and there is much food-for-thought in that message, if we truly wish to understand the full meaning in 'living in the now' or 'dying to the moment').

Following upon the final Bamboos, this tenth Bird's Beak is its 'swan-song' also and on this, its last appearance, it conveys the final, perfect example of the harmonious and balanced union of opposites in daily living.

Life now has more simplicity and is lived in accordance with the rhythms, patterns and cycles of the seasons, as close to plants, birds, animals and other creatures as our lives will allow. Needing little, loving much, our observation of, and connection with Nature, as well as with the nature of those we have come to know and love on our Journey, has furthered insight into our own nature, and we find that the more contact we have with this way of living, the happier we become. Now, in this final summing up and expression of the open and closed Bird's Beak hands, we go beyond the glorious sound made by birds, to a further exploration of the *Ch'i*, the breath of life, which makes that sound possible.

We have long been incorporating the breath with each T'ai Chi movement: the passive *yin,* 'in' breath harmonising with the yielding, retreating and rising movements; the active *yang* 'out' breath rhythmically directing those that are strong, outward or downward flowing. We have found that, whilst our normal respiratory system works in a ratio of 1 : 4 (there being eighteen breaths drawn a minute for every seventy-two beats of the pulse), we have been so deepening and lengthening the breath that we have greatly increased the time it takes to do each movement, improved our lung capacity, strengthened the heart and circulatory system and thus invigorated the whole body. Moreover, when so directed by this calm, deeper breathing, we are led into such inner harmony that the mind is also at peace.

We learn that the one still-point, the small pause which occurs between each breath (and which is slightly-longer at the end of the 'out' breath, as if the lungs were relaxing prior to preparing themselves for the next, vital intake of oxygen), is allocated – in esoteric terms – to a place of wisdom and stillness and this confirms what we have already learnt, for, as we silently perform the slow, deeply-balancing movements and breathe in harmony with them, we again experience the group energy which is akin to a complex web which supports and binds us together and which differs from the energy gained from solo practise. Like birds which fly in group formation, we are linked together by what appear to be invisible elastic threads that form a totality of vibrating air currents which, again like migrating birds, support and give energy to the weaker ones amongst us. By breathing in harmony with our own body's movements and simultaneously moving in harmony with each other, we sense a group soul, which manifests in the air and integrates us both individually and collectively. This group soul then so binds us together in the silence, that it has us emerging from the Form revitalised, smoothed out, joyously-together in mind and spirit, smiling at each other in friendship and deeply grateful for the spiritual links which have been forged between us. Such a situation then becomes another metaphor for life, for we are not only bound to each other by the invisible bonds of breath and energy, but by everything that moves forward out of stillness and quietly lives in wisdom.

Some participants then continue the silence as they quietly move away. Others, speaking, convey in quiet tones only that which has meaning for them and then give the necessary pauses that allow others to quietly respond, in turn. Thus, as birds convey their messages to other birds and creatures, we communicate with each other, either silently, or otherwise.

In summation, this final Bird's Beak stance yet again conveys the duality of 'sound and silence' in speech, as well as the breaths that make this possible. One hand remains open to portray the ever-present *Ch'i* in the infinity of air and the other closes to portray the ever-poignant silence that follows upon the sound that breath has conveyed. The central *tan t'ien* of equilibrium is firmly-established, the breathing is in balance, and the mind is calm – for the quantum leap has been taken and we are 'at one' with the universe. Then, after an almost breathless, hushed expectancy - as if that small still-point between the breaths were infinitely long – we find we have to take a very long in-breath and an equally long step, as Life, or Kuan Yin, or our fate as decreed by the stars, moves us towards our destiny.

79 THE SNAKE CREEPS DOWN INTO WATER (SQUATTING SINGLE WHIP)

Entering-further into the Waters of Wisdom and confirmation of the vital component of non-differentiation

> *"There is a tremendous reservoir, as it were, which if the human mind can touch it, reveals something which no intellectual mythology – invention, supposition, dogma – can ever reveal."[1]*

The language and symbolic nature of the unconscious is unlimited and has to be so because of the diversity of oral language and imagery. It can conjure-up everything and everyone that we have ever known and, whilst we may not always recognize them, they represent aspects of ourselves that are significant. It can offer-up dreams to convey abstruse thoughts; words that seem meaningless; joyous sensations of singing or dancing, flying or wading through treacherous waters; the more-obvious feelings of love and fear, jealousy and strife and the many other, more-subtle emotions, which, whilst forming part of our human psyche, are sometimes buried so deeply that the conscious mind cannot always access or comprehend their meaning. But we must access them. They are an essential part of our psyche and it is necessary that we probe those dark areas that simmer in the depths of our inner world, in order to bring to consciousness as much as is possible of the pain and suffering we have experienced in the past. So now, as we enter into the final stages of our Journey, one of the most potent symbols of all – the Snake - glides in again with a repetition of one of the most demanding and significant movements in the whole of the Journey and, as before, allies itself to water.

Slipping into a bubbling rill, the lapping waters of a lake-side, the ripples in a stream, or any of the waters which, eventually, will flow into the depths of the ocean, the Snake now symbolizes an entry into the deep-waters of a soul that has no preferences.

[This snake was painted by a Japanese Master, in one superb,
flowing stroke of a stippled brush. Only the eyes and tongue, and
some sand thrown onto the darkened head, were added afterwards.]

We recall that the previous Snake movement symbolized 'letting-go' to the strings that proudly bound us to knowledge, analysis and intellectual achievement and that its arrival indicated that we might be drawing-nearer to that *tremendous reservoir* of serenity and wisdom which we sensed as The Source at the beginning of our Journey. But, after the Snake had drawn us up and out of those waters and into what we had believed would be the life of a New Dawn, we found ourselves immediately going into the Monkey Steps, for we had somewhat muddied those unclouded waters by our swift attachment to our conditioned thinking processes and by our desire to analyze the experience that had just occurred. Thus, there was still much work to be done on our Tiger and many repetitions had to take place.

Now the Snake returns, but we find that the movement is far-less difficult to perform and that its presence is not because we have regressed to an attachment to our left-sided, analytical brain activity, nor because we still cling to concepts and illusions, but because the Snake now shares an affinity with us: that of shedding its skin which, in this case, symbolizes a letting-go of the burdens we have been carrying in relation to 'choice'. Now, the last vestiges of separation slip away into waters that are warm, welcoming and crystal-clear and which - now that we can 'truly listen' - have a 'melody' to them that has, in fact, accompanied us throughout our lives.

The spiritual and creative forces of the Tao are paramount as the Snake leads us down into the element, which, desiring nothing for itself: *"... gives of itself freely, never questioning the form into which it must change when needed by a plant, an animal or man; with the same submissiveness it fills them all. It resigns itself selflessly to every need... in its very nature it is itself pure, it can purify, refresh, heal, strengthen, revive and clarify all things..."*[2] Water also: *"... pictures – as though in a great parable – higher qualities of man's development. Qualities such as the overcoming of rigidity in thought, of prejudice, of intolerance; the ability to enter into all things and to learn to understand them out of their own nature and to create out of polarities a higher unity... ways in which man may win through to selflessness in a pure, healthy and light-filled soul life. Just as water aids him in his entry into the earthly world, mediating to him the heavenly forces, so it can also lead him to a rebirth of his spiritual nature."*[3]

Recalling the many byways we have taken before arriving at this second 'baptism', we are reminded of the Journey's complexity and of how it seemed so difficult to be simple, to be what we are, for: *"To be what you are is in itself very arduous without trying to become something, which is not too difficult. You can always pretend, put on a mask but to be what you are is an extremely complex affair; because you are always changing; you are never the same and each moment reveals a new facet, a new depth, a new surface. You can't be all this at one moment for each moment brings its own change... You think you are very sensitive and an incident, a fleeting thought, shows that you are not; you think you are clever, well-read, artistic, moral but turn round the corner, you find you are none of these things but that you are deeply ambitious, envious, insufficient, brutal and anxious. You are all these things turn by turn and you want something to be continuous, permanent, of course only that which is profitable, pleasurable. So you run after that and all the many other yous are clamouring to have their way, to have their fulfilment. So you become the battle-field and generally ambition, with all its pleasures and pain, gaining, with envy and fear. The word love is thrown in for respectability's sake and to hold the family together but you are caught in your own commitments and activities, isolated, clamouring for recognition and fame, you and your country, you and your party, you and your comforting god.*

So to be what you are is an extremely arduous affair; if you are at all awake, you know all these things and the sorrow of it all. So you drown yourself in your work, in your belief, in your fantastic ideals and meditations. By then you have become old and ready for the grave, if you are not already dead inwardly. To put away all these things, with their contradictions and increasing sorrow, and be nothing is the most natural and intelligent thing to do. But before you can be nothing, you must have unearthed all these hidden things, exposing them and so understanding them. To understand these hidden urges and compulsions, you will have to be aware of them, without choice, as with death; then in the pure act of seeing, they will wither away and you will be without sorrow and so be as nothing. To be as nothing is not a negative state; the very denial of everything you have been is the most positive action..."[4]

These words plunge us further into the depths of our psyche, so that we can *"unearth all these hidden things, expose them and so understand them"*. We recollect the many robes of camouflage, the many masks that we have imposed upon ourselves and others, of how ego-boosting they were and artificial, illusory and spiritually destructive. We see how the state of being *without choice* could lead to the splendid merging of opposites, of one race with another; of science and psychology with religion and mysticism, of the sacred with the secular, and that these two words also apply to the natural with the supernatural; heaven with earth, spirit with matter. We understand that, if human consciousness is to merge with 'no-thing-ness', it has to acknowledge that the energies of the Universe unite all that is, and that The Field of the limitless Source of the ordered cosmos of infinite waves, testifies to this in the same way as does every holographic cell in our body. So, the human mind, which, hitherto, has been regarded as proof of our superiority and which has been so elevated by its ability to make choices, is absorbed into an existence that, by virtue of its non-discriminatory nature, is raised by the mystics to be the highest level of spiritual awareness.

Such 'Absorption in the Divine', as it is sometimes called, can be epitomized by the monastic life, and the sense of wonder which the sight of some Cistercian monks in public worship inspired in Thomas Merton, has been most-beautifully described by him, in pure Taoist terms: "... *I was amazed at the way these monks ... were... absorbed and transformed in the liturgy. The thing that was most impressive was their absolute simplicity. They were concerned with one thing only: doing the things they had to do, singing what they had to sing, bowing and kneeling and so on when it was prescribed, and doing it as well as they could, without fuss or flourish or display. It was all utterly simple and unvarnished and straightforward, and I don't think I had ever seen anything, anywhere, so unaffected, so un-selfconscious as these monks. There was not a shadow of anything that could be called parade or display.*"[5]

Moreover: "*Certainly one thing the monk does not, or cannot, realize is the effect which these liturgical functions, performed by a group as such, have upon those who see them. The lessons, the truths, the incidents and values portrayed are simply overwhelming.*

For this effect to be achieved, it is necessary that each monk as an individual performer be absolutely lost, ignored, overlooked.

And yet, what a strange admission! To say that men were admirable, worthy of honor, perfect, in proportion as they disappeared into a crowd and made themselves unnoticed, by even ceasing to be aware of their own existence and their own acts. Excellence, here, was in proportion to obscurity: the one who was best was the one who was least observed, least distinguished. Only faults and mistakes drew attention to the individual.

The logic of the Cistercian life was, then, the complete opposite to the logic of the world, in which men put themselves forward, so that the most excellent is the one who stands out, the one who is eminent above the rest, who attracts attention.

But what was the answer to this paradox? Simply that the monk in hiding himself from the world becomes not less himself, not less of a person, but more of a person, more truly and perfectly himself: for his personality and individuality are perfected in their true order, the spiritual, interior order, of union with God, the principle of all perfection...

The logic of worldly success rests on a fallacy: the strange error that our perfection depends on the thoughts and opinions and applause of other men! A weird life it is, indeed, to be living always in somebody else's imagination, as if that were the only place in which one could at last become real!"[6]

Now we see how we live through the image others make of us, as well as in our own imagination, and of how this governs us. We delve even-deeper into 'nothingness' and ponder-upon how attached we have become to our huge collection of spiritual wares, as well as to our intellect. We see how any desire for spirituality – especially when viewed as a further acqui-sition – removes us from its simplicity and understand that: "*The totality of consciousness must empty itself of all its knowledge, action and virtue; not empty itself for a purpose, to gain, to realize, to become. It must remain empty though functioning in the everyday world of thought and action. Out of this emptiness, thought and action must come... This emptiness is beyond time and space; it's beyond thought and feeling. It comes as quietly, unobtrusively, as love; it has no beginning and end. It's there unalterable and immeasurable.*"[7]

So, the ego dissolves as we sink into that which cannot be altered or measured. Only when there is no sense of ourselves 'being or doing anything', when there are no roles to fulfill, no psychological games to play, no need for the image-maker and nothing to seek, gain, or lose, can such dissolution take place and boundless, inner-freedom be attained. The monk is released from self-consciousness, enters into spirit and the true, inner conversion of water and spirit takes place, for:

> *"The man of Tao*
> *Remains unknown*
> *Perfect virtue*
> *Produces nothing*
> *'No-Self'*
> *Is 'True-Self.'*
> *And the greatest man*
> *Is Nobody."[8]*

Now the processes of enlightenment are almost fulfilled. No more will there be long periods of ego-activity interspersed with a few interludes of peace. Instead – apart from one essential, meditational Retreat – dramatic move follows upon dramatic move with an uninterrupted spiritual intensity which could only be assimilated by a being that is free from the impurities of dualistic thought and has the capacity for total acquiescence.

Effortlessly and with joy at this final renunciation, we submerge ourselves into the Waters of Wisdom that symbolize the highest qualities of human spirituality and, in so doing, we become weightless, unearthly, as if no-thing – and are transformed. That heavy cloak, that burden of our desire for a higher, more transcendental version of knowledge, religion, or even spirituality, slips off our shoulders and we find ourselves as if magnetically-drawn upwards on a journey towards the stars. As we prepare to rise, however, we sense that something vital is missing, something that we must carry with us as an essential link with our earthly nature, a substance which will keep us in touch with the source of our mortal, human condition. So, first with one hand, then with the other, we scoop-up some earth – and only then do we rise upwards.

Photo used with permission of Cheng Man Ching Enterprises, LLC

80 STEP UP TO FORM
THE SEVEN STARS

*The power of the Seven Stars; our proximity to the Source
and the Home of the Taoist Immortals*

> *"Is it not of great significance that the world of the stars
> permeates all movements of water, that water infuses all earthly
> life with the events of the cosmos, that all life processes are
> through water intimately connected with the course of the stars?
> Wherever there is moving water… everywhere it is illumined
> by the world of the stars. Thus water becomes an image of the
> stream of time itself, permeated with the rhythms of the starry
> world. All the creatures of the earth live in this stream of time, it
> flows within them, and, as long as its flows, sustains them in the
> stream of life."[1]*

It is night. We rise up and out of water and we fly towards the stars.
The sky seems so dark, so still, the earth below so far. We absorb the
darkness, its enveloping depth, its immensity, and experience something
akin to the peace of the Stillness known so long ago. We fly as if weightless, formless, nebulous, but – will our identity be lost forever? We feel
the earth in our hands and are comforted.

The stars shed their light and become familiar and we feel like a
new-born babe scooped-up out of the waters of the womb. Lifted out
and up and away from the Waters of Wisdom, it is as if we are enfolded
in swaddling clothes made of shimmering star-dust. We float higher
and the stars become larger, brighter and we reach out towards them
with our spirit, with wonder and joy at their existence, with gratitude
for their illumination. One set in particular beckons, one constellation
that is used by navigators of every nation, one group which can easily
be located and recognised no matter what the season, nor the time of

night and - as we rise even-further - we find we have been travelling through space towards a place which could not have been otherwise, a place which forms the most important constellation in the whole of the Northern night sky. For this is the Home of the Immortals, known as Ursa Major, the Great Bear, whose seven stars form the ladle-shaped Great or Northern Dipper and which – also known as the Wagon, the Wain, the Plough, the Bushel and the Chariot – has been singled out for myths and legends in places as widely unconnected and scattered as Lapland is from Lhasa.

As one writer envisaged it: *"In the far north .... there is a high and paradisal place, peopled by an assembly of beings of superhuman longevity and wisdom. They have associates and contacts at lower levels. Access to it is difficult. This is the place where earth rises to join the celestial centre, the pole of heaven. Here is the axis of the sky, and above is the power that keeps it turning. The visible and sovereign sign of that power is the great constellation of seven stars, which possess a divine life, and circle in the centre without setting.*

Our disc-shaped earth has a sacred centre which is in union with this centre where the heavens are pivoted. As above, so below."[2] Thus it is said that the Great Bear: *"... sets in motion and keeps the heaven turning in due season."*[3]

As marker to the pole of heaven, which in northern latitudes never sets, other legends have it that these seven luminaries are the sources of power which drive the system of the life-producing circle of the zodiac and, thus, operate the seven most important orbs in the whole of the universe: the Sun and the other major planets (or 'wanderers', for 'planet' means 'wanderer'), which travel across the heavens as Moon, Mercury, Venus, Mars, Jupiter, and Saturn. Similarly, the immense significance of this great constellation and its place in cosmic influence, is borne-out by ancient Chinese documents which state that the Seven Stars (*Tseih Sing*) of the Great Bear were associated with the celestial palace of the Lord on High, *Shang Ti*; with *Shou Lao*, the high-domed 'Star God of Longevity', and with no-less-than the celestial mountain paradise itself, *Tien Shan*, home of the Taoist Immortals,[4] towards which many Immortals travelled in their celestial boat.

308

Painting of 'Seven Immortals in a boat'

The Great Bear thus occupies: *"...a prominent position in the Taoist heavens as the aerial throne of their supreme deity, Shang Ti, around whom all the other star-gods circulate in homage."*[5]

The Chinese also consider that the three stars of the Great Dipper's handle, known as the 'Jade Scales', determine the weighing and measuring of divine justice, and the 'measuring of the seasons'[6] ('measure', in Chinese, having the same sound as 'constellation'). Thus, the Seven Stars are honoured as the great motivators of the heavens as they revolve around the Pole-star; as the balancers of the weal and woe of life; as the rulers of the four quarters of the sphere; as the separators of *yin* and *yang*, and as the governors of the lengths of the seasons, thereby fulfilling many of the Universal Laws.

There is more to learn about the heavens and our earth than all this, however, for we now find that we are floating and almost stationary and are so close to the stars that we find we share many characteristics with them, for none is the same as another, they each have diverse characters and individual natures, each forms connections with the others and, as each star is born, changes, develops, evolves and dies, each makes its own contribution. They have, moreover, all helped to shape life on Earth and have transformed the human race's understanding of the Universe.[7] As we learn more about the stars, however, we find we have also become acutely-aware of the earth we are carrying and, crossing our arms away from the body to more-carefully hold onto such a precious cargo, we find that a powerful emphasis is being placed on those hands and that they and their content have become the rounded symbols of heaven and earth and of the strong connection between both those spheres. Then, whilst ruminating upon this (for it seems to be a confirmation of the influence 'consciousness' has upon 'matter'), we feel a small, but powerful 'tug' in our palms and realise that the energy in the earth is slowly drawing our awareness downwards and that this small, but vital 'pull' is confirming a different, more-elemental link between the earth below and the heavens to which we had been travelling. For the stars of the heavens are linked with the seven metals of earth, by the qualities and powers that the stars confer upon them and so we see that this is of great significance, for the sun and the six major planets, all of which, as has been said, are motivated by the Seven Stars, have correspondences in the earth with the seven main metals mined by man. As gold is linked with the Sun and silver with the Moon, so is Mercury (quicksilver) related with the planet of that name; copper with Venus; iron with Mars; tin with Jupiter and lead with Saturn.[8] And, since – through their powerful terrestrial energies and health-sustaining properties – we are as much influenced in body and mind by those seven metals as by the primordial cosmic set of their seven, corresponding, celestial forces, we are as connected to the metals of the earth and the stars in the skies, as the earth is linked to the heavens through the Pole that unites them.

These powerful astral and earthly influences then offer a further link with the number seven by what has already been mentioned as the seven psychic centres, or *choils*, cavities, wheels or *chakras*, three of which were described in Chapter 69. As the whirling cosmic-energy centres, which are distributed throughout – and powerfully affect – the human body, their driving energy is powered by the *Ch'i*, which, once transmuted into the highest form of spirituality in the Third Treasure of *Shên*, is of such importance in our Journey. Moreover, the Chinese and the Hindu perception of these seven *choils* is almost identical, since it is propounded in both systems that, when the energies of these forces are harmoniously activated to their highest capacities - primarily from specifically chosen, deep-breathing exercises - the rest of the body and all the senses will become activated and free-flowing; physical health and mental equilibrium will be greatly enhanced and, in time, mystical union will occur. Each psychic centre is thus transformed into the purest spiritual energy of 'bright spirit' and, eventually, all centres will be activated upwards through the body, from the *choil* at the base of the torso, to the highest wheel at the crown of the head. Then, when total spiritual fulfilment has taken place, the higher energies will lead the practitioner on towards the realm of the Seven Stars and the home of all the deities of the planetary system: the Paradise of the Taoist Immortals itself.

Jung too conveyed the importance of this seven-starred 'chariot' in the sky when he said that it is a *'model of the structure of the self'*[9] and it is in this light that we can gauge the full depth and range of symbolic meaning in the many titles of this Journey and, not least, the current one. For, as the most notable constellation and guide in the heavens, the Seven Stars are of vital importance to us, since it is towards the true centre of the heavens that they point and it is towards the true centre of ourselves that we have ever-been travelling. Moreover, not only do they point the way to that Pole of Heaven to which we aligned ourselves at the Commencement of this Journey, but that process has been furthered by virtue of its 'ladle' scooping us up towards that resonating sounding board of our own truth and because the T'ai Chi's 'silken thread' (which is 'attached' to that seventh, highest *chakra*), connects us to the Pole Star, so that we may be drawn, spiritually, ever-upwards. Thus, despite the tribulations of Tiger's enduring presence, we have never been severed from the Seven Stars, and their existence has guided our whole Journey towards this Home of The Immortals and to those celestial beings who, having been raised to such a sovereignty of perfection that they transcend the ordinary laws of Nature, fulfil those of the universe.

Still transformed by the Waters of Wisdom, still floating between heaven and earth and still with the metals of the earth in our hands, we sense that all the seven psychic centres of our earthly state are there to awaken us to the consciousness that all things are linked together in that eternal web of the Field of Energy and – as we float, suspended between the two spheres – we see that this has been confirmed a thousand-fold.

Primary Reality, which was so clearly conveyed to us at the beginning of the Stillness, has now become a reality to us. It has always existed and the totality of its immensity has been incomprehensible, but, with the realisation that the energy of each of the Seven Stars harnesses, controls and guides each of the seven main planets in the Zodiac - as well as the changing Seasons and ourselves - we are more-than content. For, with our seven psychic centres providing the link between their corresponding star-vibrations in the heavens and the 'stars' of the earth, we are closer to spiritual fulfilment than ever before and can sense why that light dusting of stardust still envelops us. We also sense that, at some future time, we will again be drawn to – and may even be re-united with - the Seven Stars themselves.

Meanwhile, being made of the same substances as they are: of earth and air, fire and water, spirit and matter, we now, most finely and most delicately, apprehend that:

> *"All things by immortal power*
> *Near or far*
> *Hiddenly*
> *To each other linked are*
> *That thou can't not stir a flower*
> *Without troubling of a star."*[10]

and that the time of floating gently in space is over. Now we must return to earth so that another transformation can take place. Another – and very-different - aspect of our relationship with Tiger is on the horizon and we must be ready. Before this final preparation, however, and with a most extraordinary sense of wonder, we find that we, ourselves, have formed the outline of the Great Bear's dynamic juxtaposition of stars, this *"model of the structure of the self"*, and

have, indeed, fulfilled the title of this movement, for we have: "Stepped up to FORM the Seven Stars"!*

*Astronomers will tell us that the 'head' of The Great Bear is formed by the two stars which point directly to the Pole Star, whilst, in the T'ai Chi movement they are placed at our feet. There can be no doubt, however, that the ancients, who named this movement, were as content as is the author to use the star at the end of the Bear's tail, to relate to our own head. Moreover, the two fists in the movement are not two of the Bear's seven stars, but only one, since it is a double star and is described by Sir Robert Stawell Ball, LL.D., as 'The Beautiful Telescopic Double Star', p.24, "The Story of the Heavens", Cassell & Co, Ltd., London, Paris & Melbourne, 1893.

81 Retreat and Prepare to Ride Tiger

The Retreat as a final Preparation; the wonder of our earthly, erring humanity, and Tiger as the Transcendental Agency

In this difficult world, to stop rushing around,
to sit on soft grass, and know the true ground,
to switch off the world and come back to the earth,
to move with great stillness and yet know sweet mirth,
to let the pure eye see a star, or a face,
a leaf or a blossom – and this exquisite place –
to know that the light of the Tao's in a bee,
and to know that not anything comes from the 'me'.

We were so close and yet so far and, Janus-like, we could see both ways. Ahead lay the poignant, exquisite Taoist Paradise. Behind lay the extraordinary beauty of the earth that we know so well. But, even as we began to form the shape of the Seven Stars, we had felt that sensation in our hands, that small but potent tug, as if the very metals contained in the earth they held were drawing us back to where they had come from, to the depths of soil, to the rocks and caverns, to all the hills and valleys and mountains that they had left behind. And then, even as we drew closer to the outline of the Great Bear itself, the stars ceased to exert their magnetism, the tiny tug became stronger and we began to understand why it had seemed so vital to carry that earthly element with us. Instinctively, we had wanted to retain some part of what we now saw pertained to our mortal, erring, earth-based humanity. Despite the overwhelming power of the call from the heavens, we had not been ready for such an 'absorption into the divine', and the reason for this had lain in our hands. We could not be parted from the earth, we were still connected to it, it was the very ground of our being, but we also realised that we must return those 'stars' of the earth, back to the earth.

So now we sink back. The earth's magnetic energies are deeply-connected to those we are holding, and, hand-in-hand, as it were, they gently, slowly, carefully, lower us back to the ground. But before we reach it, we open our hands and return the earth to the earth, for it has it served its purpose and must be where it belongs. Then, once that re-union has been made, we find why we, too, must land, for the wisdom inherent in the Order of the T'ai Chi titles is guiding us and there is more to be done.

Now we see how each aspect of our Journey has offered opportunities for self-knowledge so that, eventually, we could be in charge of the damaged ego and then do something momentous: we could "Ride the Tiger". Such a preparation has had to be total, has had to occur on every level and has entailed much work, through purifying the physical body, sensitising the mind, clarifying and learning how to deal with the emotions, heightening our psychic and other sensory abilities and giving light to the spirit. And the ability to Ride the Tiger now is near. Proximity to the Source, to the 'pole of heaven', has showered us with illuminating starlight, but it has also revealed that a final Preparation on one more contemplative Retreat must first take place.

So we step back and part the arms in a wide, dramatic and powerfully-dualistic sweep – both slantingly-upwards and diagonally-downwards – as if rending the Veil of Illusion which had had us imagining that we were ready for union with the Seven Stars. But, we are also expressing our gratitude for the manifold blessings that were so recently-bestowed upon us and are affirming both the wonder of our spiritual response to the divine, as well as our imperfect humanity and, thus, are ready for the Retreat.

The monk, the nun, the hermit, the recluse, all those who, either wholly or partially, act upon their need for meditative contemplation and silence are – by virtue of their Retreat – in the process of being in charge of the ego, so that each time it becomes necessary to Ride the Tiger, they may be more-skilled at doing so – and we ponder upon this. We also recollect how, long ago, we had understood that the Tiger would always be with us and that we should embrace it and cradle it in our arms, whilst, paradoxically, we also had to learn how to banish it. Now, another paradox is clarified, for Zen teachings say that, in the world of ordinary, earth-bound mortals, "80% is perfection", and that, whilst undoubtedly there are a few extra-ordinary and deeply spiritual beings on this planet, there is no fully-realised or perfected person on earth, no fully-enlightened or immortal soul amongst us. For, if they were so illumined, they would have been transformed into those such as Kuan Yin or any of the other Bodhisattvas or angels who, invisible to our eyes, but clearly-evident in their ministrations, offer guidance to us as they weave in and our of our lives or direct us from their home in the celestial paradise.

There are, however, a few mortal, but spiritually-empowered, 'pointers' in each generation who help us uncover our imbalances through psycho-analytical or meditational and self-knowledge processes - and we do well to heed them as much as we would a Boddhisattva - but we also need to bear in mind that Jung, himself a 'pointer' of some magnitude, once said: *"... only the most naive of attitudes assumed that the analytical process was aimed at resolving the problems of life. In essence, life was problematical, and men derived their purpose from living it as if in answer to the problem it posed."*[1] Moreover, rarely in the psycho-analytic field is the ego offered up as being the source of the problems of life as a whole.

But now, in response to this, we find that the Tiger stirs. Now, whilst on Retreat, a small paw reaches out, a small claw moves forward, a low purr is heard, an eye becomes visible, a tail-tip lightly lifts, swishes and tilts, and a somewhat subtle, but no less transparent Tiger begins to question this. It does not want to be offered up as being the "source of the problems of life", it is proud of its 'divinely-inspired, spiritual efforts' to overcome itself and, simply by our having a goal of perfection, simply by our yearning and striving for spiritual success, we find that the Tiger has harnessed this endeavour for its own empowerment.

We have made sufficient contact with the Seven Stars, however, for their power to prove the stronger. Sinking into even-deeper meditation, we connect with that which is always, quietly, awaiting release: the alert, spiritual intelligence of the Tao. Compassion then stirs in us for all the mistakes of humanity and we cease to strive, but blend with the Tao, which never strives. We cease to 'go against the grain of things' and, whilst gently acknowledging Tiger's endeavours, retreat further into ourselves, relinquish the goal of egolessness and surrender entirely. And the Tiger retracts its claw, draws back its paw and settles back into slumber.

Then it is that we realise that 'being earthed, being ordinary' is wonderful and that we no longer need be concerned as to whether we Ride the Tiger or not. We no longer need be in charge of anything. We have understood how to live peacefully with the Tiger, our own, as well as those of others. We can step back and yet still belong, realising that such peace, such stillness, will come of its own accord. We can accept that, as stillness follows movement and activity follows rest, so will 'bad' thoughts follow 'good' ones, 'good thoughts' follow 'bad', for each thought is inevitably and inextricably interwoven with its opposite and will always be so for as long as we are mortal. We only need 'choicelessness' to observe them as they slip and slide and pass through the mind, for it is only our limited intellect that turns away from them or labels them as 'likes' or 'dislikes' and removes us from the simplicity of 'becoming the observed', without interference from the observer.

The Retreat then brings us to that peaceful, internal place where we can accept what we are, exactly as we are. Our deep spiritual urge, together with our conditioning and subsequent insecurities, had placed us on this Journey and where we were wrong was in imagining that we – and others - were wrong, which, by implication, meant that the human condition was wrong and even – by inference – that the Tao itself, was wrong…! But, where we were most in error was in having a belief in 'perfection', instead of recognising that all we need is to flow with life, without desiring it to be anything other than how it is.

So now there is some clarity, some perception of the intricacies of the repetitive, but ever-changing self. Some modifications have been made to the psyche, some insights and self-knowledge gained. Fundamental change has eluded us and we have not attained enlightenment, but with all the years of probing and, ultimately, through the grace of contact with the Seven Stars, the ordinary, erring human has emerged who can benefit from the unchanging spiritual essence within, as well as accept the constantly shifting dualities which are part of our 'pole of heaven'. And, having recognised Tiger's self-praise in the spiritual quest, and how it had even allowed us to imagine that we had vanquished it, we see that the spiritual path is, possibly, more beset with traps than any of the secular ones and that its greatest ensnarement is when, feeling so close to spiritual liberation, we imagine that we may, perhaps even 'soon', be permanently inhabiting the very realms of the Seven Stars themselves.

Thus we come to an understanding that: *"parallel straight lines meet only in infinity"* and that this is: *"...not only a religious but a great psychological truth. The great opposites in life, man, things, or even inanimate matter, wherever body and antibody meet through their very opposition ultimately form a common transforming substance. They did steer a strange parallel and irreconcilable course until forced to join each other by some transcendental agency which is an expression of infinite meaning."*[2] In effect, our own parallel lines: the one being our human, dualistic nature and the other being the sense of that *'infinite meaning'* in the Field of the Tao, had been transcended when, for example, we had been in-step-with the Tao in the final Bamboos and, later, when, in those few exalted moments, we had been so close to the Seven Stars - for it was at those times that we had slipped off the harness of our human frailties and had experienced union with the Way of the Tao. In the deepest sense, however, it had been the Tiger that had been the *'transcendental agency'* which had united those two paths. It had been our companion throughout our lives, padding along by our sides and disclosing itself as our shadow when we had blocked ourselves from the light and, because it had caused great inner turmoil, we had been forced to deal with the pain it caused. Without its existence, however, we would never have been moved towards that tremendous urge for inner clarity and truth, nor been led towards some proximity to the divine.

With this in mind, we now find that there is no need to strive. Through stepping back and opening ourselves up to the most profound influences of heaven *and* earth, the Preparation is complete. We can let go to striving; we can let go to the idea of perfection and, by letting go, we suddenly find that we *are* "Riding the Tiger"!

82 Turn Around and Ride the Tiger

In charge of the Tiger

"*Let go! Let go! Let go! Let go! Let go! Let go! Let go!*" – seven times over we these words (one for each of the Seven Stars!) and "*Surrender!*" we say, and we do! And laughter ripples up from our centre and we are filled with joy! For, although the long Journey has been fuelled by our striving for perfection, and our endeavours have been sincere, such total acceptance of the hardships inherent in the Universal Laws has ensured that such striving has no further significance and the difficult physical movement of Riding the Tiger is made all the easier because of it.

We lightly draw back the forward leg. Like dancers trained to focus on a specific point in space, we turn our head towards where we wish to land. We prepare to swing that leg in a wide, horizontal arc, and, having then shifted our focus onto the silken thread at the crown of the head, we rise up and swing the leg as we pivot on the other foot. Sometimes called: "Turn with a hundred-times-trained leg", the reason why is clear: we may-well have to practise the movement a hundred times over, before perfecting the lightness and lack of effort it requires. Or, perhaps, the preparation we have had for the necessary 'lightness', will ensure that we can Ride the Tiger a hundred times over again. However long it takes, or however many more times we have to do it, is irrelevant. What is important is that we understand that we *can* Ride the Tiger – if we do not try too hard. Having absorbed and applied the technicalities and having done the preparation by ceasing to strive in order to achieve, this very difficult movement can be effected smoothly and easily and we can fly around in its crescent-moon swing with light-hearted weightlessness, neither wobbling nor 'falling-off' – and find we can achieve it best of all, *if we do not mind 'falling off'*.

The same applies to the movement's spiritual components. If we try to control the ego with goal-filled effort or are troubled when we fail, we can try a hundred times over and it will still be to no avail. There will be no transformation, and the Tiger will continue to ride us. So, as in the 'Kicking Section', we synchronise the movements with their psychological and spiritual counterparts. When drawing back the forward leg, we further the movement by relinquishing any 'striving to get it right' or fear of non-achievement. When we turn the head and choose where we plan to land, we view ego's interference from a wider perspective. When we swing the leg around in its far-reaching arc, our focus on the crown of the head re-affirms our connection with the Pole Star. And, when all these things coincide, we can 'let go' and Ride the Tiger with lightness and ease.

The movement marks the near-fulfilment of this long, self-probing, spiritual quest, for it is now clear that, when conditioned fear no longer imposes self-protective thoughts onto any action we take or speech we make, we are Riding the Tiger. When we no longer desire life to be different from how it is, we are Riding the Tiger. When we recognise that the spiritual essence of a person can be stronger than the damaged ego and that the Tiger is fearful of contact with such essence, we are Riding the Tiger. When we perceive to what degree the Tiger has endeavoured to survive by attaching itself to the past and has fought with every means possible to divert us from contact with that fine focus of the reality of the 'now', we are Riding the Tiger. And when the self is untroubled by rejection or self-image and we can observe without the observer, we are Riding the Tiger with great skill indeed.

Now, that little Bird of Consciousness, that little sparrow which, to the Chinese, is also known as the Messenger of the Goddess, appears again. Long, long ago, the small child reached out for it and now, after much travail, we connect with that child again with unselfconscious awareness. The ever-shifting, specious mask that so often covered the open, crystal-clear face of self-awareness, comes off and stays off. The higher realms of *Shên* reveal how The Supreme Intelligence of the universe is available to all, so that, regardless of our limitations, we can be committed to life and participate in it so deeply that, frequently, there is mystical union with what we perceive. By such 'letting-go' we can become what we see, whether it be rabbit or river, a snail or its trail. There is no dividing line, no separation. *Ching* is transmuted into *Ch'i*, *Ch'i* into the higher realms of *Shên*. Insight makes tangible the full meaning of the *wu-wei* of life, which derives from a clear perception of what has to be done and how it has to be done, as much as from the stillness of a heart that has no motive for personal gain. Life is lived with the minimum of effort and we use the requisite amount of energy for any action required. Once the action is over, there is no need to dwell upon it, no troubled post-mortems need take place. The Journey has been offering these Taoist teachings from its inception, but it has taken a long time to put the wisdom of such simplicity into practise.

Now our joys arise from the knowledge that 'enough' is richness indeed. Our contentment comes from the goodness inherent in our relationship with – and responsibility towards – all that is. We honour Life and thus are ready for its fullness and by unhesitatingly committing ourselves to everything that it offers, find that it proffers supremely-spiritual riches and aids and abets us in our undertakings. Once responsible and responsive in this way, we live in freedom, and are whole-heartedly available for service to others, for:

> *"Man at his best, like water,*
> *Serves as he goes along:*
> *Like water he seeks his own level,*
> *The common level of life,*
> *Loves living close to the earth,*
> *Living clear down in his heart,*
> *Loves kinship with his neighbors,*
> *The pick of words that tell the truth,*
> *The even tenor of a well-run state,*
> *The fair profit of able dealing,*
> *The right timing of useful deeds,*
> *And for blocking no one's way*
> *No one blames him."[1]*

83 Hands Down and Sweep ('Pluck') the Lotus

Plucking the lotus of joy and spiritual fulfilment

Imagine a small island. Its shores are covered with fine soft sand and, on a clear, sun-filled day, its turquoise blue and crystal clear waters shimmer with tiny bright specks of sunlight. Beneath the waters there are shallows and depths, rocks and crevices, small valleys and slopes, and all are teeming with the life of sea plants, multi-coloured fish and other sea creatures of various sizes and shapes.

On such a bright, clear day, much of what is below the waters is visible, but when the sun is lost to the clouds and the waters are dark, laden with storm or tossed by tempest, nothing can be seen below the surface. Much can be seen on land, however, for groves of bamboo sway nearby and pine trees whisper on its undulating hills. Exotic flowers, sweet-scented jasmine and much trailing honeysuckle abound in the valleys, whilst an almost-impenetrable jungle occasionally comes into view. A magnificent white peacock, a golden rooster and some elegant cranes all walk where they will on their firmly-planted, but delicate feet, and even some mythical, magical phoenixes are seen to appear, as if out of the mists of time, trailing their glory behind them. Other, diagonally-flying, birds – and many, many sparrows – alight on branches, open their beaks in exquisite sound and convey messages of great import to all other birds, creatures and plants – for everything in Nature can penetrate the meaning of all that is offered to them.

Other creatures roam this island: powerful tigers with young cubs, wide-stepping bears and delicate deer, chattering monkeys, untamed horses and slithering snakes (one of which is white), and some of these creatures slip through the hazards of the jungle as they heed the call of a Goddess who leads them through the morass to the many gateways of beauty and wisdom that can be found in the most unexpected of places.

But, when the tempest rages and the skies open with fierce, annihilating rain, then it is that the bamboos and trees, the bushes, the intertwining flowers and the twisting jungle foliage, all toss and sway at the behest of the storm, and the birds, animals and creatures seek their shelter and there remain, until the turmoil is over. All that is, except the tiger, which still can roam and roar at will, because, when wet, simply shakes itself dry in seconds…

There also is a lake in the heart of this island with crystal-clear waters of incredible purity, and mud below of great depth and density. Sometimes the sweet strains of a lute are heard from somewhere nearby; sometimes the Seven Stars, or some gently-waving clouds, are reflected in its waters. Sometimes a human meditates-upon those reflections and much is divined. At other times, veneration occurs, for, out of that mud and upwards through the shimmering water, grows one perfect, solitary plant which culminates in an exquisite flower. Its roots are deeply embedded and emerge from what appears to be a chaos of tangled, twisted growth and the roots themselves are immensely thick and tough. But, out of those resilient, entangled, mud-encrusted roots, the solitary plant moves upwards, infinitely slowly, towards the light of the sun-filled heavens, towards the cosmic power of the moon, towards the luminous, gleaming pole-star of the night. And, even as the pole-star relates to heavenly power, so this plant symbolises ultimate fulfilment: for it is the Lotus of Perfected Wisdom, the Flower of Timeless Purity.

Such an island has already been partly-described in the Gripping the Tiger's Ears' section, when its inhabitants and their unique characteristics were offered as aspects of the Self. Now the analogy surfaces again as the Lotus is added to all the other features and attributes of the island's abundance of life and immense variety of forms, since all of these – and much more – can be seen as parts of ourselves. For, whilst the island as a whole is as unique as any thumb-print, our island is composed of all that encompasses the whole of humanity and, in an attempt to fathom the causes of the powerful undercurrents and meaningful depths that have so disturbed us throughout this Journey, we – like the lotus – have ever-been travelling towards the light and in the process have endeavoured to discern as many aspects of our inner life as were perceptible to the inward-gazing eye. Because we saw ourselves as separate from other islanders, however, alone and isolated, and because we dwelt so often in our shadow-filled shallows, we rarely looked deeply-enough to penetrate the areas below conscious awareness and thus remained unaware that, below the waters, we are as irrevocably connected to each other by vast land-masses, as much as we are linked to everything else that exists.

On occasion, however, when basking in the sun and warmly at peace – or when the inner light was particularly bright and we became conscious of our manifold blessings – some of those inter-connections, some of the teeming life and the immense variety of forms below the surface, became clearer and we united with others and a glow of warmth radiated between us. That warm inner light then began to penetrate the mud of our human depths, and the Lotus of Wisdom that abides, invisible, in the darkness of the unconscious realms, took root and slowly, slowly moved upwards towards the source of the light. Then, if we paused long-enough to allow the mud to settle and looked with greater penetration into the truth of ourselves, we sometimes discovered even-more about the nature of the waters and the connecting land-mass, and united with clarity to some of the deeper, hitherto inaccessible areas within ourselves and each other – and this led to further growth for the Lotus. We also discovered that, by allowing these unconscious truths to penetrate the conscious mind, the islander's ego weakened and the Lotus grew stronger and that, from working on the long, immensely slow process of self-realisation and from deepening the perceptions that result in greater understanding, the Lotus grew even-further in beauty and wisdom. And, when we experienced the purity of a love that over-flows with compassion and protective tenderness, the Lotus moved closer towards its ultimate flowering and fulfilment.

It is because of all this that, in Eastern traditions, the Lotus has for so long been sacred and its journey been symbolic of human spiritual awakening and growth - for the analogy between its muddy roots and our mortal confusions is obvious. Moreover, since the mud is almost impenetrable and the roots are strong and deeply embedded in their earthly environment, it takes great blows to release them from their almost unbreakable adherence to their apparently chaotic environment.

And, yet, despite such a seemingly-obstructive beginning, despite such slowness of movement, and despite such absence of clarity surrounding it, the plant continues to grow until its stalk becomes a pillar like the axis of the world, in readiness for the throne of the flower itself. Then the full blooming of this multi-petalled 'Flower of Light' is revealed, the perfected result of the interaction of the forces of the active *yang* sun upon the yielding *yin* waters of the lake and the muddy earth below. Symbolising our slow, spiritual evolution out of the most complex of human conditions, it eventually reaches its fulfilment.

The Lotus symbolises even-more than this, however, for it conveys the perfection of our world and all that abides in it, because its leaves, the circumference of its petals, its many seeds and all its fruit are circular. It symbolises 'timelessness', because each flower produces buds, flowers and seeds *simultaneously* and thereby offers the past, the present and the future in the totality of one single moment. It symbolises night and day, for its petals open with the dawn of the sun and close with its departure, and, from all of this, it conveys both the wheel of the ever-changing cycles of existence and yet the timelessness of immortality itself.

Now as we move nearer to the end of our Journey, we stand by that lake in the centre of that island and enact the T'ai Chi movement. With heightened awareness of its symbolism and significance, we carefully place the stalk of this unique flower between the toes of a forward-ly-placed foot – and our hands remain facing down. We then swing-up that foot to the left, swoop-up our hands to the right and then, in a swift, sweeping movement, attempt to unite our toes and hands so that we can 'Pluck' the lotus stalk upwards and carry it away. But, in the T'ai Chi class – and in metaphorical terms – we so often miss, connect so rarely, that the notable silence in the room which reveals the lack of the slapping sound which should accompany the swift contact of hands with foot, becomes so palpable that again we bubble over with laughter at our imperfections.

On attempting the movement again, however, we find that there is a magical antidote to this lack of connection. If we look up to the heavens and focus the mind upon the Seven Stars *as we perform the movement*,

we accomplish it with success, thus revealing to what extent the mind can accurately judge the distance between foot and hand, as well as the importance of maintaining our link with the heavens by not allowing the Monkey to *think* (with panic) about the movement. And then, having finally succeeded in Plucking the Lotus, we can fully participate in all the beauty, joy and freedom already offered to us as a result of our ability to Ride the Tiger and partake of the myriad riches of the spiritual state.

Now, the Tiger neither roars nor restrains us and the Monkey ceases to meddle in our minds. Now, we can pluck this flower of Timeless Wisdom without the resistance which so often arises, when, finally nearing a resolution to a deeply-threatening situation, we prefer to 'leave well-enough alone' in order to remain with our inadequacies, because they are so familiar.

We then recognise that the growth of our inner lotus never could have been forced by the chemicals of the intellect and that the flower could only grow organically, in its own time, at its own pace and as it was destined to grow. For then – and only when ready - could we have plucked this flower of life *fully* and with joyfulness. It may take courage and strength to make the attempt and a very long time before we have the capacity to follow the movement through to its ultimate fulfilment, but any such reluctance is understandable, for - in the very moment of plucking the flower from its roots - we are severing the links with our past, with the mud which is our past, with the damage to the ego which is our past and with our separatist individuality. Moreover, once those links are severed, we cannot go back, nor – long term - can we hold back, for if we do not pluck this glorious, shimmering gift in all its beauty, all the suffering, all the apparent chaos, all the pain, all the seeming losses, all that we have perceived as the confusion and misery of our lives, becomes meaningless. Ultimately, there is no choice, the 'dark night of the soul' eventually does lead to the 'dawn of enlightenment' and, if we can pluck that Lotus stalk and use it as a spiritual arrow, we can achieve something we would not have thought possible: we can transform Tiger's power, from moment-to-moment, with the shaft of the Lotus itself.

84 Shoot Tiger With Bow

Instant transformation of Tiger's power with the arrows of spiritual consciousness

As the lion-tamer first seeks to understand the nature of the animal being handled, establish a rapport with it, and only then attempts to master it with the swish of a whip, so have we had to learn the nature of our own Tiger, embrace it as an honest friend who holds-up to us the mirror of truth, and only then attempt to master it with one swift stroke.

Now we come to a movement which reveals that our recent ability to both Ride the Tiger and Pluck the Lotus has liberated us into spiritual freedom and, with much training behind us, we now arrive at a vital movement which indicates that we can annul Tiger's power *at the very moment* when it enters into consciousness.

The movement is called "Shoot Tiger with Bow" and, once having mastered it, we need give no more than a moment's recognition of Tiger's presence, before taking action and defeating it with the arrows of light. Had we not Plucked the Lotus, however, such action would not have been possible, for we would not have the shaft of the lotus stalk to use as our arrow and would not have known the pure joys of instant spiritual freedom which results from its use. Thus, each time Tiger returns to its island, we swiftly recognise its presence, take up our lotus stalk, use it as our spiritual arrow of enlightenment, deliver it with accuracy and skill, and *transform the mind from moment to moment.*

Shooting the Tiger with Bow thus means *instant* transformation and this was clarified by Krishnamurti, when he wrote: *"To bring about some kind of order in daily life, that is transformation; not something extraordinary, out of this world. When one is not thinking clearly, objectively, rationally, be aware of that and change it, break it. That is transformation. If you are jealous watch it, don't give it time to flower, change it immediately. That is transformation. When you are greedy, violent, ambitious, trying to become some kind of holy man, see how it is creating a world of tremendous uselessness... and if you go into it very deeply, transformation means never having a thought of becoming, comparing; it is being absolutely nothing".[1]*

Such a movement also confirms that – despite the joy and freedom inherent in Plucking the Lotus and using its stalk with precision – the brain inevitably will continue with some of its conditioned reactions and function in the same way as does the rest of the body, but that – if our 'will' as 'intention' remains inviolate – a mutation in the mind can occur which gives access to that wider, all-pervading and all-knowing wisdom that empowers *direct* perception with resulting – appropriate - action. Shooting the Tiger thus is not a clever trick of the mind, nor a feat of the imagination, but an instant response to a spiritual perception that reveals how dangerous it is for the Tiger to invade the inner reservoir, that peace-filled space within - and that such a swift awareness of ego's presence then does the work of the banishment by enabling the action of Shooting the Tiger to be swift, clean and simple.

"Putting the Government in exile" is how another Indian spiritual teacher spoke of it*, recognising that the Tiger is never eliminated entirely from the human condition and that Shooting the Tiger does not cause Tiger's permanent 'death', but only removes it from consciousness at the moment when it lands-upon what it considers to be its own, considerable territory.

So, we banish the Tiger in order that our inner and outer life can be in harmony with our natural state, or what the Chinese call the "uncarved block". No falsity or contrivance need mar its simplicity, nothing extraneous need overlay its essence, and although it might seem to the Tiger that such living costs no less than everything it normally considers essential, such banishment can ensure that we can creatively balance our lives on a daily basis.

The preparation for Shooting the Tiger has been infinitely slow, and has occurred through a complex process of spiritual evolution, but its fulfilment has arrived – and has happened suddenly. The journey to that point can be explained: *"... in true Taoist fashion by reference to water. Bringing cold water to the boil is a gradual process; yet, at a certain*

*Pherozshah Dorabji Mehta

temperature, the change from non-boiling to boiling is sudden. In other words, for those not fortunately gifted with unsought intuition, preparation for attaining it is gradual and often arduous, but the intuition or illumination, when it comes is, of course instantaneous. "[2] These experiences thus arise in those few moments in time when, either unsought or as a result of our spiritual, meditational work, the mind is ego-free.

Other similar – though usually-unbidden - illuminations have been experienced by men and women of every tradition and creed. Known as wonder-filled 'epiphanies' in the West, they are known in the East as *satori* and, in China, as the '*wu*' of *wu-wei*, whilst: a State of Grace, the Hand of God, Contact with Essential Mind, an experience of Transcendent Peace Descending are just some of the many descriptions of these divine states. And, whilst nearly all such experiences are of short duration, they can remain forever in the mind and, in some instances, have shaped a whole way of life. All contribute towards a state of awe and wonder, as well as enlightenment, however, and, in the context of the T'ai Chi, relate to the spiritual results that can arise from absorbing the meaning in the movement we are about to make.

Physically, Shooting Tiger with the Bow of our lotus shaft indicates that we are using a smaller, Oriental bow and arrow than its large, Occidental counterpart, for, when using the latter, most archers stand. Our T'ai Chi posture indicates something other than this, however, for our legs are widely-placed, both hands are raised in a curve, and the eyes are assessing the position of a target on the ground below. We therefore realise that there must be another, somewhat unexpected factor to contend with, for - since it is unlikely that the target is poised on the ground, quietly awaiting our arrow - it is palpably clear that we must be riding an animal, be it horse, donkey, ox or ass, and that aiming with economy of effort and precision of aim at a moving target is vital, if we are to succeed.

Thus, since our Tiger can be as swift in the mind as any animal in full gallop and can appear in many guises, the last of the Ten Essential Points, "Seek Serenity in Action" is what is needed now. So, we follow all the precepts and focus with 'intention' and only then take aim and unleash our arrow. And yet, for all our awareness of what is needed, for all our experience, and for all our proximity to the Source, sometimes, somehow – as in Plucking the Lotus – we miss. Undeniably, accuracy is not easy when riding on, as well as aiming at, a swiftly-moving animal, but perhaps our 'intention' was blurred, or we were still re-acting to life instead of utilising our lotus shaft with *wu-wei*? Perhaps the Tiger was too quick for us, or maybe the Tiger was doing the shooting!? Or, as often happens in the T'ai Chi itself (which, after all, is a metaphor for life and sometimes appears to be so complex that we 'forget how to do it', or we keep our understanding of its meaning as if in parenthesis, separately contained from daily living, un-released and unrealised), perhaps we had no faith in our ability to master the action? We continue to utilise the remaining opportunities which life gives us to practise our spiritual archery, however, and – given that we are, by now, deeply aware that we are shooting at our own ego - just sometimes we focus with ease and swiftly grasp the lotus shaft, aim with a clear perception of the target and then – with superb precision – let fly the inner arrow. The action is seamless, our aim is true and there is joy from the sweet resonance of accuracy.

85-86 Circle Fist and Body; Twisted Step; Deflect Downwards; Strike (Intercept) and Punch; Withdraw (Yielding) and Push

The spirit of androgyny fulfilled; the Wonderful Hand of No-Form; the eleventh and final Gateway to Wisdom and a vision of the Nameless

The Journey of the Spirit has been described to us in a multitude of ways, either through the words offered by those who, themselves, have had some capacity for psychological wholeness and spiritual grace and who have experienced some of the attributes of the mystical state, or through the inspirational guidance offered by Taoism. From much of this, we have been led to understand that our inability to easily-incorporate those teachings into daily life relates to the imbalance of the proportions of *yin* and *yang* in our psyche and this was confirmed by Carl Gustav Jung, who spent a life-time in the study of these imbalances. He was in accord with the Taoist perception that - as he termed it in his concept of 'individuation' - *full* realisation of the *yang* masculine and *yin* feminine archetypes within us was the imperative, and he also recognised, as does Taoism and other spiritual teachings, that a yearning for such 'harmony within duality' is the foundation from which we spiritually transform and grow.

Such androgyny is perceived as the blending of the masculine and feminine principles in consciousness and an embrace of both in thought and action. And, whilst few fulfil this potential (perhaps because our conditioned consciousness is so strongly influenced by our gender), it is, nevertheless, considered in many spiritual traditions that psychological one-sidedness need not be a permanent factor of human existence, but can be seen as a transient – albeit necessary – stage of our long journey towards self-awareness. Thus, it could be said that the duality inherent in the masculine and feminine principles emerges from the Oneness of the Great Void; that they then form the physical, mental and emotional foundation for the duality and differentiation which is our human condition; that psychological androgyny is the next stage which leads to the unfolding of spiritual non-differentiation and that, once this has been achieved, such unity and sense of wholeness lead on to the final Return to the Source of Oneness again.

Much, therefore, has already been said on this Journey about duality and much work has been done, by various processes, in order to achieve a degree of harmony within it. We have learnt that today is not as yesterday; that tomorrow will be unlike either - and to cling to neither of them by doing only what is required and then leaving it behind. We have learnt to yield to change as radically as each day does to the day before and to the day to come. We have learnt that female intuition can sense when to respond with masculine clarity and that male action can incorporate female pliability and, thus, how to refrain from inappropriately intruding female intuition upon circumstances that require a masculine, rational response, and vice versa. We have seen that 'expectation' and 'hope' and 'coming to conclusions' are concepts to be avoided and that, although repetitions occur in our lives that may have similar foundations – and that we are drawn to 'the familiar' – there always will be 'change within no-change'. We have recognised the importance of answering to life with a freshness, a fluidity, a simplicity and a spontaneity, as if in an ever-shifting continuum of adaptability that is without self-conscious or stereotyped role-playing, and we have learnt about *wu-wei*, or action that is free from the Tiger. Thus, whilst duality will ever-remain an integral part of the cosmic ordering of the Seven Stars, we recognise that all that we have learned enables the opposites in life to coalesce as time and events dictate, whilst androgyny can be used creatively as an integral part of the human condition, as well as a preparation for union with the Field, or Source, of cosmic order.

Now our Tiger is just a dot on the horizon (or, more often than not, only a memory), and our view of the world no longer contains the dilemma caused by the divisive nature of choice. Now, we can discover whether all that we have attained, can be sustained, and we exemplify this by putting into the T'ai Chi's physical form some of the psychological and spiritual processes referred to above, for they have produced a chemical change in the body as well as a mutation of mind which is greater than the sum-total of *yin* and *yang* combined.

A short series of movements now takes place, the titles of which imply that Tiger is still in control, still active and - if we had not been prepared for 'change within no-change' – we would have wondered at their inclusion at this late stage of the Journey. Instead, all the *Fist and Twist, Deflect, Strike, Punch and Push* movements we now portray indicate that, finally, we have fulfilled the Supreme Ultimate *Use* of the *Chüan*. The Tiger, and all its potent elements, has been transformed by the powerful energy of *Shên* into the 'transcendental agency' mentioned previously, and this spiritual energy is now utilising, instead of neutralising, the Tiger, in the same way as it did in the recent Ride the Tiger and Pluck the Lotus movements. Now, all the *yang* elements in these current movements have been absorbed into their opposite, whilst those of the open-handed *yin* movements that follow have done the same, thereby indicating that a powerfully-androgynous shift of emphasis has taken place.

Now, we enact these familiar movements from such a different perspective that we slip into these oft-repeated actions with a warm and happy consciousness that pervades our being and with such a softness and a strength that any observer might find it difficult to distinguish between the *yin* and *yang* emphases in these complementary opposites - for they have sinuously evolved into what we now understand to be the foundation of the Form. Through the combination of both 'gender' qualities, we now are wholly balanced and our final wave-like Withdrawal and Push represents the Universal Law of the union of opposites and of the use of energy in its purest form. Action is then utterly effective and simple and altruistic reciprocity arises in its wake.

This then clarifies the meaning of the whole Journey and, whilst experiencing such rhythmic equilibrium, it is as if we are enfolded in an impartial and beautifully-harmonised aura of wholeness which reminds us of how we felt when, so recently, we were enveloped in stardust. For, there is 50% *yang* and 50% *yin* in all the actions, instead of, as hitherto, a clearly-identifiable Tiger-filled *yang* emphasis on those movements that either preceded or followed-upon those that are clearly spiritual and softly *yin*. There is an equality of firm 'intention' within and pliable 'yielding' without and, when such a fusion of opposites in action occurs, it is known as the "No-Form of the Empty Hand", or the "Wonderful Hand of the T'ai Chi Ch'üan".

Now there is no necessity to strike or punch, in the same way as – previously - we no longer felt the need to kick-out at life or even Ride the Tiger and, when portraying all this, we appear to float in a heightened stream of energy that has arisen from the realms of utter simplicity - and yet we are also 'grounded'. Furthermore, when we practise the rare but Wonderful Hand of No-Form, we can be all forms and all ways, for we have reached a place in the psyche where we have become No-Form, without loss of essence. The personal identity which had made us feel separate and different from others has dissolved and a being has evolved which is filled with light. 'Oneness' becomes our foundation and it is said that a butterfly alighting upon that Wonderful Hand would find no base from which to take off...

The palm of the hand (which closes to form the *Ch'üan* of the fist) is known to the Chinese as "The Palace of Work" - and there is no doubt we *have* worked hard on the *Ch'üan*. But now we are ready to fulfil the state of the No-Form of the Wonderful Hand outside the T'ai Chi class room and are given another example of this which is similar to those already given in Chapter 46: some students were walking and talking along a corridor in an American university, when, on turning a corner, they found that they were about to 'bump into' a professor who was coming from the opposite direction. Instead of causing a collision, and possibly some physical damage, they found that they had moved against what they later described as being 'only a coat' and this was because the professor – who was also a T'ai Chi expert – had so swiftly assessed the situation and so easily slipped out of it, that it was as if he had not been there at all. He had developed the art of 'No Form'; had put it into practise the moment it was needed, and then gone on his way.

Another example of No-Form comes from Chuang Tzu:

"If a man is crossing a river
And an empty boat collides with his own skiff,
Even though he be a bad-tempered man
He will not become very angry.
But if he sees a man in the boat,
He will shout at him to steer clear,
If the shout is not heard, he will shout again,
And yet again, and begin cursing.
And all because there is somebody in the boat.
Yet if the boat were empty,
He would not be shouting, and not angry.

If you can empty your own boat
Crossing the river of the world,
No one will oppose you,
No one will seek to harm you."[1]

Our androgynous spiritual energy has thus brought other good results, for we, too, can dissolve into the moment, *as and when needed,* as if, externally, we were wearing a *yang,* impenetrably-protective and colourful coat that could de-materialise instantly into a *yin,* gossamer-like silken cloak, which – though hitherto imbued with all the colours of the rainbow – can suddenly becomes as amorphous as a cloud. *Yang* can unfold into *yin,* and *yin* into *yang,* as and when required, and thus we can be both. Through the use of instinctual discipline and the perfected coordination of both sides of the brain, we can symbolise the harmony of heavenly intervention and earthly concordance, in the most androgynous of ways. Moreover, when we have mastered the movements of the T'ai Chi 'to the Right', each side of the brain and each side of the body is fully-operational, whilst the same applies when we have learnt how to reverse the movements by doing them 'To the Left'. When, then, we form two lines, facing each other, in order to do what is known as the "Mirror Version", with one group doing it to the Right and the other to the Left, we further this androgyny, for then we become totally aware of ourselves, as well as of everyone else for the entire 25 minutes of the Long Form, and all the colours and all the movements flow together in unison, and in the same direction.

Now, we gladly take what life is offering and live with a spontaneous, open-hearted and serene response to the problems that life imposes. With this enactment of the penultimate stages of our Journey, we are ready for the final stage. We came from the Void and to the Void we

338

must return and, with our final Push, the eleventh and final Gateway to Wisdom opens to reveal the indescribable beauty, serenity and depth of stillness at the heart of Enlightenment. Then, with this overwhelming moment of realisation – and almost blinded by the beauty - the immanence of 'That which is Nameless' is revealed and our joy in a vista that is both boundless and endless, is beyond anything that, hitherto, we could ever have imagined.

87-88 THE GRAND TERMINUS: CROSS HANDS, THE CONCLUSION OF THE T'AI CHI CH'ÜAN, AND THE END OF THE JOURNEY

The P'o and the Hun souls, and the Return to the Source

"But consider the Tao, which transcends both finite and infinite. Since the Tao is All and nothing lies outside it, since its multiplicity and unity are identical, when a finite being sheds the illusion of separate existence, he is not lost in the Tao like a dew-drop merging with the sea; by casting off his imaginary limitations, he becomes immeasurable. No longer bound by the worldly categories, 'part' and 'whole', he discovers that he is coextensive with the Tao. Plunge the finite into the infinite and, though only one remains, the finite, far from being diminished, takes on the stature of infinity. Mere logicians would find fault with this, but if you perceive the hidden meaning you will laugh at their childish cavils. Such perception will bring you face to face with the true secret cherished by all accomplished sages - glorious, dazzling, vast, hardly conceivable! The mind of one who Returns to the Source thereby <u>becomes</u> the Source. Your own mind, for example, is destined to become the universe itself!"[1]

The man who spoke those words was one who was old and wise and whose inner vision was as serene and vast as it was exalted. He was a Taoist who lived in the last century and, although recognized by others as an Immortal, had been driven from his mountain retreat and now lived his life as a layman in an unobtrusive dwelling in a large capital city. His name was *Tsêng Lao-wêng* and the man to whom he spoke

- a Buddhist seeker of great erudition and spiritual advancement - had sought him long and from afar.

The snow had been heavy and the journey difficult, but, on arrival at the house, the seeker was offered neither tea nor warmth, but was directed by a servant to sit in the same room as the Taoist layman and two other men, whilst they meditated in unmoving and deep silence. There he remained, tired, cold, hungry and thirsty – and even somewhat impatient at this long delay in finally speaking with the Master whom he had sought for so long – when, slowly, a change took place within him and his exhaustion was forgotten and he began to experience such heightened sensations of well-being and buoyancy that he understood them to be "*...a strikingly intense form of the joy that comes from being in the presence of a person of great mystical achievement.*" An exquisite happiness then enveloped him, together with a feeling that the "*...entire cosmos, lovely, shining and beautifully ordered, was somehow contained within the narrow confines...*" of his own head.[2]

This experience did not last – although its significance did - and, as our own journey leads us towards this mystical Source, we too consider the words of this Master and of how it is said that the Tao transcends life and death, the finite and the infinite and what unutterable bliss there must be in merging oneself with all that is, has been, and ever will be and, thus, be "*destined to become the universe itself*".

We sense how the numinous exists throughout the universe and how the mystic, the sage, the monk at prayer – and those such as the Buddhist seeker - all have revealed how profound has been their yearning for that which can never be known by the rational mind; how deep has been their search for the sublime impact of contact with its nameless essence, how great has been their thirst for that which is inscrutable – and that even those whose lives may appear to have been arid and without worth, may well-have been blessed with such a divine calling and had experienced, at least in part, a sense of that ineffable 'something' which is not bound by death.

There also have been the many mystics of many faiths who, after long periods of meditation and prayer, have described what they experienced as a Union with the Sublime or a Return to the Source and have spoken of their awareness of a perfect identification with what, in essence, is nameless. Their words of elation, bodily lightness, sensations of bliss, radiance, ecstasy, joy, of being surrounded by brilliance and light – and the intensity inherent in their descriptions of the Absolute – clearly have indicated a freedom from ego that is almost palpable. Accounts of their lives, too, reveal how abundant is their gay serenity, their wisdom and compassion, their inner harmony and simplicity of action, and of how impervious they are to cold, heat, hunger, human error or even woe – for they see divinity in all things. Thus, their world: *"... loses its terrors; laughter comes so easily that accomplished adepts are frequently mistaken for simpletons. Death is no more to be feared than dropping off to sleep on a summer afternoon. As the mind, no longer fettered by duality, joyously recognizes its unity with pure, bright, illimitable Mind — the Tao, the Godhead — there comes a sense of being able to soar throughout the universe at will."*[3]

None of this implies that the end of our mortal lives need be death-bound and, thus inspired by these and many other accounts of the mysterious, yet ever-possible union with the Nameless Source, the information derived from them not only confirms that the blessings of a profound spiritual life on this earth are founded on reality, but that (as if such riches were not enough), when union with the Tao or the Ultimate, one's Buddha nature, Atman, the Divine, Christ, or *Sunyata* has been attained and sustained, bliss there can be after death, as well.

The Chinese tradition in this is no different, but their view of life after death varies from many other traditions in that they speak of two souls – the *(yin) P'o* and the *(yang) Hun* – which unite at birth and, on death, can continue so; can be separated on death and then re-united some time thereafter, or can be parted forever if the *Hun* soul has achieved a state of supreme holiness and purity.

The first soul, the *P'o*-soul, stems from the earth and is the heavier and darker of the two. Arriving in the womb from the moment of conception, it is the only soul in the child throughout gestation and, thus, is the first of the two souls to inhabit the body. It relates to the corporeal form and to all the bodily functions and sensations, from which all physical growth occurs. It is earth-bound and, because the generative system (the *Ching* or essence, as the first of the Three Treasures) depends upon it in order to function, it is this soul which continues the physical survival of mankind on earth.

On death, the *P'o*-soul may linger awhile at the grave of the deceased and, it has to be said, can cause some disquiet to family members if the funeral arrangements or filial sacrifices are not as they should be. If all is well, however, it eventually sinks down to the earth from whence it came and, together with the physical body, rests in the Realms of Shade and there, sometimes, disintegrates. If the *P'o*-soul has inhabited a person of ill-repute, however, who has despised or despoiled it, it can descend and then return in the form of an undesirable ghost, demon or perfidious animal spirit and many and varied are the possible permutations devised by the human mind to account for the, sometimes, ghoulish visitations which can harass the living, whilst highly-ingenious methods are used by the Chinese to negate the effects of these most unwelcome arrivals on hearth and home.

At birth, the soul of the second *yang* category, the *Hun*-soul, comes forth from the 'great emptiness' of cosmic breath and, on entering the body to unite with the *P'o*-soul, manifests in the first cry of the new-born infant. As the 'breath soul' and vitality itself, it lives in the eyes when open during the day as an expression of our health and consciousness, and is housed in the liver at night, when the eyes are closed and we sleep. As *Ch'i*, it is, thus, the second of the Three Treasures to arrive and the first soul to depart the body on our last breath. However, if spiritually un-evolved and the person has lived in ignorance of – or denied – the spiritual components of her or his individuality, immediate dissolution must be the fate of the *Hun*-soul on death, for, having transmuted into the lower aspects of *Shên*, it must then descend to await, and then unite with the *P'o*-soul on the latter's arrival, when both might then disintegrate. In contrast, if some degree of spiritual purity has been attained by the individual, the *Hun*-soul can survive as spirit after death for varying lengths of time; can be concerned about those it leaves behind and can be available and called back by the voices (the breath) of its kith and kin. Such contact is only deemed possible, however, if the members of the family or friends have used the processes of meditation and fasting to focus their thoughts and feelings on those who have departed;

have recalled how they spoke, joked, thought, felt and behaved in general, and, thereby, have gained access to their ways.

The vital spiritual force and the movement toward eventual union with the divine thus are due to the components of the *yang, Hun*-soul, whilst the bodily form, functions and senses are governed by those of the *yin, P'o*-soul. The two souls are united at birth by breath and consciousness, and are separated when, in time, we die; can be re-united with each other immediately, or at varying intervals, thereafter, or not at all, whilst it is also believed that the longest time a more highly-evolved *Hun*-soul can survive after death is five generations, since it can be accessed through the living memory of those who, like many a Chinese, have survived into great longevity.

This, then, accounts for the aspect of the *Hun*-soul of a more-evolved being, for, being the lighter of the two souls (as the heavens are to the earth), it can rise upwards from the fontanel, the Thousand-petalled Lotus area (which is shaved by monks in order for cosmic light to enter or leave the body), into the light of the upper air, to there become beneficent spirit, fairy, glad ghost, angel or joy-filled genie and thus can continue in a spiritual form as the purer components of the deceased's personality and individual essence and even by the name by which the departed was known in the family group.

Much has been written about the *Hun*-soul in relation to how long it can survive as *Shên* or spirit after its 'owner' has died, but it is clear that the Chinese believe that its ultimate destination occurs when the person whose body it has inhabited has evolved into the highest form of the Third Treasure of *Shên* as cosmic spirit, for then - having become one of those Immortals who choose to fly freely between heaven and earth in recognizable human-form on any creature of their choice, and can change their gender and garb at will - they can, in appropriate guise, exert their considerable marvel-working powers on our well-being and spiritual development on earth.

But, what propels them so serenely between the Taoist Paradise and our earthly world? It would seem that they have a divine combination of choices, for: if their 'chariot' of crested crane, flowing-tailed phoenix, or magnificent dragon (which is considered the most-venerable of all creatures) has not wings of its own, they can draw-upon the energies of all seven of their whirling, psychic-energy *choils* to propel them upwards to the Seven Stars, and use the magnetic pull of the seven star-metals in the earth to gently lower them down again; can deploy any available slip-stream of energy, breath of wind or gust of rain, according to the direction required; float on a passing cloud, or harness the incredibly-powerful magnetic energy of the North and South extremities of the earth's axis to transport them directly to and from the heavens! And, since such flights have been described as: *"... floating off at times to merge with the primordial condition beyond the universe of form"*, it can be seen that such 'flying' *"... is a state of consciousness in which all sense of self and other, of heaven and earth has vanished..."*.[4] And thus flew:

> *"Lo, the Immortal, borne by spirituality,*
> *His hand grasping a lotus flower,*
> *Away to Time everlasting,*
> *Trackless through the regions of Space!*
> *With the moon he issues from the Ladle,*
> *Speeding upon a favourable gale; ...*
>
> *Now passed beyond the bounds of mortality..."*[5]

Thus, if full and final spiritual Realization and Union with the Source has become the very ground and essence of the being, the finite will merge with the infinite - as described earlier by the Taoist sage, *Tsêng Lao-wêng* - and the *Hun*-soul then can transmute into a *Pu Sa*, or an Immortal and be perpetually immersed in the Tao, taking up residence with the Star God of Longevity in the Region of the Seven Stars and continuing forever as a purified, free, ethereal *Shên* spirit residing in the Taoist Paradise.

As a result of all this, Taoists do not necessarily believe in the Buddhist Theory of Reincarnation, since (pragmatically) it is considered that the ever-increasing pyramid-structure of human population-growth makes the sheer mathematics of the concept of one deceased person's soul entering into the body of another who is newborn, unrealistic, whilst (spiritually), due to their belief in two souls; that heaven and earth are eternal, and that Immortality is a spiritual condition which unites *both* spheres when the *Hun* soul has achieved its highest fulfilment, it is immaterial as a concept. What they do believe, however, is that vast galaxies arrive, new stars are born, that we come from the stars and return to their source.

From all this it can be seen that, for the sage and the mystic, the Tao holds more ecstasy, mystery and fulfillment than can ever be known by the corporeal self in its often misguided, ego-filled *P'o*-soul - or even by the spiritually-evolving *Hun*-soul - and that the further the being moves into emptiness and unknowing, the more he or she can be transformed into blissfully-receptive instruments for the union with the universe that is the source of our being.

Now in the T'ai Chi Ch'üan, we turn to the North again to where the Seven Stars have ever-been guiding us and, with arms spreading wide, we reach out to all the opposites of existence before drawing them in towards ourselves in an embracing movement of pure, untainted joy. Uniting creation and dissolution, life and death, we finally depict an entry into the realm of the axis of heaven, the mid-way point of balance, the place between the rising and the setting sun. Crossing our hands in front of our chest in a sublime moment of grace acquired, we turn our palms outwards and then raise them up to the luminous splendour of the stars, to the greatest and most sublime sources of power and influence on earth. The evolution of the *Hun*-soul into the highest form of

Shên, the purest of spirit, is thus portrayed and, in a wonderfully-fulfilling movement of consciousness, we convey its final journey to the heavens by symbolically returning it to the Source of All Being.

Then, with equally sublime awareness, we move our hands downwards to convey the *P'o*-soul to its final, earthly realm.

Joyfully, gently, these final movements portray the departure of both souls in the most movingly-graphic perfection of physical symbolism. In a state of pure fulfillment, we find that the Journey, which slowly has taken us from emptiness into form, from form into emptiness, now delivers us in spirit towards the vast and ultimate Source from which, in truth, we have never been severed. In deep repose, we stand in the Stillness, as at the beginning of our Journey, and experience the profound peace of the circle of spiritual energy, which is both around and within us. We have come full circle and are re-united with the seamless state of the womb of the Tao. Enveloped by the Stillness, we have completed the whole of the Form, just to end it as and where we were when first we began. Having travelled far, we now find that 'home' is where we really are.

Integrated and inter-connected, the transformation - which is empowered by the ever-changing, ever-renewable energy of the universe - is complete. We stand, encircled by the cosmic aura, and the more we lose corporeal awareness and enter into the world of spirit, the further the invisible energy extends outwards in ever-widening dimensions. Time and space no longer signify. Dissolving, dissolving, dissolving the body, we enter into and become ever-widening circles of light, at-one with the stars themselves.

And then it is that we sense how the mind, the essence, the spirit of being, the infinite and the finite, all unite within the Source and become one with the Universe, the true nature of which can only be known to those sublime and exalted beings who, having realized it for themselves, reside at its heart.

APPENDIX A

Within the

|

UNIVERSE

|

there exists the seamless

|

SOURCE

|

and the

|

STILLNESS

|

of the

|

Indescribable Way

|

of

|

TAO

|

which manifests in

|

ONE-NESS   NON-DUALITY   WHOLENESS

|

from which arises

|

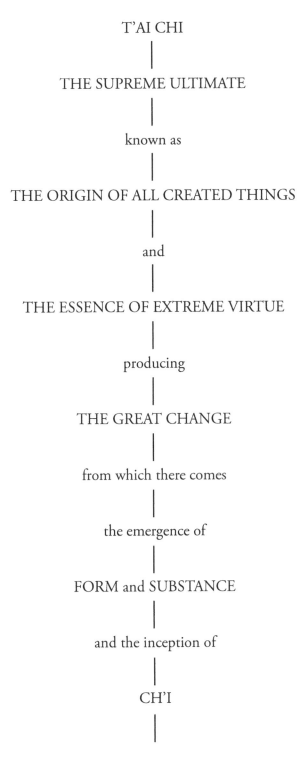

T'AI CHI

|

THE SUPREME ULTIMATE

|

known as

|

THE ORIGIN OF ALL CREATED THINGS

|

and

|

THE ESSENCE OF EXTREME VIRTUE

|

producing

|

THE GREAT CHANGE

|

from which there comes

|

the emergence of

|

FORM and SUBSTANCE

|

and the inception of

|

CH'I

|

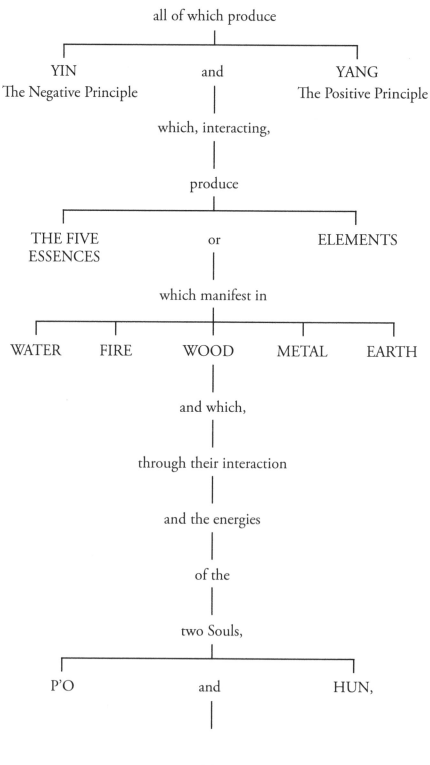

all of which produce

YIN   and   YANG
The Negative Principle   The Positive Principle

which, interacting,

produce

THE FIVE   or   ELEMENTS
ESSENCES

which manifest in

WATER   FIRE   WOOD   METAL   EARTH

and which,

through their interaction

and the energies

of the

two Souls,

P'O   and   HUN,

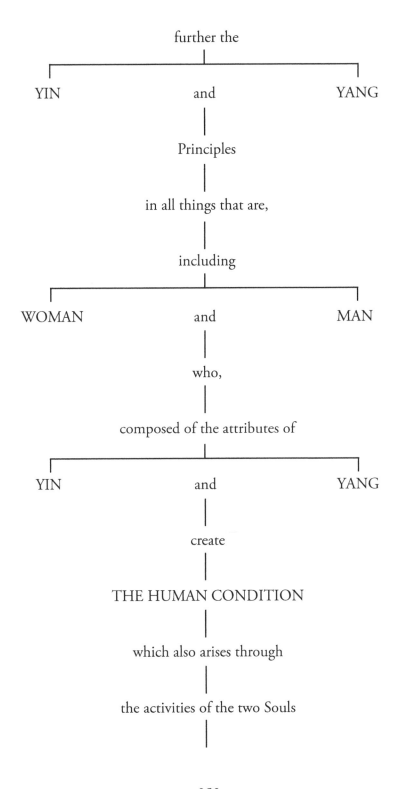

further the

YIN   and   YANG

Principles

in all things that are,

including

WOMAN   and   MAN

who,

composed of the attributes of

YIN   and   YANG

create

THE HUMAN CONDITION

which also arises through

the activities of the two Souls

and the

|

THE THREE SPIRITUAL ENERGIES

|

of

|

CHING: the energy of the HEART,

|

manifesting in the

|

GENERATIVE FORCE;

|

CH'I: cosmic energy, the life force

|

manifesting as

|

BREATH,

|

and

|

SHêN: higher consciousness,

|

or cosmic ('bright') spirit,

|

manifesting as

|

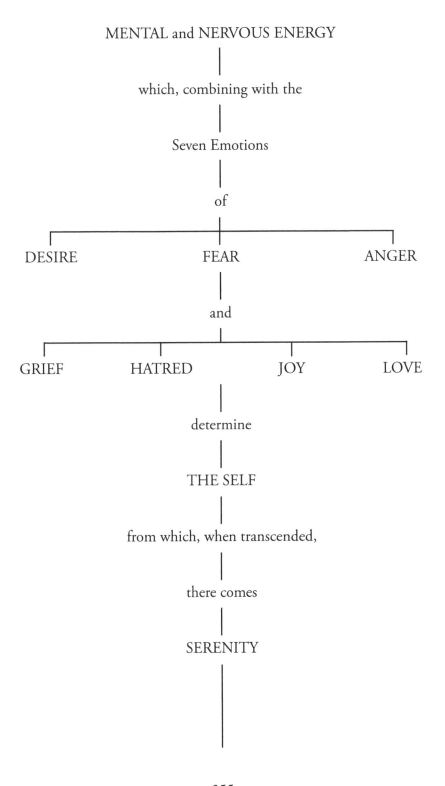

MENTAL and NERVOUS ENERGY

|

which, combining with the

|

Seven Emotions

|

of

DESIRE   FEAR   ANGER

|

and

GRIEF   HATRED   JOY   LOVE

|

determine

|

THE SELF

|

from which, when transcended,

|

there comes

|

SERENITY

out of which arises

ONE-NESS　　　　　NON-DUALITY　　　　　WHOLENESS

and the

Indescribable Way

of

TAO,

together with the

STILLNESS

within the seamless

SOURCE

of the

UNIVERSE

Appendix B

THE TEN ESSENTIAL POINTS OF MASTER _YANG_ CHING-PU

1   Suspend your head from above and keep it up straight.

2   Lower your chest and lift your upper back.

3   Loosen your waist.

4   Distinguish between solidness and emptiness.

5   Drop your shoulders and lower your elbows.

6   Apply your will (as 'intention'), and not your force.

7   Co-ordinate your upper and lower body movements.

8   Unify your internal and external movements.

9   Apply absolute continuity to your movements.

10   Seek serenity in activity.

References

Please note that, despite extensive research, some copyright references could not be obtained and these are marked with an asterisk. If further information is available about their copyright ownership, kindly contact the publisher of this book.

1   Ssu-K'ung T'u, Lotus and Chrysanthemum: an anthology of Chinese and Japanese poetry, p.63, "Motion", Joseph Lewis French (sel.ed.), H.A. Giles (transl.), Liveright Publishing Corp., New York, 1934.*

Chapter 1

1   Bohm, David, The Holographic Paradigm and other Paradoxes: exploring the leading edge of Science, Wilber, Ken (ed.), pp.21-22, Shambhala, Boulder, and London, 1982.*
2   Ibid, p.22, believed to be out of print.

Chapter 2

1   Lao Tzu, The Way of Life according to Lao Tzu, Bynner, Witter (transl.), No.6, p.28, Capricorn Books, New York, 1962, reprinted with Permission from The Witter Bynner Foundation for Poetry.
2   Chuang Tzu, The Way of Chuang Tzu, "Action and Non-action", Merton, Thomas (transl.), p.80, George Allen and Unwin Ltd., London, 1970, copyright © 1965 by The Abbey of Gethsemani. Reprinted by permission of New Directions Publishing Corp. N.Y.

Chapter 3a

1   Lao Tzu, The Way of Life according to Lao Tzu, No.25, Bynner, Witter (transl.), p.40, Capricorn Books, New York, 1962, reprinted with Permission from The Witter Bynner Foundation for Poetry.

Chapter 3b

1 Lao Tzu, *The Way of Life according to Lao Tzu*, Bynner, Witter (transl.), No.76, p.73, Capricorn Books, New York, 1962, reprinted with Permission from The Witter Bynner Foundation for Poetry.

2 Blofeld, John, *The Secret and Sublime: Taoist Mysteries and Magic*, p.176, © George Allen and Unwin Ltd., 1973. Reprinted by permission of HarperCollins Publishers Ltd. (U.K) and by Dutton, a division of Penguin Group (USA) LLC.

Chapter 4

1 Li Po and Tu Fu, *Li Po and Tu Fu*, Cooper, Arthur © (select. & transl. with introduction and notes), p.224, Penguin Books, Harmondsworth, 1973, reproduced by permission of Penguin Books Ltd.

2 Ibid.

Chapter 5

1 Jung, C.G., excerpt from *Memories, Dreams, Reflections*, p.414, © Fontana Paperbacks, London, 1983, reprinted by © permission of HarperCollins Publishers Ltd. (UK) and translation copyright © 1961, 1962, 1963 and renewed 1989, 1990, 1991 by Random House LLC. Used by permission of Pantheon Books, an imprint of the Knopf Doubleday Publishing Group, a division of Random House LLC. All rights reserved. Any third party use of this material, outside of this publication, is prohibited. Interested parties must apply directly to Random House LLC for permission.

2 Lao Tzu, *The Way of Life according to Lao Tzu*, Bynner, Witter (transl.), No.35, p.47, Capricorn Books, New York, 1962, reprinted with Permission from The Witter Bynner Foundation for Poetry.

Chapter 6

1 Yang Wan-li, *Heaven My Blanket, Earth My Pillow – poems from Sung-Dynasty China,* "Walking in the Office Garden on a Warm Spring Day", Jonathan Chaves (transl.), p.61, published by John Weatherhill Inc. New York, 1975 and reprinted with permission by White Pine Press, 2004.

2 Lao Tzu, *The Way of Life according to Lao Tzu*, Bynner, Witter (transl.), No.16, p.34, Capricorn Books, New York, 1962, reprinted with permission from The Witter Bynner Foundation for Poetry.

3 Ibid. No.10, p.30.

Chapter 7

1   Koo, Linda chih-ling, abstract from: *Nourishment of Life – Health in Chinese Society*, p.77, The Commercial Press Ltd., Hong Kong, 1982.

2   Ibid.

Chapter 8

1   Williams, C.A.S. *Outlines of Chinese Symbolism and Art Motives*, p.285, "Musical Instruments", published by © Dover Publications, Inc. New York, 1976, reprinted with their permission.

2   Wilhelm, Richard (transl.) *I Ching or Book of Changes*, No.16, p.68, Routledge & Kegan Paul, London, 1975. Reprinted by permission of Princeton University Press.

3   Williams, C.A.S. *Outlines of Chinese Symbolism and Art Motives*, p.285, "Musical Instruments", published by © Dover Publications, Inc. New York, 1976, reprinted with their permission.

4   Ibid. p.283.

5   Wang Wei, *Lotus and Chrysanthemum: an anthology of Chinese and Japanese Poetry*, p.110, "In a Retreat among Bamboos", Joseph Lewis French (sel./ed.), Witter Bynner and Kia Kang-hu (transl.), Liveright Publishing Corp. New York, 1934, reprinted with permission from The Witter Bynner Foundation for Poetry.

Chapter 9

1   Cooper, J.C., *Taoism, the Way of the Mystic*, p.10, The Aquarian Press, Wellingborough, 1972. Wildside Press/Borgo Press (USA) and others unable to locate copyright details for USA* but reprinted by © permission of HarperCollins Publishers Ltd. (U.K.)

2   Wilhelm, Richard (transl.) *I Ching or Book of Changes*, Book II, The Material, pp.342-343, Routledge & Kegan Paul, London, 1975. Reprinted by permission of Princeton University Press.

3   Blofeld, John, *Gateway to Wisdom*, p.56, George Allen & Unwin, London, 1980, reprinted by © permission of HarperCollins Publishers Ltd. (U.K.), U.S.A.*

4   Lao Tzu, *The Way of Life according to Lao Tzu*, Bynner, Witter (transl.), No.23, pp.38-39, Capricorn Books, New York, 1962, reprinted with permission from The Witter Bynner Foundation for Poetry.

5   Leggett, Trevor, *Zen and the Ways,* p.127 and p.130, Routledge & Kegan Paul Ltd., London, 1978, reprinted with permission from publishers: Charles E. Tuttle, North Clarendon, USA.

6   Lao Tzu, *The Way of Life according to Lao Tzu,* Bynner, Witter (transl.), No.42, p.52, Capricorn Books, New York, 1962, reprinted with permission from The Witter Bynner Foundation for Poetry.

Chapter 10

1   Cooper, J.C., *Taoism, the Way of the Mystic,* p.100, The Aquarian Press, Wellingborough, 1972. Wildside Press/Borgo Press (USA) and others unable to locate copyright details for USA* but reprinted by © permission of HarperCollins Publishers Ltd (U.K.).

2   Chuang Tzu, *The Way of Chuang Tzu,* "Three Friends", Merton, Thomas (transl.), pp.54-55, George Allen and Unwin Ltd., London, 1970, copyright © 1965 by The Abbey of Gethsemani. Reprinted by permission of New Directions Publishing Corp. N.Y.

3   Granet, Marcel, *The Religion of the Chinese People,* Maurice Freedman (transl.), p.109, Basil Blackwell & Mott Ltd. Oxford, 1975.

4   Leggett, Trevor, *Zen and the Ways,* p.229, Routledge & Kegan Paul Ltd., London, 1978, reprinted with permission from publishers: Charles E. Tuttle, North Clarendon, USA

5   Ssu-K'ung T'u, *Lotus and Chrysanthemum: an anthology of Chinese and Japanese poetry,* p.55, "Tranquil Repose", Joseph Lewis French (sel.ed.), H.A. Giles (transl.), Liveright Publishing Corp. New York, 1934.*

Chapter 11

1   Krishnamurti, J., *Education and the Significance of Life,* p.91, published by Victor Gollancz Ltd., London, 1959, with permission from the Krishnamurti Foundation Trust.§

2   Cameron, David Cashel, Sydney, Aust., unpublished, 1968, with his permission.

Chapter 12

1   Hong Kingston, Maxine, *The Woman Warrior, Memoirs of a girlhood among ghosts,* p.29, Picador edition by Pan Books Ltd., 1981.

2   Krishnamurti, J., *Krishnamurti's Journal,* pp.22-23, published by Victor Gollancz Ltd., London, 1982, with permission from the Krishnamurti Foundation Trust.§

3   Abstracted from the Radio Times, 2 April, 2013, p.91, "Young Drivers in Numbers".

Chapter 13

1   Lao Tzu, *The Way of Life according to Lao Tzu*, Bynner, Witter (transl.), No.43, p.53, Capricorn Books, New York, 1962, reprinted with permission from The Witter Bynner Foundation for Poetry.
2   Lutyens, M., *Krishnamurti, the Years of Fulfilment*, p.15, published by John Murray, London, 1983, with permission from the Krishnamurti Foundation Trust Ltd.§

Chapter 14

1   Wilhelm, Richard (transl.) *I Ching or Book of Changes*, No. 52, p.201, Routledge & Kegan Paul, London, 1975. Reprinted by permission of Princeton University Press.

Chapter 15a

1   Pogson, B., *In the East my Pleasure Lies*, p.110, Stuart & Richard, London, 1950.

Chapter 15c

1   Austin, R; Levy, D., and Ueda, K., *Bamboo*, p.13, Weatherill, New York and Tokyo, 1981, believed to be out of print.*
2   Ibid. p.16.
3   Goodall, J.A., (Sel. & Annot.), *Heaven and Earth – 120 album leaves from a Ming Encyclopedia: San-ts'ai t'u-hui*, 1610, p.129, Lund Humphries, London, 1979. Believed to be an 'orphan work'.*

Chapter 16

1   Cooper, J.C., *An Illustrated Encyclopaedia of Traditional Symbols*, abstracted from p.50, "Deer", © Thames & Hudson Ltd., London, 1978.
2   Chuang Tzu, *The Way of Chuang Tzu*, "Perfect Joy", Merton, Thomas (transl.), pp.99-100, George Allen and Unwin Ltd., London, 1970, copyright © 1965 by The Abbey of Gethsemani. Reprinted by permission of New Directions Publishing Corp. N.Y.

3   Cooper, J.C., *An Illustrated Encyclopaedia of Traditional Symbols,* abstracted from p.50, "Deer", © Thames & Hudson Ltd., London, 1978.

Chapter 17

1   Blofeld, John, *Gateway to Wisdom,* pp.133-135, George Allen & Unwin, London, 1980, reprinted by © permission of HarperCollins Publishers Ltd. (U.K.) U.S.A.*

2   Ibid.

3   Krishnamurti, J. *The Collected Works – The Mirror of Relationship,* Vol III, 1936-1944, pp.215-216, published by Kendall Hunt Publishing Co., Iowa, 1991, with permission from the Krishnamurti Foundation Trust Ltd.§

4   Abstracted from: "Hollywood: a Celebration of the American Silent Film", Episode 6: "Swanson and Valentino", 1980.

Chapter 18

1   Chuang Tzu, *The Way of Chuang Tzu,* "The Fasting of the Heart", Merton, Thomas (transl.), pp.52-53, George Allen and Unwin Ltd., London, 1970, copyright © 1965 by The Abbey of Gethsemani. Reprinted by permission of New Directions Publishing Corp. N.Y.

Chapter 20

1   Yang Wan-li, *Heaven My Blanket, Earth My Pillow – poems from Sung-Dynasty China,* "Bamboo Hermitage", p.84, Jonathan Chaves (transl.), published by John Weatherhill Inc. New York, 1975 and reprinted 2004. With permission by White Pine Press.

Chapter 22

1   Blofeld, John, *The Secret and Sublime: Taoist Mysteries and Magic,* p.167, George Allen and Unwin Ltd., 1973. Reprinted by permission of HarperCollins Publishers Ltd. (U.K) and by Dutton, a division of Penguin Group (USA) LLC.

2   Chuang Tzu, *The Way of Chuang Tzu,* "The Need to Win", Merton, Thomas (transl.), p.107, George Allen and Unwin Ltd., London, 1970, copyright © 1965 by The Abbey of Gethsemani. Reprinted by permission of New Directions Publishing Corp. N.Y.

Chapter 24

1 Wen-Shan Huang, *Fundamentals of Tai Chi Ch'uan,* abstracted from pp.31-52, South Sky Book Co., Hong Kong, 1974.

Chapter 25

1 Krishnamurti, J. *Beyond Violence,* p.118, published by Harper & Row, New York, 1973, with permission from the Krishnamurti Foundation Trust Ltd.§

Chapter 26b

1 Cooper, J.C., *An Illustrated Encyclopaedia of Traditional Symbols,* abstracted from p.17, "Bamboo", © Thames & Hudson Ltd., London, 1978.

2 Austin, R; Levy, D., and Ueda, K., *Bamboo,* p.17, Weatherill, New York and Tokyo, 1981, believed to be out of print.*

Chapter 27

1 Lawrence, D.H., *Pansies – Poems by D.H. Lawrence,* "Being Alive", p.114, Martin Secker, London, 1930, reprinted by permission of Pollinger Limited (*www.pollingerltd.com*) on behalf of the Estate of Frieda Lawrence Ravagli.

Chapter 28

1 Laotse, *The Wisdom of Laotse,* Harris, Iverson L, (transl.), p.8 (from *Golden Threads in the Tapestry of History,* by Kenneth Morris in an address given 1955), Point Loma Publications, Inc. San Diego.

2 Cooper, J.C., *An Illustrated Encyclopaedia of Traditional Symbols,* abstracted from p.38, "Clouds", © Thames & Hudson Ltd., London, 1978.

3 Chuang Tzu, *The Way of Chuang Tzu,* "The Empty Boat", Merton, Thomas (transl.), p.115, George Allen and Unwin Ltd., London, 1970, copyright © 1965 by The Abbey of Gethsemani. Reprinted by permission of New Directions Publishing Corp. N.Y.

4 Bohm, David, *The Holographic Paradigm and other Paradoxes: exploring the leading edge of Science,* Wilber, Ken (ed.), p.208, Shambhala, Boulder, and London, 1982, believed to be out of print.*

Chapter 29

1 Cooper, J.C., *An Illustrated Encyclopaedia of Traditional Symbols,* abstracted from pp.129-130, "Phoenix", © Thames & Hudson Ltd., London, 1978.

Chapter 30

1 Wen-Shan Huang, *Fundamentals of Tai Chi Ch'uan,* abstracted from p.231, South Sky Book Co., Hong Kong, 1974.

Chapter 38

1 Lao Tzu, *The Way of Life according to Lao Tzu,* Bynner, Witter (transl.), No.55, p.60, Capricorn Books, New York, 1962, reprinted with permission from The Witter Bynner Foundation for Poetry.

2 Krishnamurti, J. *Beyond Violence,* p.74, published by Harper & Row, New York, 1973, with permission from the Krishnamurti Foundation Trust Ltd.§

3 Ibid. p.77.

Chapters 39-45

1 Lawrence, D.H., *Last Poems* (Ed. by Richard Aldington), "Healing", p.97, Martin Secker, London, 1933, reprinted by permission of Pollinger Limited (*www.pollingerltd.com*) on behalf of the Estate of Frieda Lawrence Ravagli.

2 Horney, Karen, *Our Inner Conflicts – a Constructive Theory of Neurosis,* p.41, Routledge & Kegan Paul Ltd., London, 1964, with permission from W.W. Norton & Company, Inc.

3 Lawrence, D.H., *Pansies – Poems by D.H. Lawrence,* "Ego-bound", p.67, Martin Secker, London, 1930, reprinted by permission of Pollinger Limited (*www.pollingerltd.com*) on behalf of the Estate of Frieda Lawrence Ravagli.

4 Fordham, Frieda, *An Introduction to Jung's Psychology,* pp.21-22, Penguin Books Ltd., Middlesex, 1961, with © permission from Sarah Bennet and Julia Mackinder.

5 Ibid. pp.61-62.

6 Post, van der, Laurens, *Jung and the Story of our Time,* p.25, Penguin Books, Harmondsworth, 1983 and Chatto and Windus, reprinted by permission of the Random House Group Ltd. (UK) and copyright

© 1975 with permission of Vintage Books, an imprint of the Knopf Doubleday Publishing Group, a division of Random House LLC. All rights reserved.

7   Lao Tzu, *The Way of Life according to Lao Tzu*, Bynner, Witter (transl.), No.79, p.75, Capricorn Books, New York, 1962, reprinted with permission from The Witter Bynner Foundation for Poetry.

Chapter 46

1   Lawrence, D.H., *Pansies – Poems by D.H. Lawrence*, "Sea-weed", p.59, Martin Secker, London, 1930, reprinted by permission of Pollinger Limited (*www.pollingerltd.com*) on behalf of the Estate of Frieda Lawrence Ravagli.

2   Murphy, Carol R., *The Sound of Silence – Moving with T'ai Chi*, p.27, Pamphlet 205, January, 1976, with permission from Pendle Hill, Wallingford, Pennsylvania.

Chapter 47

1   Murphy, Carol R., *The Sound of Silence – Moving with T'ai Chi*, p.23, Pamphlet 205, January, 1976, with permission from Pendle Hill, Wallingford, Pennsylvania.

2   Krishnamurti, J., *Krishnamurti's Journal*, p.71, published by Victor Gollancz Ltd., London, 1982, with permission from the Krishnamurti Foundation Trust.§

3   Ibid., p.72.

4   Blofeld, John, *The Secret and Sublime: Taoist Mysteries and Magic*, p.184, George Allen and Unwin Ltd., 1973. Reprinted by permission of HarperCollins Publishers Ltd. (U.K) and by Dutton, a division of Penguin Group (USA) LLC.

5   Goodall, J.A., (Sel. & Annot.), *Heaven and Earth – 120 album leaves from a Ming Encyclopedia: San-ts'ai t'u-hui*, 1610, p.85, Lund Humphries, London, 1979. Believed to be an "orphan" work.*

Chapter 48a

1   Hesse, Hermann, *The Journey to the East*, trans. Hilda Rosner, p.41, Panther Books, Granada Publishing Ltd., London, 1985, with permission from Peter Owen Ltd. London, and copyright © 1956 by Hermann Hesse reprinted by permission of Farrar, Straus and Giroux, LLC.

2   Thakar, Vimala, *Silence in action,* p.80, published by Mrs. E.A.M. Frankena-Geraets and Mr. L.E. Frankena, Holland, 1968, with permission from Stichting Bookfund Vimala Thakar Holland.

Chapter 48b

1   Blofeld, John, *The Secret and Sublime: Taoist Mysteries and Magic,* pp.175-176, George Allen and Unwin Ltd., 1973. Reprinted by permission of HarperCollins Publishers Ltd. (U.K) and by Dutton, a division of Penguin Group (USA) LLC.

Chapter 49

1   Tanner, Tony, abstract from review: "Life Worship", on "Phoenix II – works by D.H. Lawrence"*

2   Sung Yu, *Lotus and Chrysanthemum: an anthology of Chinese and Japanese poetry,* p.51, "The Philosopher", Joseph Lewis French (sel.ed.), H.A. Giles (trans.), Liveright Publishing Corp. New York, 1934.*

Chapter 50

1   Williams, C.A.S., *Outlines of Chinese Symbolism and Art Motives,* p.225, "Horse", published by © Dover Publications, Inc. New York, 1976, reprinted with their permission.

2   Post, van der, Laurens, *The Night of the New Moon,* pp.75-77, published by Chatto and Windus, reprinted by permission of The Random House Group Ltd.

3   Post, van der, Laurens, *Jung and the Story of our Time,* pp.29-30, Penguin Books, Harmondsworth, 1983 and Chatto and Windus, reprinted by permission of the Random House Group Ltd. (UK) and copyright © 1975 with permission of Vintage Books, an imprint of the Knopf Doubleday Publishing Group, a division of Random House LLC. All rights reserved.

4   Lao Tzu, *The Way of Life according to Lao Tzu,* Bynner, Witter (transl.), No.69, p.70, Capricorn Books, New York, 1962, reprinted with permission from The Witter Bynner Foundation for Poetry.

Chapter 52

1   Cooper, J.C., *An Illustrated Encyclopaedia of Traditional Symbols,* abstracted from pp.129-130, "Phoenix", © Thames & Hudson Ltd., London, 1978.

2   Post, van der, Laurens, *Jung and the Story of our Time*, p.19, Penguin
    Books, Harmondsworth, 1983 and Chatto and Windus, reprinted by
    permission of the Random House Group Ltd. (UK) and copyright © 1975
    with permission of Vintage Books, an imprint of the Knopf Doubleday
    Publishing Group, a division of Random House LLC. All rights reserved.

Chapter 53

1   Greene, Liz, *Relating – An Astrological Guide to Living with Others on a
    Small Planet*, p.233, The Aquarian Press, Wellingborough, Northants., ©
    1986, with permission from Red Wheel/Weiser, LLC Newburyport, MA
    and San Franciso, CA, *www.redwheelweiser.com*.
2   Ibid., p.234.
3   Ibid., p.233.
4   Sunday Times, "Things that go bump in the sea", lst September, 1985.
5   Jung, C.G., Excerpt from *Memories, Dreams, Reflections*, p.416, ©
    Fontana Paperbacks, London, 1983, reprinted by © permission of
    HarperCollins Publishers Ltd. (UK) and translation copyright © 1961,
    1962, 1963 and renewed 1989, 1990, 1991 by Random House LLC.
    Used by permission of Pantheon Books, an imprint of the Knopf
    Doubleday Publishing Group, a division of Random House LLC. All
    rights reserved. Any third party use of this material, outside of this
    publication, is prohibited. Interested parties must apply directly to
    Random House LLC for permission.
6   Lawrence, D.H., *Last Poems* (Ed. by Richard Aldington), "The Four",
    p.48, Martin Secker, London, 1933, reprinted by permission of Pollinger
    Limited (*www.pollingerltd.com*) on behalf of the Estate of Frieda
    Lawrence Ravagli.

Chapter 54

1   Post, van der, Laurens, *Jung and the Story of our Time*, p.208, Penguin
    Books, Harmondsworth, 1983 and Chatto and Windus, reprinted by
    permission of the Random House Group Ltd. (UK) and copyright © 1975
    with permission of Vintage Books, an imprint of the Knopf Doubleday
    Publishing Group, a division of Random House LLC. All rights reserved.
2   Ssu-K'ung T'u, *Lotus and Chrysanthemum: an anthology of Chinese and
    Japanese poetry*, p.56, "Refinement", Joseph Lewis French (sel.ed.), H.A.
    Giles (transl.), Liveright Publishing Corp. New York, 1934.*

Chapter 55

1   Cooper, J.C., *Taoism, the Way of the Mystic*, p.31, The Aquarian Press, Wellingborough, 1972. Wildside Press/Borgo Press (USA) and others unable to locate copyright details for USA,* but reprinted by © permission of HarperCollins Publishers Ltd. (U.K.)

2   Claremont de Castillejo, Irene, *"Dilemma of Levels"*, pp.14-15, Guild Lecture No.101, May, 1959, with permission from The Guild of Pastoral Psychology, London.

3   Ibid., p.16.

4   Anandamayi Ma, the Essential Sri, *Life and Teachings of a 20th Century Indian Saint*, pp.50-51, Atmananda (trans.); Alexander Lipsky (Biog.), Joseph A. Fitzgerald (Edit.), Motilal Banarsidass Publishers Pvt Ltd. Delhi, 2007, with permission from World Wisdom, Bloomington, USA.

Chapter 56

1   Govinda, Lama Anagarika, *The Way of the White Clouds*, p.25, The Overlook Press, Peter Mayer Publications, Inc., Woodstock and New York, 2005, also published by Century, reprinted by permission of the Random House Group Ltd.

Chapter 57

1   Lawrence, D.H., *Last Poems* (Ed. by Richard Aldington), "Phoenix", p.73, Martin Secker, London, 1933, reprinted by permission of Pollinger Limited (*www.pollingerltd.com*) on behalf of the Estate of Frieda Lawrence Ravagli.

Chapter 58

1   Lawrence, D.H., *Last Poems* (Ed. by Richard Aldington), "Change", p.73, Martin Secker, London, 1933, reprinted by permission of Pollinger Limited (*www.pollingerltd.com*) on behalf of the Estate of Frieda Lawrence Ravagli.

2   Blofeld, John, *The Secret and Sublime: Taoist Mysteries and Magic*, pp.182-183, George Allen and Unwin Ltd., 1973. Reprinted by permission of HarperCollins Publishers Ltd. (U.K) and by Dutton, a division of Penguin Group (USA) LLC.

3   Field, Joanna, *A Life of One's Own*, pp.14-15, Penguin Books, Harmondsworth, 1955, with permission from Taylor & Francis Books (UK).

4   Post, van der, Laurens, *Jung and the Story of our Time*, p.133, Penguin Books, Harmondsworth, 1983 and Chatto and Windus, reprinted by

permission of the Random House Group Ltd. (UK) and copyright
© 1975 with permission of Vintage Books, an imprint of the Knopf
Doubleday Publishing Group, a division of Random House LLC. All
rights reserved.

5   Lawrence, D.H., *Last Poems* (Ed. by Richard Aldington), "Seekers",
p.142, Martin Secker, London, 1933, reprinted by permission of
Pollinger Limited (*www.pollingerltd.com*) on behalf of the Estate of
Frieda Lawrence Ravagli.

Chapter 59

1   Lawrence, D.H., *Last Poems* (Ed. by Richard Aldington), "Salvation",
pp.89-90, Martin Secker, London, 1933, reprinted by permission of
Pollinger Limited (*www.pollingerltd.com*) on behalf of the Estate of
Frieda Lawrence Ravagli.

Chapter 60

1   Lawrence, D.H., *Pansies – Poems by D.H. Lawrence,* "To let go or to hold
on -?", pp.18-19, Martin Secker, London, 1930, reprinted by permission
of Pollinger Limited (*www.pollingerltd.com*) on behalf of the Estate of
Frieda Lawrence Ravagli.

Chapters 61-66

1   Blixen, Karen, *Out of Africa,* p.244, Penguin Books, London, 2011 and
Gyldendal, Copenhagen, 1937, by permission of Penguin Random
House (USA) and © by agreement with Gyldendal Group Agency.

2   Lawrence, D.H., *Last Poems* (Ed. by Richard Aldington), "The Work of
Creation", p.28, Martin Secker, London, 1933, reprinted by permission
of Pollinger Limited (*www.pollingerltd.com*) on behalf of the Estate of
Frieda Lawrence Ravagli.

3   Mullikin, Mary Augusta and Hotchkis, Anna M., abstracted from *The
Nine Sacred Mountains of China,* Vetch and Lee, Hong Kong, 1973*

Chapters 69a-69b

1   Lawrence, D.H., *Last Poems* (Ed. by Richard Aldington), "The
Rainbow", p.31, Martin Secker, London, 1933, reprinted by permission
of Pollinger Limited (*www.pollingerltd.com*) on behalf of the Estate of
Frieda Lawrence Ravagli.

2   Post, van der, Laurens, *Jung and the Story of our Time,* p.50, Penguin Books, Harmondsworth, 1983 and Chatto and Windus, reprinted by permission of the Random House Group Ltd. (UK) and copyright © 1975 with permission of Vintage Books, an imprint of the Knopf Doubleday Publishing Group, a division of Random House LLC. All rights reserved.

3   LeShan, Lawrence, *Clairvoyant Reality,* pp.65-66, Turnstone Press, Wellingborough, Northants. © Lawrence Leshan 1974.

4   Ibid., p.34

5   Ibid., pp.36-37

6   Ibid., p.56

7   Austin, R; Levy, D., and Ueda, K., *Bamboo,* p.24, Weatherill, New York and Tokyo, 1981, believed to be out of print.*

Chapter 70

1   Lawrence, D.H., *Phoenix – the posthumous Papers of D.H. Lawrence,* "Birds", p.67, William Heinemann Ltd., London, 1936, edited and with an Introduction by Edward D. McDonald, reprinted by permission of Pollinger Limited (*www.pollingerltd.com*) on behalf of the Estate of Frieda Lawrence Ravagli.

Chapter 71

1   Yang Wan-li, *Heaven My Blanket, Earth My Pillow – poems from Sung-Dynasty China,* p.22-23, Jonathan Chaves (transl.), published by John Weatherhill Inc. New York, 1975 and reprinted 2004, permission by White Pine Press.

2   Williams, C.A.S., *Outlines of Chinese Symbolism and Art Motives,* p.441 and 443, "Written Characters", published by © Dover Publications, Inc. New York, 1976, reprinted with their permission.

3   Cooper, J.C., *An Illustrated Encyclopaedia of Traditional Symbols,* abstracted from pp.85-86, "Horse", © Thames and Hudson, London, 1978.

4   Lieh Tzu, *Taoist Teachings from the Book of Lieh Tzu,* Giles, Lionel (trans.), p.114, John Murray, London, 1947.

5   Cooper, J.C., *An Illustrated Encyclopaedia of Traditional Symbols,* abstracted from pp.85-86, "Horse", © Thames and Hudson, London, 1978.

6   Capra, Fritjof, *The Turning Point – Science, Society and the Rising Culture,* pp.326-327, Wildwood House Ltd., 1982, © reprinted by permission

of HarperCollins Publishers Ltd. (UK) and of Simon & Schuster, Inc. (USA). All Rights Reserved.
7   Ibid. p.329-330.

Chapter 72

1   Lawrence, D.H., *Phoenix – the posthumous Papers of D.H. Lawrence,* "Reptiles", p.67, William Heinemann Ltd., London, 1936, edited and with an Introduction by Edward D. McDonald, reprinted by permission of Pollinger Limited (*www.pollingerltd.com*) on behalf of the Estate of Frieda Lawrence Ravagli.
2   Lao Tzu, *The Way of Life according to Lao Tzu,* Bynner, Witter (transl.), No.21, p.37, Capricorn Books, New York, 1962, reprinted with permission from The Witter Bynner Foundation for Poetry.

Chapters 73-76

1   Lao Tzu, *The Way of Life according to Lao Tzu,* Bynner, Witter (transl.), No.64, p.66, Capricorn Books, New York, 1962, reprinted with permission from The Witter Bynner Foundation for Poetry.

Chapter 77

1   Cooper, J.C., *Taoism, the Way of the Mystic,* p.113, The Aquarian Press, Wellingborough, 1972. Wildside Press/Borgo Press (USA) and others unable to locate copyright details for USA* but reprinted by © permission of HarperCollins Publishers Ltd. (U.K.)
2   McTaggart, Lynne, *The Field,* p.xvi, Element, as a © imprint of Harper Collins, London, 2003 reprinted by permission of HarperCollins Publishers Ltd. (UK) and copyright © 2002 reprinted by permission of HarperCollins Publishers (USA)
3   Ibid., p.31.
4   Ibid., p.xx.
5   Ibid., p.31.
6   Ibid., p.32

Chapter 79

1   Lutyens, Mary, *Krishnamurti, the Years of Fulfilment,* p.224, published by John Murray, London, 1983, with permission from the Krishnamurti Foundation Trust.§

2   Schwenk, Theodor, *Sensitive Chaos – the Creation of flowing forms in Water and Air,* Olive Whicher and Johanna Wrigley (trans.); Water Roggenkamp (illust.), p.98, Verlag Freies Geistesleben Publishers, Stuttgart, and Rudolf Steiner Press, London, 1965, with permission from Rudolf Steiner Press, Temple Lodge Publishing, Forest Lodge.

3   Ibid., p.99.

4   Krishnamurti, J. *Krishnamurti's Notebook,* pp.201-202, published by Victor Gollancz Ltd., London, 1976, with permission from the Krishnamurti Foundation Trust.§

5   Merton, Thomas, *The Seven Storey Mountain,* p.329, Sheldon Press, London, 1983, with permission of SPCK Publishing.

6   Ibid., p.330.

7   Krishnamurti, J., *Krishnamurti's Notebook,* pp.89-90, published by Victor Gollancz Ltd., London, 1976, with permission from the Krishnamurti Foundation Trust.§

8   Chuang Tzu, *The Way of Chuang Tzu,* "The Man of Tao", Merton, Thomas (transl.), p.92, George Allen and Unwin Ltd., London, 1970, copyright © 1965 by The Abbey of Gethsemani. Reprinted by permission of New Directions Publishing Corp. N.Y.

Chapter 80

1   Schwenk, Theodor, *Sensitive Chaos – the Creation of flowing forms in Water and Air,* Olive Whicher and Johanna Wrigley (trans.); Water Roggenkamp (illust.), p.68, Verlag Freies Geistesleben Publishers, Stuttgart, and Rudolf Steiner Press, London, 1965, with permission from Rudolf Steiner Press, Temple Lodge Publishing, Forest Lodge.

2   Ashe, Geoffrey, *the Ancient Wisdom,* pp.141-142, MacMillan London Ltd., 1977.

3   Ibid., p.130.

4   Burnham, Robert, *Burnham's Celestial Handbook,* Vol.3, p.1940, Dover Publications Inc., New York, 1978.

5   Williams, C.A.S., *Outlines of Chinese Symbolism and Art Motives,* p.371, "Stars", published by © Dover Publications, Inc. New York, 1976, reprinted with their permission.

6   Burnham, Robert, *Burnham's Celestial Handbook,* Vol.3, p.1941, Dover Publications Inc., New York, 1978.

7   Abstracted from: "Seven Ages of Starlight", T.V., BBC4, Produced and Directed by Gaby Hornsby, 25 October, 2012.

8   Ashe, Geoffrey, *the Ancient Wisdom,* p.31, MacMillan London Ltd., 1977.

9   Ibid., pp.132-133.

10 Thompson, Francis, quoted in LeShan, Lawrence, *Clairvoyant Reality*, p.44, Turnstone Press Ltd., Wellingborough, Northamptonshire, Lawrence Leshan, 1974.

Chapter 81

1   Post, van der, Laurens, *Jung and the Story of our Time*, p.132, Penguin Books, Harmondsworth, 1983 and Chatto and Windus, reprinted by permission of the Random House Group Ltd. (UK) and copyright © 1975 with permission of Vintage Books, an imprint of the Knopf Doubleday Publishing Group, a division of Random House LLC. All rights reserved.

2   Ibid., p.86.

Chapter 82

1   Lao Tzu, *The Way of Life according to Lao Tzu*, Bynner, Witter (transl.), No.8, p.29, Capricorn Books, New York, 1962, reprinted with permission from The Witter Bynner Foundation for Poetry.

Chapter 84

1   Krishnamurti, J., *Meeting Life,* compiled by Mary Lutyens, p.97, published by Arkana, 1991. With permission from the Krishnamurti Foundation Trust.§

2   Blofeld, John, *The Secret and Sublime: Taoist Mysteries and Magic*, p.193, George Allen and Unwin Ltd., 1973. Reprinted by permission of HarperCollins Publishers Ltd. (U.K) and by Dutton, a division of Penguin Group (USA) LLC.

Chapters 85-86

1   Chuang Tzu, *The Way of Chuang Tzu*, "The Empty Boat", Merton, Thomas (transl.) p.114, George Allen and Unwin Ltd., London, 1970, copyright © 1965 by The Abbey of Gethsemani. Reprinted by permission of New Directions Publishing Corp. N.Y.

Chapters 87-88

1   Blofeld, John, *The Secret and Sublime: Taoist Mysteries and Magic*, pp.209-210, George Allen and Unwin Ltd., 1973. Reprinted by

permission of HarperCollins Publishers Ltd. (U.K) and by Dutton, a division of Penguin Group (USA) LLC.

2 Ibid., p.204.

3 Ibid., p.198.

4 Blofeld, John, *Taoism – the Quest for Immortality*, p.153, Unwin Paperback, London, 1979, reprinted by © permission from HarperCollins Publishers Ltd. (U.K.)

5 Ssu-K'ung T'u, *Lotus and Chrysanthemum: an anthology of Chinese and Japanese poetry*, p.56, "Height-Antiquity", Joseph Lewis French (sel.ed.), H.A. Giles (transl.), Liveright Publishing Corp. New York, 1934.*

§ All Krishnamurti texts used with permission of the Krishnamurti Foundation Trust Ltd. Any personal views expressed are the author's own and do not necessarily reflect the views of the Krishnamurti Foundation Trust Ltd.

Appendix A

With acknowledgement to the late E.T.C. Werner for this Table of Cosmology; pp.460-462 of *Outlines of Chinese Symbolism and Art Motives*, by C.A.S. Williams, Dover Publications Inc. New York, 1976, and with gratitude to Dover Publications for permission to adapt its basic Format.

ILLUSTRATIONS

Please note that, despite extensive research, a few illustrations could not be attributed and are marked with an asterisk. If further information is available about their copyright ownership, kindly contact the publisher of this book.

Part Two

About the Author

The author was born in Holland in 1935 of Dutch-English parentage and lived in Australia during her formative years.

Her strongest early influence was her mother, Grace, who, when a student at Cambridge, became a suffragette of the less-militant kind. She imparted to her children a profound sense of social justice and a deep interest in psychology, philosophy and the Arts.

Ursula's anti-authoritarian brother, Roelof, dubbed 'Prince of the Push' at Sydney University's Libertarian Society, unwittingly provided her with a platform for the later, spiritually-based, influence of Jiddu Krishnamurti, whom she first heard speak in Sydney when she was 19 and to whose teachings she became affiliated for the rest of her life.

At the age of 24, she moved to England, made her home there and, whilst training in T'ai Chi Ch'üan, worked mainly as a personal assistant to private individuals.

An aptitude for her study of T'ai Chi was influenced by early sporting activities. She had already broken a world swimming record by the age of 10 and at High School was elected Sports Captain. She received prizes for English Literature, acted in children's radio programmes, studied piano and ballet and won a medal for ballroom dancing. Her love of all forms of dancing, especially to jazz music, has stayed with her throughout her life.

Buddhism became another influence, through her annual teaching of T'ai Chi at the Buddhist Society's Summer School in the 1980s. The courtesies and gentle art of the Japanese Tea Ceremony added a further dimension.

It was Taoism, however, that became the strongest influence, and it was this facet of Eastern philosophy that was woven into her 30 years' teaching of the slow, meditative T'ai Chi form of exercise.

Ursula also travelled widely and, late in life, married an Australian anthropologist, who introduced her to ecology and social anthropology and to the discovery of a profound joy in step-motherhood. She leads a fully-organic life-style and lives in the Hampshire countryside with two cats, a fox, some moles and visiting deer.

'The Tiger's Mouth –
a Taoist Journey towards the Source'
can be purchased direct from the publisher:

Wordzworth Publishing
www.wordzworthpublishing.com

Lightning Source UK Ltd.
Milton Keynes UK
UKOW06f1923181115

263002UK00003B/9/P